Vygotsky and the
Social Formation of Mind

Vygotsky and the
Social Formation of Mind

James V. Wertsch

Harvard University Press
Cambridge, Massachusetts
and London, England

This book has been digitally reprinted. The content
remains identical to that of previous printings.

Library of Congress Cataloging in Publication Data

Wertsch, James V.
    Vygotsky and the social formation of mind.

    Bibliography: p.
    Includes index.
    1. Vygotskiĭ, L.S. (Lev Semenovich), 1896-1934.
2. Cognition—Social aspects. 3. Psycholinguistics—
Social aspects. 4. Semiotics—Social aspects. I. Title.
BF109.V95W47 1985   153'.092'4 [B]   85-7619

ISBN 0-674-94351-1 (paper)

To Mary

Foreword

It was with great pleasure that we accepted the invitation of our friend James Wertsch to write a foreword to this book on Lev Semenovich Vygotsky, one of the greatest psychologists of the first half of the twentieth century. In examining Vygotsky's cultural-historical approach to the origins and development of higher mental functions and consciousness, Wertsch has not limited his analysis to psychology. Rather, he has correctly viewed this approach as a general theory of culture, an approach that is rooted in Russian culture of the first decades of the twentieth century. This is the context in which the "phenomenon of Vygotsky" must be understood.

Vygotsky stands before us not as an isolated phenomenon or puzzle but as a representative of the most important and, in many respects, most significant period in our society's culture and science. Several points in his approach reflect the atmosphere of creativity in which he lived and worked. For example, his notion of the semiotic or symbolic nature of higher mental functions and consciousness is very closely tied to the theory and practice of Russian symbolism, which appeared most strikingly in poetry, painting, theater, and film during this period. As has been noted by theorists of art and philosophy, such as V. V. Ivanov, A. F. Losev, and B. F. Asmus, symbolism emerged in opposition to naturalism in art. This protest against naturalism is quite apparent in the works and verses of A. Belyi, A. Blok, O. E. Mandel'shtam, B. L. Pasternak, and many other, and in the works and performances of V. E. Meierkhol'd and S. M. Eisenshtein. For Vygotsky, who was a great connoisseur of art, this opposition took the form of a protest against empiricism in psychology.

A second problem central to the approach outlined by Vygotsky and his followers is that of development. Vygotsky's Russian contemporaries—the evolutionist-biologist V. A. Vagner and A. N. Severtsov—were producing remarkable ideas in this area. Vagner insisted that there must be a significantly tighter connection between psychology and general biology, especially evolutionary theory. He identified the dangers of too close a tie between psychology and physiology, a tie that could lead psychology down the wrong path. We can now say that his fears were not unfounded and that the theory of conditional reflexes was not the best thing for psychology. At that same time, Severtsov appealed to mental reality to explain evolutionary processes, viewing mind as a factor in evolution. Vygotsky stated that "the biological significance of mind is a necessary condition of scientific psychology" (1982, p. 76).

A third influence on Vygotsky was the study of physiology. During the years when he was working, new antihomeostatic directions in physiology proper were being formulated, above all in the work of A. A. Ukhtomskii and N. A. Bernshtein. These scholars argued that there is a class of functional, as opposed to anatomical-morphological, organs in the human body. This view is now known as the physiology of activation. It is fully consistent with Vygotsky's idea that in the development of psychology a psychological physiology (not to be confused with the classical psychophysiology of sense organs) is more important than a physiological psychology. Vygotsky himself viewed higher mental processes as functional systems or organs. It is worth noting that at present there is an increasingly close rapprochement between the physiology of activation, as developed by Bernshtein's followers, and the psychological theory of activity, as developed by the Vygotskian school.

The problems of thinking and speech and of the origins and functions of consciousnesses occupied a major place in Vygotsky's scientific quests. Leading Soviet scholars such as G. G. Shpet, N. Ya. Marr, and M. M. Bakhtin worked in these areas. They were all concerned with the origins of language, which they correctly considered the substance of consciousness. Such investigators undoubtedly had an important influence on the development of Vygotsky's ideas about the formation of higher mental functions and consciousness. Specifically, in his works we find the problematics of the external and internal, the idea of the connection between actions and signs, the notion that the strata of being and signs in consciousness genetically precede its genuinely reflexive strata, and finally an understanding of dialogicality and polyphony in consciousness.

In old Russia psychology, especially experimental psychology, was significantly less developed than in the West. In coming to psychology from the study of literature and art, Vygotsky energetically began to master the various traditions of psychology from all parts of the world. His understanding was transformed in a creative recasting of the theories of behaviorism, Gestalt psychology, functional and descriptive psychology, genetic psychology, the French sociological school, and Freudianism.

Of course, Vygotsky did more than collect facts from all these traditions and disciplines. He considered the information he collected through the prism of his own conceptual scheme, which he never considered complete. In this connection it is important to note that Vygotsky was a staunch advocate of dialectical and historical materialism. He was one of the creators of Marxist psychology. For Vygotsky, Marxist philosophy was not a dogma or a doctrine in which one could find answers to concrete questions in psychology. Rather, in mastering Marxism he assumed that a psychologist could assimilate a general method of scientific research, which could then be applied to concrete problems. In this connection Vygotsky wrote, "I don't want to discover the nature of mind by patching together a lot of quotations. I want to find out how science has to be built, to approach the study of mind having learned the whole of Marx's method" (1982, p. 421).

This book provides a quite complete presentation of Vygotsky's theory and of Vygotsky himself. Wertsch has chosen the most difficult and least developed, as well as the most fascinating, point of Vygotsky's theory as the object of his own experimental research, namely, the mechanism of cultural development of behavior. This mechanism is the transition from interindividual activity to intraindividual activity. This general explanation by Vygotsky has been superbly operationalized by Wertsch and transformed into an instrument of microstructural and microgenetic investigation of the formation of higher mental functions that lie in the child's zone of proximal development.

It may be appropriate to make one suggestion; that is, it is worth paying more attention to Vygotsky's position that "meaning is the internal structure of a sign operation" (1982, p. 160). Zaporozhets expressed this idea much more strongly, calling meaning the crystal of action. The solution to the problem of the external and internal lies in this idea: action and meaning (sense) are two sides of a single coin. This provides the key to explaining why followers of Vygotsky turned to analyses of object-oriented action and only much later returned to the problem of meaning and consciousness. This route gave rise to the psychological theory of activity, a new and quite natural stage in the development of the cultural-historical theory.

In conclusion, we will say a few words about "Vygotskian perspectives" and the "zone of proximal development." His school is no longer called the cultural-historical school; more frequently one hears of the psychological theory of activity as developed by the Vygotsky-Leont'ev-Luria school. This name is largely adequate, since over the course of many years the representatives of this school have focused more on problems of action and activity than on problems of sign, meaning, symbol, and consciousness, which have remained in the shadows. The elaboration of the structure of activity and of voluntary movements and actions is no doubt a major accomplishment of this group. With the recent publication in Moscow of the sixth volume of Vygotsky's *Collected Works,* his theory of the cultural-historical development of higher mental functions and of consciousness, as he himself formulated it, has gotten a second wind. Therefore Wertsch is correct in emphasizing Vygotsky's cultural-historical theory.

One can say that in the zone of proximal development of Vygotsky's school lies the solution to the extremely complex problem of the structure and functions of consciousness and the mechanism of its formation. One hardly needs to point out that successful resolution of this problem will be significant not only for the fate of human culture, but, as the author of this book has demonstrated so well, for the fate of human civilization. It is obvious to us that competition between American and Soviet scholars to resolve problems of the structure and formation of consciousness is a much more worthy pursuit than competition to create the means for destroying human civilization.

Finally, let us say a few words about Vygotsky as a person. According to the testimonials of our teachers, he was a kind person, ardently demanding of others and of himself. In him, one saw mind, feeling, and will all harmonized in such a way as to make him a genuine scholar, whose life and work served as a model for several generations of Soviet psychologists. One can see the consciousness, personality, and activity of a great scholar in this passage:

The very attempt to approach the soul scientifically, the effort of free will to master the mind, to the extent it is not clouded or paralyzed by mythology, contains in itself the entire past and future path of psychology because science is the path to truth, albeit one that passes through periods of error. It is namely this to us, the path of our science: in struggle, in surmounting mistakes, in difficulties, in an inhuman struggle with thousand-year-old prejudices. We do not want to be Ivans who do not remember their relatives. We do not suffer from illusions of grandeur, thinking that history begins with us. We do not want to receive from history a trivial name. We want a name on which the dust of centuries settles. In this we see our historical right, an indication of our historical role, the claim of realizing psychology as a science. (1982, p. 428)

In these words is expressed a respect for the centuries-old science of psychology and for the scholars who created it. It is appropriate that James Wertsch, with similar respect, has recognized the scientific creation of our fellow countryman Lev Semenovich Vygotsky.

V. P. Zinchenko   V. V. Davydov
USSR Academy of Pedagogical Sciences, Moscow

Preface

This volume grew out of several trips I made to the USSR between 1975 and 1984. I was fortunate to begin these trips at a time when several of Vygotsky's colleagues and students were still alive. My discussions with such outstanding personalities and scholars as A. R. Luria, A. N. Leont'ev, D. B. El'konin, A. V. Zaporozhets, and L. I. Bozhovich provided much of the inspiration and information I needed to undertake this project. It is impossible for me to convey how important these people have been in helping me understand Vygotsky as a person and as the creator of an account of human consciousness.

As these figures passed from the scene, I came to rely more heavily on the next generation of Soviet scholars for much of my information. In this connection V. P. Zinchenko and V. V. Davydov have played an especially important role. They have spent countless hours explaining their interpretation of Vygotsky's ideas.

Many individuals in the West have also been essential in my efforts to complete this work. At the risk of leaving out several who deserve mention, I wish to thank in particular Michael Cole, Patricia Greenfield, Michael Holquist, Maya Hickmann, John Lucy, Ben Lee, Sylvia Scribner, Addison Stone, and Susan Sugarman. They have provided me with the encouragement, as well as the critical commentary, required to present ideas from one scientific tradition to readers from another.

To say that colleagues in the USSR and the United States have assisted me in understanding Vygotsky's ideas does not mean that they agree with everything I have said in this volume. With regard to the first four chapters, where I have outlined basic themes in Vygotsky's writings, some differ with me at least in the emphasis they would give to various points. In the final four chapters, where I have attempted to extend Vygotsky's ideas, some of my colleagues have gone so far as to raise concrete objections to the idea that my claims are part of Vygotsky's approach. For example, it has been suggested that "Vygotsky and Beyond" would be an appropriate subtitle for chapter 8. Such comments point out that the final responsibility for my interpretations and extensions of Vygotsky's ideas must remain with me.

I also wish to thank the many organizations that have supported me over the past decade. The International Research and Exchanges Board, the American Council of Learned Societies, and the Fulbright Commission have made possible my various trips to the USSR. The Institute of Psychology and Institute of Linguistics of the USSR Academy of Sciences, the Pushkin Russian Language Institute, and the Department of Psychology at Moscow State University have provided the hospitality and material support to carry out my research while in the USSR. The Spencer Foundation, Northwestern University, and the Center for Psychosocial Studies have supported the empirical research that I and several of my students have conducted in connection with Vygotsky's ideas, research that is reported here in chapters 3 and 7. The seemingly endless typing and retyping of this manuscript was cheerfully undertaken by Kathleen Pucci and other members of the staff of the Center for Psychosocial Studies.

Over the years that I have worked on this volume I have come to view it not only as a project in academic research but as an exercise in intercultural understanding. I have continually been impressed by the differences that separate Western and Soviet views of human mental functioning. The differences I have in mind are not of the sort that characteristically arise in the mutual recriminations of political rhetoric. Rather, they are fundamental differences in assumptions about issues such as the role of social forces in the formation of the individual. Such differences need not be a source of misunderstanding. Instead, they can provide everyone with a challenge to grow. It is my deepest hope that this volume can contribute in some small way to this process.

Contents

Vygotsky and the
Social Formation of Mind

Note on Russian Names

Readers of English have become accustomed to spellings such as "Vygotsky" and "Luria" rather than more precise but cumbersome transliterations such as "Vygotskii" or "Vygotskij" and "Luriya" or "Lurija." Therefore the names of relatively familiar figures will be spelled in their anglicized form. However, for less familiar names—Shchedrovitskii, for example—the more precise transliteration practices used in standard publications, such as *Soviet Psychology,* will be followed.

CHAPTER 1

Vygotsky:
The Man and His Theory

L ike the humanities and other social sciences, psychology is supposed to tell us something about what it means to be human. However, many critics, including such eminent members of the discipline as J. S. Bruner (1976), have questioned whether academic psychology has succeeded in this endeavor. One of the major stumbling blocks that has diverted psychology from this goal is that psychologists have too often isolated and studied phenomena in such a way that they cannot communicate with one another, let alone with members of other disciplines. They have tended to lose sight of the fact that their ultimate goal is to contribute to some integrated, holistic picture of human nature.

This intellectual isolation is nowhere more evident than in the division that separates studies of individual psychology from studies of the sociocultural environment in which individuals live. In psychology we tend to view culture or society as a variable to be incorporated into models of individual functioning. This represents a kind of reductionism which assumes that sociocultural phenomena can ultimately be explained on the basis of psychological processes. Conversely, sociologists and social theorists often view psychological processes as posing no special problems because they derive straightforwardly from social phenomena. This view may not involve the kind of reductionism found in the work of psychologists, but it is no less naive. Many aspects of psychological functioning cannot be explained by assuming that they derive solely and simply from the sociocultural milieu.

This disciplinary isolation is not attributable simply to a lack of cooperation among various scholars. Rather, those interested in social phenomena and those interested in psychological phenomena have defined their objects of inquiry in such different ways that they have almost guaranteed the impossibility of mutual understanding. For decades this problem has been of concern to those seeking to construct a unified social science. Critical theorists such as T. Adorno (1967, 1968) and J. Habermas (1979) have struggled with it since the 1940s. According to Adorno, "the separation of sociology and psychology is both correct and false" (1967, p. 78). It is correct because it recognizes different levels of phenomena that exist in reality; that is, it helps us avoid the pitfalls of reductionism. It is false, however, because it too readily "encourages the specialists to relinquish the attempt to know the totality" (p. 78).

Keeping sight of this totality while examining particular levels of phenomena in social science is as elusive a goal today as earlier in the twentieth century. Indeed the more progress we make in studying particular phenomena, the more distant this goal seems to become. My purpose here is to explicate and extend a theoretical approach that tried to avoid this pitfall—the approach of the Soviet psychologist and semiotician Lev Semenovich Vygotsky (1896–1934).

Vygotsky, of course, did not make his proposals in order to deal with today's disciplinary fragmentation, but many of his ideas are relevant to the quandaries we face. To harness these ideas, they must first be interpreted in light of the milieu in which they were developed. Hence I shall explicate the cultural and historical setting in which Vygotsky worked and then extend his ideas in light of theoretical advances made during the half-century since his death.

Vygotsky is usually considered to be a developmental or educational psychologist. Much of what I shall have to say, however, is based on the assumption that it is incorrect to categorize him too readily as a psychologist, at least in today's restricted sense. It is precisely because he was not *only* a psychologist that he was able to approach this discipline with a fresh eye and make it part of a more unified social science. In fact the Soviet philosopher and psychologist G. P. Shchedrovitskii (October 13, 1981—conversation) has argued that one of the main reasons for Vygotsky's success in reformulating psychology in the USSR is that he was not trained as a professional psychologist.

Under normal circumstances an outsider is not given the opportunity to reformulate a discipline such as psychology in a major country. Vygotsky, however, did not live in normal circumstances: he entered adulthood just as his country was experiencing one of the greatest social upheavals of the twentieth century—the Russian Revolution of 1917. This event provided two decades or so of what is perhaps the most exciting intellectual and cultural setting of our time. It was largely because of this setting that Vygotsky was able to develop his ingenious ideas and that these ideas could have a significant impact.

A Biographical Sketch

Vygotsky's biography can be divided into two basic periods: the first, from his birth in 1896 until 1924, the year in which he made his initial appearance as a major intellectual figure in the USSR; the second, from 1924 until his death from tuberculosis in 1934.

Information about Vygotsky's early life is sketchy. Other than family records and reminiscences, especially those of his older daughter, Gita L'vovna Vygotskaya,[1] the only major source of information about Vygotsky's early life is K. E. Levitin (1982), who in turn gathered much of his information from one of Vygotsky's childhood friends, Semen Dobkin.[2] Vygotsky was born on November 17, 1896,[3] in Orsha, a town not far from Minsk in Belorussia. When he was about a year old, his family moved to Gomel, a somewhat larger town in Belorussia, where he spent his childhood and youth. His father, who had finished the Commercial Institute in the Ukrainian city of Khar'kov, was a department chief at the United Bank of Gomel and a representative of an insurance society. His mother was trained as a teacher but spent most of her life raising eight children. Together this couple made the Vygodsky family one of the town's most cultured. The rather stern disposition and bitter ironic humor of Vygotsky's father contrasted with the very gentle personality of his mother. It was apparently from her that Lev Semenovich acquired his initial knowledge of German[4] and his love for the poet Heine.

The picture that emerges from information about Vygotsky's early years is one of a happy, intellectually stimulating life—in spite of the fact that, like other members of his family, he was excluded from several avenues of opportunity because he was Jewish. In tsarist Russia being Jewish meant living in restricted territories, being subject to strict quotas for entering universities, being excluded from certain professions, and several other forms of discrimination. These circumstances were undoubtedly the source of much of the elder Vygodsky's bitterness. He and his wife, however, seem to have provided a warm and intellectually stimulating atmosphere for their children, which is evident from Dobkin's comment that Vygotsky's

> father's study was often at the children's disposal. There, they arranged all sorts of meetings and would go there to be alone for a while or to meet with a small group of friends. The dining room was also a place for communication as there was invariably lively and interesting conversation during the obligatory evening tea at a large table. Talks over the samovar were one of the family traditions which played an important role in the formation of the mentality of all the children, especially the older ones.   (Levitin, 1982, pp. 24–25)

Instead of attending public schools, Vygotsky studied with a private tutor for several years and then finished his secondary education in a Jewish gymnasium. He profited enormously from his early years of study with his tutor, Solomon Ashpiz. Ashpiz's pedagogical technique was apparently grounded in a form of ingenious Socratic dialogue, which left his students, especially one as gifted as Lev Semenovich, with well-developed, inquisitive minds.

By the age of fifteen Vygotsky had become known as the "little professor" (Levitin, October 6, 1981—conversation), because he often led student discussions on intellectual matters. For example, he examined the historical context of thought by arranging debates and mock trials in which his peers played the role of figures such as Aristotle and Napoleon. These debates were a manifestation of one of Vygotsky's main interests during that period of his life—philosophy.

While still a child in Gomel, Lev Semenovich also began to show fervent interest in the theater and in literature. Of the former his sister said, "I don't think there was any period in his life when he did not think or write about the theatre" (Levitin, 1982, p. 20). With regard to the latter Dobkin reported, "Literature, especially his favourite poetry, always gave him much solace in life and always engaged his attention" (ibid., p. 20). Dobkin also reports that as a schoolboy Vygotsky "was forever citing favourite verses" (p. 27). Like all Russian children, Lev Semenovich knew a great deal of Pushkin's poetry, but in contrast to most of his schoolmates who usually preferred the lyric verses, he preferred Pushkin's more serious, even tragic, passages. In addition, he loved the poetry of Blok, especially the "Italian Poems," which have a tragic air.

When reciting poetry, Vygotsky had the habit of singling out the lines that he felt captured the essence of the poem and skipping the remaining ones. For example, from Pushkin's "Mozart and Salieri" he recited only the beginning lines: "They say: there is no justice here on earth. But there is more—hereafter. To my mind this truth is elementary as a scale." This is by no means the end of Salieri's monologue. While much of the continuation is quite significant, Lev Semenovich recited only these lines, saying they were sufficient to grasp the essence. This notion of the heightened significance of an abbreviated linguistic form was destined to play an essential role in his account of language and mind.

Vygotsky graduated from his gymnasium in 1913 with a gold medal. Though widely recognized as an outstanding student, he had great difficulty entering the university of his choice—largely because he was Jewish. The first problem he encountered was the "deputy's examinations," so called because they were attended by a deputy or representative of the province, who had the decisive say. The deputy, usually a teacher from the public gymnasium, was often quite anti-Semitic.

During this period there was a quota on the number of Jews who could enter Moscow and Saint Petersburg universities: no more than 3 percent of the student bodies could be Jewish. As Levitin (1982, pp. 27–29) points out, this meant that all the Jewish gold medalists and about half the silver medalists would be admitted. Since Lev Semenovich had every reason to expect a gold medal, his matriculation to the university of his choice seemed assured.

Midway through Vygotsky's deputy examinations, however, the tsarist minister of education decreed a change in procedures by which Jews would be chosen for Moscow and Saint Petersburg universities. The 3 percent quota was maintained, but Jewish applicants were now to be selected by casting lots, a change apparently designed to dilute the quality of Jewish students at the best universities. Dobkin remembered Lev Semenovich's response to this change. Lev

> showed me the newspaper with the report about the new circular, which meant a great misfortune for him personally and for his whole family since it dashed his career plans and hopes of getting a university degree.
>
> "There," said Lev, "now I have no chance."
>
> The news seemed so monstrous to me that I replied quite

sincerely: "If they don't admit you to the University it will be a terrible injustice. I am sure they'll let you in. Wanna bet?"

Vygotsky, who was a great bettor, smiled and stretched out his hand. We wagered for a good book.

He did not make a single mistake on his final exams and received a gold medal . . .

And then the incredible happened: late in August, the Vygodskys received a cable from their friends in Moscow telling them that Lev had been enrolled at the University by the draw. On the same day, he presented me with a volume of Bunin's poetry inscribed "To Senya in memory of a lost bet." (Levitin, 1982, pp. 28–29)

Lev Semenovich's parents insisted that he go into medicine at the university. At the time this seemed to be a good path, since for Jews medicine guaranteed a modest but secure professional life. Vygotsky was more interested in history or philology, but these departments were devoted primarily to training secondary-school teachers, and as a Jew he was forbidden to be an employee in the tsarist government. Lev Semenovich was also interested in law, but court officials (with the exception of lawyers) could not be Jewish in tsarist Russia. Thus Lev Semenovich entered the university in Moscow in medicine. However, according to Dobkin, "hardly a month passed before he transferred to the law department" (ibid., p. 29). Apparently Lev Semenovich planned to become a lawyer, one of the few professions that would allow him to live beyond the pale.

In 1914, while in Moscow as a student, Vygotsky also began attending the Shanyavskii People's University, an unofficial school that sprang up in 1911 after a minister of education had expelled most of the students and more than a hundred of the faculty from Moscow University in a crackdown on an antitsarist movement. Many of the best professors in Moscow had been the victims of this expulsion. As a result Shanyavskii University was a more interesting institution at that time than Moscow University. Vygotsky's majors there were history and philosophy.

Vygotsky graduated from Moscow University in 1917 with a degree in law. Although he received no official degree from Shanyavskii University, he profited greatly from his studies in psychology, philosophy, and literature. He returned to Gomel after his graduation to teach literature and psychology.

Very little information is available about the impact of the 1917

Revolution on Lev Semenovich. Innumerable personal and historical accounts have documented the massive changes introduced into the lives of everyone involved, and one must assume that Vygotsky was no exception. As A. R. Luria (1979) has documented, the Revolution profoundly changed disciplines such as psychology as well. Whole new realms of inquiry were opened, and opportunities for younger scholars,[5] were greater than had previously been imaginable.

Lev Semenovich continued living in Gomel's relatively peaceful setting for seven years after his return in 1917. With his cousin David Vygodsky he taught literature at a school in Gomel. He also conducted classes on aesthetics and the history of art in a conservatory and gave many lectures on literature and science. Furthermore, he organized a psychology laboratory at the Gomel Teacher's College, where he delivered a series of lectures that provided the groundwork for his 1926 volume, *Pedagogical Psychology*.

Dobkin recalls that he, Lev Semenovich, and David Vygodsky began publishing inexpensive copies of great literary works in 1918. This venture was dubbed "Ages and Days," and its trademark was composed of a sphinx and a butterfly. After existing long enough to produce two volumes, it was closed down because of the paper shortage that was by then affecting Gomel as well as the rest of the country. Lev Semenovich's two partners in this business left Gomel soon afterward; Vygodsky went to Petrograd in search of work, and Dobkin to Moscow to further his studies.

At the time of Dobkin's departure in 1920, Vygotsky was in poor health. The disease that was eventually to kill him, tuberculosis, had begun to take its toll. It was already a serious enough threat to Vygotsky's life in 1920 that he spent a brief period in a sanatorium and asked one of his former professors from Shanyavskii University to publish his collected manuscripts in the event of his death. He recovered from this bout of tuberculosis, however, and continued his projects in Gomel. In 1924 he married Roza Smekhova. They had two daughters.

Between his graduation from the university and his move to Moscow, Lev Semenovich somehow managed to fit a great deal of reading into his hectic schedule of teaching, public lectures, publishing, and writing. Among the authors that figured prominently in Vygotsky's readings were poets such as Tyuchev, Blok, Mandel'shtam, and Pushkin; writers of fiction such as Tolstoy, Dostoevsky, Bely, and Bunin; and philosophers such as James and especially Spinoza. He also read the writings of Freud, Marx, Engels, Hegel, Pavlov, and the Russian philologist Potebnya.

In retrospect all this work seems to have been preparation for an event in 1924 that was to change Vygotsky's life irrevocably. This turning point, which separates the two major periods of Vygotsky's biography, was his appearance on January 6, 1924, at the Second All-Russian Psychoneurological Congress in Leningrad. There he made a presentation, "Methods of Reflexological and Psychological Investigations."[6] Several of Vygotsky's future students were at the meeting and later fondly recounted the electrifying effect this unknown young man had on the conference. According to Luria,

> when Vygotsky got up to deliver his speech, he had no printed text from which to read, not even notes. Yet he spoke fluently, never seeming to stop and search his memory for the next idea. Even had the content of his speech been pedestrian, his performance would have been notable for the persuasiveness of his style. But his speech was by no means pedestrian. Instead of choosing a minor theme, as might befit a young man of twenty-eight [sic] speaking for the first time to a gathering of the graybeards of his profession, Vygotsky chose the difficult theme of the relation between conditioned reflexes and man's conscious behavior . . . Although he failed to convince everyone of the correctness of his view, it was clear that this man from a small provincial town in western Russia was an intellectual force who would have to be listened to. (1979, pp. 38–39)

Vygotsky's brilliant performance so impressed the director of the Psychological Institute in Moscow, K. N. Kornilov, that he immediately invited this "Mozart of psychology" (Toulmin, 1978) to join himself and others in restructuring the institution. Lev Semenovich accepted and later that year left Gomel to begin his new career. Upon his arrival in Moscow, he lived for a period in the basement of the Experimental Psychology Institute. Dobkin recalled that Vygotsky's room contained archives of that institute's philosophical section, including reports on ethnic psychology. Vygotsky plunged into reading these archives, which made up the walls of his new living quarters, thereby continuing his education.

In 1925 Lev Semenovich completed his dissertation, "The Psychology of Art." During the fall of that year he received permission to have a public defense, but a renewed and serious bout of tuberculosis made that impossible. Recognizing this fact, the qualifying commission excused him from a public defense, and he was passed. The origins of Vygotsky's dissertation stemmed from as early as 1916, when he had completed a lengthy manuscript on *Hamlet*. According to Dobkin, Lev Semenovich had actually begun the manuscript as a schoolboy when seeing *Hamlet* had left a great impression on him. The early versions were Vygotsky's "most closely guarded secret" (Levitin, 1982, p. 32) during that period of his life.

The years between 1924 and 1934 were extremely busy and productive for Vygotsky. Soon after his arrival in Moscow, Aleksandr Romanovich Luria (1902–1977) and Aleksei Nikolaevich Leont'ev (1904–1979) joined him as students and colleagues. Together these three became known as the "troika" of the Vygotskian school. Several other students and followers eventually joined the school, but it was Luria and Leont'ev who were destined to be the major developers of Vygotsky's ideas after his death.

Luria's initial encounter with Vygotsky reflected a respect bordering on awe. Such an opinion is not uncommon among those who worked with Vygotsky. He seems to have had a profound impact on the lives of almost all his students and colleagues. Roza Evgenevna Levina (May 3, 1976—conversation) recalled her first contact with Vygotsky as being completely overwhelming. She and four other students who were to become followers of Vygotsky were in their third year at the university in Moscow when they met him. They were between twenty-one and twenty-three years of age at the time, and Vygotsky was thirty. But from an intellectual perspective he seemed "several generations older." Levina recalls taking notes on Vygotsky's ingenious (and often spontaneous) lectures and understanding them only years later. Another of his students, P. Ya. Gal'perin (1984), has recounted how "all of Moscow came running" to hear Vygotsky's clinical diagnoses and how students sometimes listened to his lectures through open windows because the auditorium was completely packed.

The almost messianic impression that Vygotsky made is borne out in many other observations as well. For example, Luria, one of the most prominent neuropsychologists of the twentieth century, said, "All of my work has been no more than the working out of the psychological theory which [Lev Semenovich] constructed" (1978), and of his own professional life Luria said, "I divide my career into two periods: the small and insignificant period before my meeting with Vygotsky and the more important and essential one after the meeting" (Levitin, 1982, p. 159).

The excitement that Vygotsky generated among his students and colleagues is perhaps impossible to appreciate in today's setting. They were totally dedicated to the man and to his ideas. According to Luria, "The entire group gave almost all of its waking hours to our grand plan for the reconstruction of psychology. When Vygotsky went on a trip, the students wrote poems in honor of his journey. When he gave a lecture in Moscow, everyone came to hear him" (1979, p. 52).

What generated such excitement and enthusiasm among Vygotsky's followers? At least two essential factors were involved. First, the genius of Vygotsky. His mind absorbed a huge amount of diverse information and analyzed it in accordance with an evolving set of guiding principles. But the same can be said of many people who have not had Vygotsky's impact; it alone cannot explain his influence. One must also appreciate the importance of a second factor, the social and political environment of the USSR during the two decades between the Russian Revolution of 1917 and the beginning of the Stalinist purges. This period, especially after the end of the Civil War in 1922, was one of upheaval, enthusiasm, and energy unimaginable by today's standards. People such as Vygotsky and his followers devoted every hour of their lives to making certain that the new socialist state, the first grand experiment based on Marxist-Leninist principles, would succeed. When one appreciates the life-giving energy provided by this environment and by the commitment of intellectuals to the creation of a new society, Vygotsky's work and influence become easier to understand.

The last decade of Vygotsky's life was extraordinarily hectic and productive. He joined the Psychological Institute of Moscow University in the modest position of junior staff scientist (or staff scientist, 2nd class, as the rank was then known). The year before his arrival in 1924 the directorship of this institute had passed from G. I Chelpanov to Kornilov. The major reason for the change was that Kornilov was viewed as a "materialist" devoted to developing a Marxist psychology, whereas Chelpanov had been labeled an "idealist." Kornilov's takeover signaled the seriousness and dedication with which scholars were then trying to employ Marxist principles when approaching issues in psychology (as well as in other disciplines).

Vygotsky viewed his task in this new institutional setting as twofold. First, he wanted to reformulate psychological theory along Marxist lines. This theme in Vygotsky's writings is sometimes dismissed by Western readers as mandatory lip service to something he did not really believe. This was absolutely not the case with Vygotsky. Although

Soviet psychology was later to suffer from immersion in a dogmatic political climate (compare Tucker, 1971; Kozulin, 1984), Vygotsky died before this condition became a pervasive fact of life. His belief in Marxist principles was honest and deep. According to Luria, "Vygotsky was . . . the leading Marxist theoretician among us . . . in [his] hands, Marx's methods of analysis did serve a vital role in shaping our course" (1979, p. 43).

Vygotsky's second goal after 1924 was to develop concrete ways for dealing with some of the massive practical problems confronting the USSR—above all, the psychology of education and remediation. Typically the USSR has had great faith in scientific solutions to practical problems. At the time Vygotsky was working, the practical problems for psychology included massive illiteracy (which has been almost completely overcome today), cultural differences among the peoples who were all eventually supposed to become Soviet (as opposed to Uzbek, Ukrainian, and so on), and an almost total absence of services for those who were mentally retarded or otherwise unable to participate in the new society. While working at Kornilov's institute, Vygotsky expanded his horizons in practical issues by examining problems of defectology (*defektologia*).[7] In particular, he was concerned with children who were hearing impaired, mentally retarded, or (in current terminology) learning disabled. In 1925 he began to organize the Laboratory of Psychology for Abnormal Childhood in Moscow. In 1929 this became the Experimental Defectological Institute of Narkompros (People's Commissariat for Education), and after Vygotsky's death, the Scientific Research Institute of Defectology of the Academy of Pedagogical Sciences. Vygotsky was the first director of this institute and continued to be heavily involved in its workings until his death.

In addition to carrying out the work needed to create a new institute (the difficulty of which was exacerbated by the relative chaos that still existed in the USSR), Vygotsky conducted empirical research. Levina (May 3, 1976—conversation) recalls that she and other students of Vygotsky searched the neighborhood of the institute for children who could serve as subjects in their studies. They temporarily used this method of "subject selection" because it was unclear which bureaucracy had the power to give them permission to enter the kindergartens.

Besides his administrative activities Vygotsky also lectured and wrote. In 1925 he produced the written version of his 1924 presentation at the Second All-Russian Psychoneurology Congress; between November of 1925 and the spring of 1926, while in the hospital with another attack of tuberculosis, he wrote a major philosophical critique of the theoretical foundations of psychology, "The Historical Significance of the Crisis in Psychology"; and in 1926 he published *Pedagogical Psychology*, which derived from his earlier lectures in Gomel.

Beginning in the late 1920s Vygotsky traveled extensively in the USSR to lecture and help set up research laboratories. In the early spring of 1929 he went to Tashkent (Uzbekistan) for several months to give a course and train teachers and psychologists at the Eastern Department of the First Central Asian State University. In early 1931, at the request of the newly formed psychology sector at the Ukrainian Psychoneurological Institute, Vygotsky and several colleagues moved many of their activities to the city of Khar'kov. Although this move severely disrupted their personal lives, the group readily accepted the invitation to set up a new base of operations. They viewed Khar'kov as providing a supportive atmosphere that would foster the growth of a new approach to psychology. They felt they needed a few years' respite from the hectic environment of Moscow in order to develop their ideas. Among the members of Vygotsky's school who moved to Khar'kov were Luria, Leont'ev, L. I. Bozhovich, and A. V. Zaporozhets. They were joined by such figures as P. Ya. Gal'perin and P. I. Zinchenko, who had already been living there.

Vygotsky himself did not move permanently to Khar'kov but visited this outpost of his followers on a regular basis. In addition to lecturing, writing, and organizing research during these visits, he undertook studies in medicine, especially neurology. He entered medical school and attended lectures in both Moscow and Khar'kov. His interest in medicine seems to have stemmed primarily from his interest in neurological disorders of speaking and thinking, which was manifested as early as 1929 in his writings on aphasia.

Besides his work in Khar'kov during this period, Vygotsky pursued several of his activities in Moscow with colleagues such as Levina, L. S. Slavina, and N. A. Menchinskaya. He gave lectures at the Department of Social Sciences at Moscow State University, the N. K. Krupskaya Academy of Communist Education, the Institute for Child and Adolescent Health, the Pedagogical Department of the Moscow Conservatory, and the K. Libknekht Industrial-Pedagogical Institute. Furthermore, he commuted regularly to Leningrad to work with D. B. El'konin and S. L. Rubinshtein and to lecture at the A. I. Herzen Leningrad Pedagogical Institute. Vygotsky also began to visit Poltova fairly regularly to guide the research of a group headed by Bozhovich, who had moved there from Khar'kov. He not only gave lectures in all these places but conducted clinical work and organized research activities as well. Anyone familiar with the distances between these cities and the primitive means of Soviet transportation in the 1930s can appreciate the time and energy such travel demanded. Nevertheless, like many of his cohorts, Vygotsky viewed it his duty to help build the new Soviet state.

Between 1931 and 1934 Vygotsky produced manuscripts for reviews, articles, and books at an ever accelerating pace. He edited and wrote a long introduction for the 1932 Russian translation of Piaget's volume *Le langage et la pensée chez l'enfant* (1923). His introduction was later to serve as the second chapter of his posthumous volume *Thinking and Speech* (1934).[8] Vygotsky also wrote many other pieces, including "The Diagnosis of Development and Pedological Clinics for Difficult Children" (1931a), "The History of Development of Higher Mental Functions" (1931b), "Lectures on Psychology" (1932), "The Problem of Instruction and Cognitive Development during the School Years" (1934b), "Thought in Schizophrenia" (1934c), as well as critical reviews and introductions to volumes by Bühler, Köhler, Gesell, Koffka, and Freud.

Among his research activities, Vygotsky attended a seminar in Moscow together with Luria, the linguist N. Ya. Marr, and the cinematographer S. M. Eizenshtein. Eizenshtein subsequently wrote that he loved "this marvelous man with his strange haircut[9] . . . From under this strange haircut peered the eyes of one of the most brilliant psychologists of our time who saw the world with celestial clarity" (Ivanov, 1976, p. 66).

During Vygotsky's last few years of life, he lectured and wrote at an almost frenetic pace. His daughter, Gita L'vovna (October 16, 1981—conversation), recalls his Moscow schedule as one that required him to be at work from early morning until late evening. He often did his writing after 2 A.M., when he had a few quiet hours to himself, and during the last months of his life he dictated his output to a stenographer, which is how the last chapter of *Thinking and Speech* was produced.

Throughout this period Vygotsky's bouts of tuberculosis became increasingly frequent and severe. His protracted, terrifying spells of coughing led to exhaustion for several days, but instead of resting, he tried to reach as many of his goals as possible. In the spring of 1934 his health grew much worse. His doctors insisted that he enter the hospital, but he refused because of work he needed to complete by the end of the school year. One May 9 he had a very severe attack at work and was brought home. At the end of May his bleeding began again, and on June 2 he was hospitalized in Serebryanii Bor Sanatorium. Shortly after midnight on June 11 he died. He was buried in Novo-devechii Cemetery in Moscow.

A few of Vygotsky's writings were published shortly after his death, but for political reasons a twenty-year period ensued when his work was for all practical purposes banned in the USSR. This resulted partly from the 1936 decree of the Central Committee of the Communist Party against pedology, a discipline roughly equivalent to educational psychology, especially as it concerns psychometrics. The decree was aimed at aspects of this discipline that Vygotsky himself had criticized (see Cole and Scribner, 1978), but certain of his works (for example, Vygotsky, 1935) clearly were associated with it, and so all his writings became a target of criticism. Other factors in the demise of Vygotsky's official position were the conflict between some of his claims and those found in Stalin's 1950 essay on linguistics, and the rise in the late 1940s of a form of dogmatic Pavlovianism (Tucker, 1971) that is now referred to in the USSR as "vulgar materialism."

These factors were overcome only after Stalin's death in 1953. The publication of Vygotsky's works resumed in 1956 (Vygotsky, 1956) and continues today in the USSR with the publication of six volumes of his collected works (Vygotsky, 1982a, 1982b, 1983a, 1983b, 1984a, 1984b). In all, Vygotsky produced approximately 180 works. Of these, 135 had been published in one form or another prior to the six volumes of his collected works. Several are appearing in these six volumes for the first time, but some, especially those dealing with pedology, will not appear even then.

Vygotsky's Theoretical Approach

The multiplicity of intellectual roots and research interests that characterized Vygotsky's career may suggest that any attempt to identify a core set of unifying themes in his work would be misguided. However, I would argue that it is only by identifying general themes that one can understand his approach to specific issues. The three themes that form the core of Vygotsky's theoretical framework are (1) a reliance on a genetic or developmental method;[10] (2) the claim that higher mental processes in the individual have their origin in social processes;[11]

and (3) the claim that mental processes can be understood only if we understand the tools and signs that mediate them.

Each of these themes can be fully understood only by taking into account its interrelationships with the others. Thus the very notion of origins in the second theme points toward a genetic analysis, and Vygotsky's account of social interaction and mental processes is heavily dependent on the forms of mediation (such as language) involved. Indeed much of what is unique about this approach is the way the three themes are interdefined.

While recognizing this thoroughgoing interconnection among the themes, my initial presentation of them considers each in relative isolation. Although this approach entails some artificiality, it is useful to abstract each theme from its overall framework for clarity of presentation. By isolating the themes in Vygotsky's approach, one can also gain insight into the "dynamics" that exist among them. I shall argue that they can be ordered in terms of their analytic primacy in his theoretical framework. Specifically I argue that the third theme, concerning tool and sign mediation, is analytically prior to the other two. This is so because Vygotsky's claims about mediation can generally be understood on their own grounds, whereas important aspects of the other two themes can be understood only if the notion of mediation is invoked. Thus Vygotsky defined development in terms of the emergence or transformation of forms of mediation, and his notion of social interaction and its relation to higher mental processes necessarily involves mediational mechanisms.

In addition, I believe that Vygotsky made his most important and unique contribution with the concept of mediation. At the time he was writing, other scholars had already argued for the need to use genetic analysis in the study of mind and had outlined accounts that viewed the mind as originating in social life. It was Vygotsky's contribution to redefine and extend these ideas by introducing the notion of tool and sign mediation.

During the last decade of his life the notion of mediation (*oposredovanie*) became increasingly important and well formulated in Vygotsky's theory of human mental functioning. By 1933 he went so far as to say that "the central fact about our psychology is the fact of mediation" (1982a, p. 166). L. A. Radzikhovskii has noted that this evolution in Vygotsky's thinking was paralleled by a switch from an account of mediational means closely tied to Pavlovian psychophysiology to one emphasizing meaning and the communicative nature of signs: "The concept 'stimulus-means,' which in fact always meant only that the means is not a typical stimulus (in a behavioristic conceptualization), disappears [in Vygotsky's writings]. In its place the concept *sign* becomes central for Vygotsky's theory. The term *sign* is used by Vygotsky in the sense of having meaning (1979, p. 182). Vygotsky himself recognized this change in his account of mediation. Thus in 1933 he noted that "in older works we ignored the fact that a sign has meaning" (1982a, p. 158).

It is Vygotsky's later interpretation of signs and their mediational capacities that will be the primary focus of my presentation. In his writings of this last period of his life one can see the full development of an approach that draws on his earlier studies in semiotics,[12] philology, and literary analysis. His insights into the nature of meaning in sign systems (especially human language) laid the groundwork for interpreting the genetic relationship between social and individual processes. His understanding of this relationship is the core of his approach and leads back to the issue raised at the very beginning of this chapter— the isolation of individual and social phenomena in today's social sciences. The way Vygotsky proposed to coordinate these areas of inquiry was to argue that semiotic processes are part of both and hence make it possible to build a bridge between them. This involved invoking ideas from disciplines that lie outside the social sciences as they are understood today. Vygotsky was able to do this partly because of his familiarity with a broad range of disciplines. However, his success at bridging disciplines also had much to do with the exciting social and intellectual milieu in which he lived.

Vygotsky managed to tie various strands of inquiry together into a unique approach that does not separate individuals from the sociocultural setting in which they function. This integrative approach to social, semiotic, and psychological phenomena has substantial relevance today, a half century after his death.

CHAPTER 2

Vygotsky's Genetic Method

T he fundamental claim in Vygotsky's genetic or developmental
analysis is that human mental processes can be understood only
by considering how and where they occur in growth:

> We need to concentrate not on the *product* of development but
> on the very *process* by which higher forms are established . . . To
> encompass in research the process of a given thing's development
> in all its phases and changes—from birth to death—fundamentally
> means to discover its nature, its essence, for "it is only in move-
> ment that a body shows what it is." Thus, the historical [that is,
> in the broadest sense of "history"] study of behavior is not an
> auxiliary aspect of theoretical study, but rather forms its very
> base.   (Vygotsky, 1978, pp. 64–65)

Vygotsky contrasted his genetic approach with approaches that attempt to analyze psychological phenomena without regard for their
place in development. He argued that such research can provide description but not explanation:

> Following Lewin, we can apply [the] distinction between the
> phenotypic (descriptive) and genotypic (explanatory) viewpoints
> to psychology. By a developmental study of a problem, I mean
> the disclosure of its genesis, its causal dynamic basis. By pheno-
> typic I mean the analysis that begins directly with an object's
> current features and manifestations. It is possible to furnish many
> examples from psychology where serious errors have been com-

mitted because these viewpoints have been confused. (ibid., p. 62)

The last sentence is particularly important because it reflects Vygotsky's concern with the problem of how assumptions about method influence the interpretation of psychological phenomena. He was arguing that misunderstandings often arise among researchers because they do not share assumptions about how a phenomenon should be investigated, and hence about what it *is*. For Vygotsky an essential aspect of the definition of a psychological phenomenon is its position in genetic transition. He assumed that the form of a phenomenon reflects the transformations it has undergone and the various factors that have entered into its development.

Vygotsky's point is not that psychological research which fails to use a genetic method is invalid or useless. Elsewhere in his writings he explicitly stated that such research can make an important contribution to the overall picture of psychology. However, he believed that without genetic analysis one can only describe certain aspects of psychological phenomena and cannot understand inner workings and causal dynamics. Perhaps more important for my present purposes, he believed that the failure to recognize the impact of method on the interpretation and definition of psychological phenomena can lead to confusion.

Vygotsky's major focus in genetic analysis was on developmental processes as they normally occur, but he also examined the effects of disruptions and interventions. Such procedures gave rise to several of his hyphenated terms that refer to variants of genetic analysis. In "comparative-genetic" analysis he was concerned with how the disruption of one of the forces of development would affect the evolution of overall practical and intellectual activity in humans. For example, Vygotsky studies the effects of deafness on the development of various mental functions. His approach to this issue is somewhat unique because he viewed deafness primarily in terms of how it changes a complex system of development. For this reason problems such as deafness, mental retardation, and blindness have always held great theoretical interest for Vygotsky (1981c) and his followers (for example, Leont'ev, 1948; Meshcheryakov, 1974).

Vygotsky also examined disruptions and interventions in genetic processes through the "experimental-developmental" method, which calls for an experimenter to intervene in some developmental process in order to observe how such intervention changes it. Again the primary motivation for doing this is to observe genetic processes:

> Our method may be called experimental-developmental in the sense that it artificially provokes or creates a process of psychological development. This approach is equally appropriate to the basic aim of dynamic analysis. If we replace object analysis by process analysis, then the basic task of research obviously becomes a reconstruction of each stage in the development of the process: the process must be turned back to its initial stages. (Vygotsky, 1978, pp. 61–62)

Vygotsky's claims about genetic analysis do not end with the general assertion that psychological processes must be studied in transition. In addition he had some specific ideas about the nature of development. First, he defined development primarily in terms of fundamental "revolutionary" shifts rather than steady quantitative increments. At these points of revolutionary dislocation, he argued, the very nature of development changes. Second, Vygotsky defined major transition points in development in terms of changes in the form of mediation utilized. Third, he claimed that the explanation of psychological phenomena must rely on an analysis of several different types of development, or what I shall term "genetic domains." Whereas genetic analysis is often limited to ontogenetic comparisons, Vygotsky included other types of comparisons, such as phylogenetic and sociohistorical, as well. As M. Cole and S. Scribner have pointed out, "when Vygotsky speaks of his approach as 'developmental,' this is not to be confused with a theory of child development. The developmental method, in Vygotsky's view, is the central method of psychological science" (1978, p. 7).

The Role of Qualitative Shifts

A fundamental feature of Vygotsky's genetic analysis is that he did not assume one can account for all phases of development by using a single set of explanatory principles. Instead, he argued that the critical issue is how to account for the changing relationships among multiple forces of development and their corresponding sets of explanatory principles. Thus he rejected accounts that are based on the assumption that development can be explained solely in terms of quantitative increments of some psychological unit, such as stimulus-response bonds. Instead of searching for any other single explanatory principle to account for development, he emphasized that at certain points in the emergence of a psychological process new forces of development and new explanatory principles enter the picture. At these points, he argued, there is a "change in the very type of development" (Vygotsky and Luria, 1930, p. 4),[1] and so the principles which alone had previously been capable of explaining development can no longer do so. Rather, a new set of principles must be incorporated into the overall explanatory framework, resulting in its reorganization.

Some of the clearest expositions of this point can be found in Vygotsky's critiques of existing accounts of ontogenesis. He argued that approaches which rest on a single set of explanatory principles cannot provide an adequate interpretation of change. For example, he criticized P. P. Blonskii for attempting to account for all periods of ontogenesis on the basis of physiological principles, and he criticized other investigators for basing their entire analysis on another single dimension, such as sexual maturation:

> These schemes do not take into account the reorganization of the process of development itself, by virtue of which the importance and significance of any characteristic is continually changing in the transition from one age to another. This excludes the possibility of breaking childhood down into separate epochs by using a single criterion for all ages. Child development is a very complex process which cannot be fully defined in any of its stages solely on the basis of one characteristic. (Vygotsky, 1972, p. 115)

The dominant tendencies in psychology that motivated Vygotsky's criticism of single-criterion theories were biological reductionism and mechanistic behaviorism. When considering the former, for example, he was quite critical of investigators' failure to recognize that biological principles cannot explain psychological phenomena beyond a certain level. He never disputed the role of biological factors in a complete account of ontogenesis, a point reflected in his statement that "scientific child psychology, of course, cannot be constructed otherwise than on a solid biological foundation" (1982a, p. 202).

However, he argued that beyond a certain point in development, biological forces can no longer be viewed as the sole, or even the primary, force of change. At this point there is a fundamental reorganization of the forces of development and a need for a corresponding reorganization in the system of explanatory principles. Specifically, in Vygotsky's view the burden of explanation shifts from biological to social factors. The latter operate within a given biological framework and must be compatible with it, but they cannot be reduced to it. That is, biological factors are still given a role in this new system, but they lose their role as the primary force of change. Vygotsky contrasted embryological and psychological development on this basis:

> The embryological development of the child . . . in no way can be considered on the same level as the postnatal development of the child as a social being. Embryological development is a completely unique type of development subordinated to other laws than is the development of the child's personality, which begins at birth. Embryological development is studied by an independent science—embryology, which cannot be considered one of the chapters of psychology . . . Psychology does not study heredity or prenatal development as such, but only the role and influence of heredity and prenatal development of the child in the process of social development. (1972, p. 123)

Vygotsky's argument against single-factor theories of development (theories that posit one major force of development and a single set of explanatory principles) was aimed primarily at biological reductionism and mechanistic behaviorism. His criticisms, however, also extended to representatives of another early twentieth-century school of psychology with which his ideas were much more compatible—Gestalt psychology. One of the places where this criticism appears most forcefully is in Vygotsky's introduction to a volume of Russian translations of K. Koffka's writings titled *Foundations of Mental Development* (1934). Here he argued that Gestalt psychology represented an advance over the atomistic mechanism of earlier stimulus-response theories, but that some of its proponents had slipped back into the mistake of advocating a theory that rests on a single developmental factor and a single explanatory principle. In this case the attempt was to account for all levels of psychological functioning on the basis of the notion of structure, or Gestalt, thereby overlooking the fundamental differences in explanatory principles that apply to different levels of psychological phenomena:

> What is remarkable in [Koffka's] approach is the fact that he applies the structural principle not only to the intellectual actions of the human-like apes, but also to the lower animals in Thorndike's experiments. Consequently, *Koffka sees in structures some*

primary, primordial, and essentially primitive principles of behavioral organization. [According to him] It would be a mistake to think that this principle applies only to higher, or intellectual forms of activity. It is also present in the earliest and most elementary forms of development. This debate, says the author, confirms our understanding of the primitive nature of structural functions. If structural functions are really so primitive, they must appear in the primitive behavior that I call instinctual. We see how in refuting the theory of trial and error learning Koffka was led to the conclusion *that we can apply the structural principle equally to the higher intellectual actions of human-like apes, as well as to the training of lower mammals in Thorndike's experiments, and finally to the instinctual reactions of spiders and bees.* (Vygotsky, 1982a, pp. 245–246)

In sum, one of Vygotsky's basic assumptions about the development of psychological processes is that no single factor and corresponding set of explanatory principles can alone provide a complete account. Instead, multiple forces of development, each with its own set of explanatory principles, are involved. In this account, with the incorporation of a new force into the picture, the very nature of development changes.

The Role of Mediation in Qualitative Genetic Transitions

The major transition points in Vygotsky's genetic analysis are associated with the appearance of some new form of mediation. Depending on the genetic domain at issue, this mediation may be in the form of tools or signs. In some cases developmental transitions are linked with the introduction of a new form of mediation, whereas in others they are related to a transition to a more advanced version of an existing form of mediation. The former cases are associated with the qualitative transitions in Vygotsky's genetic analysis and will be my main concern here.

In the introduction to a volume on genetic analysis, Vygotsky and Luria explained that the scheme of their essays could be presented as follows:

The use and "invention" of tools in humanlike apes crowns the organic development of behavior in evolution and paves the way for the transition of all development to take place along new paths. It creates *the basic psychological prerequisites for the historical devel-*

opment of behavior. Labor and the associated development of human speech and other psychological signs with which primitives attempt to master their behavior, signify the beginning of the genuine cultural or historical development of behavior. Finally, in child development, along with processes of organic growth and maturation, a second line of development is clearly distinguished—the cultural growth of behavior. It is based on the mastery of devices and means of cultural behavior and thinking. (1930, pp. 3–4)

Vygotsky and Luria went on to argue:

All three of these moments are symptoms of new epochs in the evolution of behavior and indications of *a change in the type of development itself*. In all three instances we have thereby selected turning points or critical steps in the development of behavior. We think that the turning point or critical moment in the behavior of apes is the use of tools; in the behavior of primitives it is labor and the use of psychological signs; in the behavior of the child it is the bifurcation of lines of development into natural-psychological and cultural-psychological development. (Ibid., p. 4)

Thus major turning points, or revolutions in development, were connected with the appearance of new forms of mediation. However, Vygotsky did not view the introduction of a new form of mediation as resulting in a form of functioning in which factors that had previously governed psychological functioning no longer operate. The point is always that the explanatory framework must be *reformulated*, not discarded and replaced, in order to take into account a new factor and its interactions with existing factors. For example, with the introduction of psychological signs in social history, the biological constitution of the organism that has resulted from evolution continues to play an important role, but psychological functioning is now governed by biological constitution *and* sign use. Thus a more complex explanatory system—one that incorporates and integrates more than one factor— must now be used to account for mental functioning. Development can no longer be explained on the basis of principles that had formerly accounted for the genesis of psychological processes (in this case, principles of Darwinian evolution). Instead, development is now attributed to principles that incorporate the new factor that has entered the picture.

Elementary and Higher Mental Functions

A fundamental distinction that underlies Vygotsky's line of reasoning about qualitative transitions and the role of mediation is the distinction between "elementary" and "higher" mental functions (1978, p. 39). Vygotsky's general strategy was to examine how mental functions, such as memory, attention, perception, and thinking, first appear in an elementary form and then are changed into a higher form. In his approach a related distinction is that between the "natural" and the "social" (or "cultural") lines of development (1960, p. 47). Natural development produces functions in their elementary forms, whereas cultural development converts elementary into higher mental processes. It is the transformation of elementary into higher functions that Vygotsky usually had in mind when he spoke of how the nature of development changes.

As Cole (1985) has pointed out, the distinction between elementary and higher mental functions has had a long history in psychology. The general distinction arose in response to the need to separate psychological phenomena that can be found in both humans and animals from those that are unique to humans. The latter are viewed as the product of the sociocultural milieu in which humans live. For this reason Vygotsky (1960, p. 15) sometimes used the terms "cultural" (versus "natural") in place of "higher" (versus "elementary") when describing mental functions. Essentially, higher processes are assumed to represent a qualitatively new level of psychological functioning. Hence, it is impossible to account for higher processes by using the explanatory principles that apply to elementary functions.

The basic outlines of Vygotsky's version of the distinction between elementary and higher mental functions can be seen in the following comments on memory (here he employed the term "natural" instead of "elementary"):

> A comparative investigation of human memory reveals that, even at the earliest stages of social development, there are two, principally different, types of memory. One, dominating in the behavior of nonliterate peoples, is characterized by the nonmediated impression of materials, by the retention of actual experiences as the basis of mnemonic (memory) traces. We call this *natural memory,* and it is clearly illustrated in E. R. Jaensch's studies of eidetic imagery. This kind of memory is very close to perception, because it arises out of the direct influence of external stimuli

upon human beings. From the point of view of structure, the entire process is characterized by a quality of immediacy.

Natural memory is not the only kind, however, even in the case of nonliterate men and women. On the contrary, other types of memory belonging to a completely different developmental line coexist with natural memory. The use of notched sticks and knots, the beginnings of writing and simple memory aids all demonstrate that even at early stages of historical development humans went beyond the limits of the psychological functions given to them by nature and proceeded to a new culturally elaborated organization of their behavior. Comparative analysis shows that such activity is absent in even the highest species of animals; we believe that these sign operations are the product of specific conditions of *social* development. (1978, pp. 38–39)

In this passage Vygotsky touched on four major criteria that he used to distinguish between elementary and higher mental functions: (1) the shift of control from environment to the individual, that is, the emergence of voluntary regulation; (2) the emergence of conscious realization of mental processes; (3) the social origins and social nature of higher mental functions; and (4) the use of signs to mediate higher mental functions.

The first characteristic that distinguishes elementary from higher mental processes is that the former are subject to the control of the environment, whereas the latter are subject to self-regulation. According to Vygotsky, "The central characteristic of elementary functions is that they are totally and directly determined by stimulation from the environment. For higher functions, the central feature is self-generated stimulation, that is, the creation and use of artificial stimuli which become the immediate causes of behavior" (ibid., p. 39). In his early work Vygotsky developed this idea by utilizing a Pavlovian model of stimulus-response connections in which higher mental functions involve an intervening link between an external stimulus and the organism's response. He argued that this reflects the fact that higher mental functions are "more complex genetically and functionally" (1960, p. 109). Pursuing this Pavlovian line of argument, he wrote:

The line common to both of these forms [that is, elementary and higher mental functions] is the stimulus-response relation. For one form the essential feature is the essentially complete determination of behavior by stimulation. For the other, the equally essential feature is *autostimulation,* the creation and use of artificial stimulus-means and the determination of one's own behavior through their use.

In all of the cases we have examined, human behavior is uniquely defined not by the presence of stimulation but by the new or changed psychological situation that is created by humans themselves. The creation and use of artificial stimuli as auxiliary means for mastering one's own reactions is the foundation for the new form of determining behavior that distinguishes higher from elementary forms of behavior. (Ibid.)

The second, very closely related, criterion that distinguishes higher from elementary mental functions is their "intellectualization," or conscious realization. This criterion has recently been examined further by researchers such as M. Donaldson (1978). Vygotsky wrote of:

higher psychological functions whose basic and distinguishing features are intellectualization and mastery, that is, conscious realization and voluntariness.

At the center of development during the school age is the transition from lower functions of attention and memory to higher functions of voluntary attention and logical memory . . . the intellectualization of functions and their mastery represent two moments of one and the same process—the transition to higher psychological functions. We master a function to the degree that it is intellectualized. The voluntariness in the activity of a function is always the other side of its conscious realization. To say that memory is intellectualized in school is exactly the same as to say that voluntary recall emerges; to say that attention becomes voluntary in school age is exactly the same as saying . . . that it depends more and more on thought, that is, on intellect. (1934a, pp. 188–189)

The third criterion that characterizes higher, but not elementary, mental functions is their social origin and social nature. Vygotsky argued that "it is not nature, but society that above all else must be considered to be the determining factor in human behavior" (1960, p. 118). He was particularly interested in how social interaction in small groups or dyads leads to higher mental functioning in the individual. For him, "this transition from a social influence external to the individual to a social influence internal to the individual . . . is at the center of our research" (1960, p. 116).

The fourth distinguishing criterion is mediation. In Vygotsky's view voluntary control, conscious realization, and the social nature of higher mental processes all presuppose the existence of psychological tools, or signs, that can be used to control one's own and others' activity. This leads once more to the conclusion that the notion of mediation is analytically prior to other aspects of Vygotsky's conceptual framework. According to Vygotsky, "The presence of *created,* along with *given,* stimuli is in our view the distinguishing feature of human psychology" (ibid., p. 109).

Thus voluntary control, conscious realization, social origins and nature, and mediation by psychological tools characterize higher mental functioning in Vygotsky's account. Elementary mental functioning, in contrast, is characterized by control by the natural environment, an absence of conscious realization, individual origins, and a lack of mediation by psychological tools.

Genetic Domains in Vygotsky's Approach

Vygotsky conducted most of his empirical research on elementary and higher mental functioning in the ontogenetic domain. His genetic analysis, however, cannot be equated with the study of child development. Indeed he specifically argued that, like other forms of development, ontogenesis can be properly understood only as part of a larger, integrated picture involving several genetic domains. In the introduction to their volume on development, Vygotsky and Luria wrote:

> Our task [in this volume] was to trace *three basic lines* in the development of behavior—the evolutionary, historical, and ontogenetic lines—and to show that the behavior of acculturated humans is the product *of all three lines* of development, to show that behavior can be understood and explained scientifically only with the help of *three different paths from which the history of human behavior takes shape.* (1930, p. 3)

Phylogenesis

Vygotsky's writings on phylogenesis focus on a comparison between higher apes and humans. Drawing heavily on the research of W. Köhler (1921a, 1921b, 1925) on tool-mediated practical activity in chimpanzees and gorillas, he viewed tool use as one of the conditions that set the stage for the emergence of higher mental functions: "the ability to invent and use tools is a *prerequisite* for the historical development of humans and already emerged in the zoological period of the development of our ancestors" (1960, p. 421).

Vygotsky's view that tool use is a *necessary but not sufficient* condition for the emergence of uniquely human higher mental functions allowed him to recognize the close phylogenetic affinity between apes and humans while insisting on the qualitative gulf that separates them. Much of his criticism of the psychological theories of his time was based on their failure to recognize the dual nature of this relationship. For example, he argued that one of the major weaknesses of reflexology and behaviorism was that these approaches implicitly attempted to reduce human behavior to animal behavior by trying to explain the former solely in terms of a "collection of habits worked out through the method of 'trial and error,' habits that are distinguished from the behavior of animals only in degree of complexity but not in principle, in qualitative terms" (ibid., p. 439). This form of reductionism results from a focus solely on the "necessary" portion of Vygotsky's formulation and a disregard for the "but not sufficient" portion.

Vygotsky also rejected the notion that the differences which separate the functioning of humans and apes could be explained entirely on the basis of phylogenetic change. This is not to say that he viewed such change as having nothing to do with the transition from apes to humans. He specifically noted that "within the confines of evolutionary theory itself one cannot ignore the fact of essential differences that exist between the human organism [and that of apes], in particular, differences in the human brain and the brain of the ape" (ibid., p. 440). However, in his view "the problem of 'animal-human' cannot be fully resolved on the basis of evolutionary theory. Evolutionary theory is only the prerequisite for the scientific construction of human psychology. It cannot encompass all of it. Human behavior must be examined from another perspective as well" (ibid., pp. 439–440).

The other perspective that Vygotsky had in mind involves forms of mediation and associated changes in social and psychological life. Vygotsky argued that the use of technical tools provides the foundation for socially organized labor activity. With the appearance of labor, the development of mental functioning is grounded in qualitatively new principles. According to Vygotsky, in order for the transformation from ape to human to be completed, "there must emerge a special, new form of adapting to nature, one that is alien to the ape—namely labor. As *Engels* showed, labor is the basic factor in the transformation of apes into humans. 'It is the first, basic condition of human existence.

This is so to such an extent that we must say in a well-known sense that labor created humans' " (1930, p. 50). This is part of the more general argument devised by Vygotsky and Luria about the relationship between types of development:

> One process of development dialectically paves the way for the following and is transformed and crosses over to a new type of development. We do not think that it is possible to place all three processes [phylogenesis, social history, ontogenesis] along a single continuum. Rather, we propose that each higher type of development begins where the preceding one finishes and serves as its continuation in a new direction. This change in direction and in mechanisms of development by no means precludes the possibility of a connection between one process and another. Indeed, it presupposes such a connection.   (ibid., p. 5)

Although Vygotsky's claims about the role of mediation by tools and speech in the development of labor can be traced to Marxist writings, especially those of Engels, he attached greater importance to the influence of semiotic phenomena than is typically found in Marxist approaches. Whereas Marx clearly emphasized the emergence of socially organized labor and production as the key to distinguishing humans from animals, Vygotsky considered the emergence of speech to be equally important. In this connection he made his most important and unique contributions but also departed in significant ways from the ideas of Marx and even Engels.

In the years since Vygotsky produced his account of the genesis of mental functions, disciplines such as primatology and physical and cultural anthropology have made advances that call into question some of his claims about phylogenesis. Of particular concern is his understanding of the relationship between phylogenetic change and the onset of culture.

Inherent in Vygotsky's account of organic evolution is the claim that it proceeds up to a point where culture can emerge, and then this evolution ceases. He envisioned virtually no overlap between the two types of genesis. Vygotsky's claims constitute what C. Geertz has termed a "critical point theory of the appearance of culture" (1973, p. 62). Such a theory views the emergence of the capacity for acquiring culture as a "sudden, all-or-none type of occurrence in the phylogeny of the primates" (ibid., pp. 62–63).

Like other scholars interested in the evolution of the human mind (for instance, Habermas, 1979), Geertz argues that recent findings in physical anthropology make critical point theories untenable. The findings show that the transition from primates to humans occurred over a much longer time span (more than four million years) than had formerly been believed. Furthermore, during early phases of this period of hominidization, certain elements of culture were in evidence with Australopithecines, such as "simple toolmaking, sporadic 'hunting,' and perhaps some system of communication more advanced than that of contemporary apes and less advanced than that of true speech" (Geertz, 1973, p. 64). Hence the beginnings of culture can be traced to a time *preceding* the point where organic evolution ceased, a finding that undermines any critical point theory.

The recognition that biological and cultural development do not occur in isolation suggests that the biological substrate of mental processes may have emerged partially *in response to* cultural pressures. Geertz's reasoning on this issue indicates a need to revise certain aspects of Vygotsky's account of change in the phylogenetic domain. Instead of assuming that organic evolution and sociocultural development are isolated processes and that the latter got under way only after the former was completed, it now becomes essential to consider the ways that organic evolution may have been influenced by early forms of culture.

Thus Vygotsky's specific claims about the nature of transition points are no longer acceptable as stated. However, this observation does not call into question the general form of his argument. In particular, it does not weaken his claim that with the emergence of sociocultural activity the very nature of development changed.

Sociocultural History

As in the case of phylogenesis, Vygotsky's claims about sociocultural history were primarily theoretical and relied on the writings of others. Yet his ideas about this genetic domain played such a central role in the formulation of his approach that in the USSR it is often referred to as the "sociohistorical" or "cultural-historical" approach to the study of mind (Smirnov, 1975; see also Luria, 1971).

In accordance with the basic theoretical tenets that underlie his genetic analysis, Vygotsky assumed that a unique set of explanatory principles applies to the domain of sociocultural history. In particular, he stressed the difference between this and the phylogenetic domain: "the process of the historical development of human behavior and the process of its biological evolution do not coincide; one is not a continuation of the other. Rather each of these processes is governed by its own laws" (1930, p. 71). Such a claim raises the issue of what principles or laws apply to sociocultural history. If the principles of Darwinian evolution are posited as governing phylogenesis, what mechanisms and explanatory principles must be incorporated into an approach to account for sociocultural change?

Vygotsky, along with other Soviet psychologists, semioticians, and philosophers working in his tradition, considered this question to be central in any attempt to construct an account of human mental processes. The first step toward an answer is reflected in the following statement by A. A. Leont'ev:

> The evolution of the species "homo sapiens" . . . has proceeded in some other different sphere than the biological, the species characteristics being accumulated not in the form of morphological changes, but in some other form. It has been a sphere of social human life, a form of the fixation of achievements of human activities in the social and historical experience of humanity . . . Man learns from the errors—and still more from the successes—of other people while each generation of animal can learn solely from its own . . . It is mankind as a whole, but not a separate human being, who interacts with the biological environment; therefore such laws of evolution as, for example, the law of natural selection become invalid inside the human society. (1970, pp. 123–124)

To account for the psychological correlates of sociohistorical change that Leont'ev has in mind here, one must invoke Vygotsky's distinction between "rudimentary" and "higher" mental functions. This dichotomy is not simply another pair of terms for the distinction between elementary and higher mental functions. Rather, it is a distinction between levels of development *within* higher mental functions. Vygotsky stated, "In our view rudimentary and higher functions are the extreme poles of one and the same system of behavior. They are its lower and higher points; they designate the boundaries within which all the levels and forms of higher functions are distributed" (1960, pp. 88–89).

It follows that rudimentary mental functions are characterized by the properties of higher (as opposed to elementary) mental functions. However, these properties, especially those of the mediational means, are manifested only in an early stage of the development of higher mental functions. In order to avoid confusion over terminology, I shall reserve the term "higher mental function" for the general type of function that contrasts with elementary mental functions. When dealing with developmental levels *within* higher mental functions, I shall employ the terms "rudimentary higher mental functions" and "advanced higher mental functions."

Clearly Vygotsky viewed rudimentary and advanced higher mental functions in terms of a genetic progression: "the structure of [advanced] higher forms appears in a pure form in these psychological fossils, in these living remnants of ancient epochs. These rudimentary [higher] functions reveal to us the previous state of all [advanced] higher mental processes; they reveal the type of organization which they once possessed" (1960, p. 108).

To assert that rudimentary and advanced higher mental functions exist in such a genetic relationship says nothing about the specific mechanism of change Vygotsky envisioned as connecting them. Not surprisingly, in order to understand Vygotsky's account of this mechanism one must once again turn to the issue of mediational means.

Sign mediation in sociocultural history is only one of several foci of analysis that Vygotsky could have chosen. As S. Scribner (1985) has noted, "all aspects of the historical progress of humankind were not of equal importance to Vygotsky. He was concerned with those forms of social life that have the most profound consequences for mental life. As we know, he thought these to lie primarily in the symbolic-communicative spheres of activity in which humans collectively produce new means for regulating their behavior" (p. 123). This focus is not necessarily the most obvious choice for someone trying to reformulate psychology from a Marxist perspective. It reflects the fact that Vygotsky gave a more central role to mediation, especially mediation by signs, than is found in most other attempts to formulate a Marxist psychology (compare Leont'ev, 1959; Seve 1978).

The basic metric by which Vygotsky measured sociocultural history was the emergence and change of psychological tools. This fact is evident in statements such as, "The behavioral development of humans is already development that is fundamentally governed not by the laws of biological evolution but by laws of the historical development of society. The perfecting of 'means of labor' and 'means of behavior' in the form of language and other sign systems that serve as auxiliary tools in the process of mastering behavior take on a primary role" (1930, p. 54).

In his account of the history of signs as mnemotechnical devises and means of calculation as well as in his explanation of the relationship between thinking and speech, Vygotsky envisioned an overarching principle of development. This principle, which I shall label the *principle of decontextualization of mediational means,*[2] replaced those of Darwinian evolution after the emergence of culture. The decontextualization of mediational means is the process whereby the meaning of signs become less and less dependent on the unique spatiotemporal context in which they are used. A focus on the decontextualization of mediational means emerges repeatedly in Vygotsky's account of the sociocultural history of higher mental functions. For him it fulfilled the fundamental requirement of his genetic analysis that different explanatory principles apply to phases of development separated by a qualitative genetic transition.

An example of this concept can be found in Vygotsky's examination of quantitative operations, or calculation. He argued that the forms of counting observed in primitives is heavily dependent on the context; that is, counting relies on the perception of concrete objects and settings. This relationship does not preclude the ability to make fine distinctions between quantities, but the distinctions are based on judgments about concrete, perceptually present objects (objects in the specific context where signs are used).

In calculation, decontextualization is tied to the emergence of a number system in which a quantity can be represented independently of any concrete perceptual context. Indeed quantity can become an abstract object itself instead of a meaning tied to a set of concrete objects. With decontextualization it becomes possible to talk about two or three without specifying two or three *what*. Systematization makes it possible to account for the meaning of mathematical signs without relying on the context of their use or application. Thus two can be defined from *within* the number system as one plus one, three minus one, four minus two, and so on.

In collaboration with his student and colleague Luria, Vygotsky conducted a set of studies that bear on the issue of decontextualization of mediational means in the genetic domain of sociocultural history. These studies were carried out in Soviet Central Asia in the 1930s. Because of the academic and political debates in the USSR during the 1930s and 1940s (see Cole, 1979), the publication of the findings from this research was delayed for several decades (Luria, 1975b).

In the West this research would usually be considered cross-cultural. But from the perspective of a Vygotskian approach it would be more appropriate to consider it "cross-historical," because Luria and Vygotsky were concerned with the influence of sociocultural institutions from one historical era on the cognitive activity of individuals whose socialization had occurred amid institutions from another era. Soviet Central Asia served as an ideal cross-historical laboratory because the population was in the midst of collectivization, a process in which they were rapidly introduced to practices and skills from societies of a different era as viewed from the perspective of historical materialism.

Luria and Vygotsky compared the performance of nonliterate subjects on a series of reasoning tasks with that of subjects who had recently acquired literacy skills. The tasks required them to do such things as categorize familiar objects or deduce the conclusion that follows from the premises of a syllogism. For example, in one task subjects were given pictures of a hammer, a saw, a log, and a hatchet and asked to say which three go together. Literate subjects were generally willing to say that the hammer, hatchet, and saw go together because they are all tools. That is, they grouped objects on the basis of abstract word meanings ("hammer," "saw" and "hatchet," but not "log," are hyponyms of "tool"). In contrast, the answers of nonliterate subjects indicated a strong tendency to group items on the basis of concrete settings with which they were familiar. Thus they might say that "the log has to be here too." Such subjects typically resisted suggestions by the experimenter that the hammer, hatchet, and saw could be grouped together—suggestions grounded in decontextualized word meanings and hierarchical relationships among them.

On the basis of his empirical findings Luria (1975b) concluded that some major differences exist between literate and nonliterate subjects in their use of abstract (that is, decontextualized) reasoning processes. His conclusions are similar to those of researchers such as D. R. Olson (1977, 1980) and L. F. M. Scinto (in press) about the effects of developing literacy in ontogenesis. Luria argued that subjects who had some experience in formal educational settings were willing to utilize decontextualized categories and assertions, whereas subjects with no such experience had much greater difficulty in doing so:

> This tendency to rely on operations used in practical life was the controlling factor among uneducated and illiterate subjects . . . The somewhat more educated group of subjects employed categorical classification as their method of grouping objects even

though they had had only a year or two of schooling. For example, when we asked them which of the following objects go together . . . a glass, saucepan, spectacles, and a bottle . . . they immediately responded, "The glass, the spectacles, and the bottle go together. They are made of glass, but the saucepan is metal." (1979, p. 71)

In his study of the subject's performance on syllogistic reasoning tasks, Luria found results analogous to those from his categorization studies: "the process of reasoning and deduction associated with immediate practical experience dominates the responses of our nonliterate subjects" (ibid., p. 79). As in the categorization experiments, higher-level performance on syllogistic reasoning tasks required subjects to use language in a decontextualized manner.

Thus Luria and Vygotsky's studies revealed a major difference between literate and nonliterate subjects in their utilization of decontextualized mediational means, in particular, language. Literate subjects demonstrated a willingness and an ability to operate with linguistic objects and a linguistically created reality. They categorized objects, accepted premises, and derived conclusions strictly on the basis of linguistic means. Nonliterate subjects did not demonstrate such tendencies. Instead, they invoked nonlinguistic, practical experience in their reasoning.

When reviewing these results, Luria sometimes argued that the emergence of theoretical reasoning can be traced to subjects' participation in the institutions of a more advanced stage of social evolution. For example, when outlining characteristics of the population in Central Asia, he asserted that "as a result of societal changes and the cultural revolution, they were integrated into a culture in a very short time. Nonliteracy was stamped out, and elementary forms of individual economic life were replaced by a collective economy. These changes could hardly help but lead to the appearance of new forms of thinking" (1981, p. 207).

It is unclear whether it was literacy per se (that is, the ability to encode and decode written text) or a generally new social institutional framework that Luria considered responsible for the new forms of thinking that concerned him. Of course the two issues are closely connected, since literacy is usually learned in a specific social institution—formal schooling. However, as investigators like H. Mehan (1979) have argued, a student is also involved in learning a set of complex role relationships, general cognitive techniques, ways of approaching problems, and the like. Therefore the question arises as to whether it is possible to separate the influence of the mastery of literacy from the influence of formal schooling.

In the past few decades several studies in anthropology and psychology have addressed this question. In some cases (for example, Cole and Scribner, 1974; Scribner, 1977; Scribner and Cole, 1981) this research was explicitly motivated by issues in Vygotsky's theoretical framework; in other cases (such as Goody, 1977) this influence is less explicit but the line of reasoning remains consistent with that proposed by Vygotsky. Much of the research has revealed and examined an implicit assumption in Vygotsky's argument, namely, that the acquisition of literacy automatically results in an increased decontextualization of mediational means. For example, Vygotsky's interpretation of the findings from his and Luria's studies in Central Asia is based on the assumption that in acquiring literacy, humans acquire the ability to utilize signs in less-context-bound ways. Indeed it could be said that they simply equated certain phases of decontextualization with literacy.

The problem is that this approach fails to recognize specific properties and types of literacy and the forms of abstraction that may derive from them. Vygotsky and his followers generally assumed that literacy is a homogeneous phenomenon that has a uniform impact on all aspects of higher mental functioning.

This set of assumptions has been questioned by Scribner and Cole (1981). Specifically, they have addressed two issues with major implications for a Vygotskian interpretation of the relationships among literacy, decontextualization, and higher mental functions. First, they explored the question of whether literacy can be equated with schooling. It may be that participation in the activities of formal schooling rather than literacy per se is what affects mental functioning. Although formal schooling and the acquisition of literacy are in most cases closely linked, it is possible to separate them conceptually and sometimes even empirically, thereby permitting concrete investigation of this issue. Second, Scribner and Cole examined the related question of whether it is possible to distinguish among forms of literacy that serve different functional roles in the life of the individual and society.

Scribner and Cole compared the performance of subgroups of Vai subjects in Liberia on cognitive tasks. Their choice of a research site was influenced by the fact that literacy and schooling are not always coterminous among the Vai. In addition to literacy in English, which is acquired in formal schooling settings, there exists literacy in Vai, "an indigenous script, transmitted outside an institutional setting and having no connection with Western-style school" (1981, p. 19). The second form of literacy is used primarily for keeping personal records and for writing commercial correspondence. Finally, many of the Vai in this study had acquired literacy in Arabic, primarily for the purpose of reading, reciting, and memorizing the Qur'an. This third form of literacy is so tightly connected with religious text activities that Scribner and Cole argue that "for most informants in our sample, 'Qur'anic' is a more appropriate description of their literate activities than 'Arabic' " (ibid., p. 83).

Since some groups of Vai are versed in only one type of literacy, Scribner and Cole had the opportunity to "disentangle literacy effects from school effects" (ibid., p. 19) by comparing several subgroups: (a) subjects who had acquired English literacy in formal schooling settings; (b) subjects who had acquired Arabic literacy in instructional settings devoted to memorizing the Qur'an; (c) subjects who had acquired literacy in a Vai syllabic writing system through informal self-instruction; and (d) nonliterates.

Findings from these comparisons are particularly relevant because Scribner and Cole examined subjects' performance on categorization and syllogistic reasoning tasks similar to those used by Vygotsky and his colleagues. The results call into question Vygotsky's assumptions about the relationships among literacy, decontextualization, and higher mental functions:

> Under conditions obtaining in Vai society, neither syllabic Vai script nor Arabic alphabetic literacy was associated with what are considered the higher-order intellectual skills. Neither literacy enhanced the use of taxonomic skills on any task designed to test categorization. Nor did either contribute to a shift toward syllogistic reasoning . . . nonschooled literacy, as we found and tested it among the Vai, does not produce general cognitive effects as we have defined them. The small and selective nature of Vai script and Arabic influences on cognitive performance precludes any sweeping generalizations about literacy and cognitive change. (1981, p. 132)

In contrast to the two forms of nonschooled literacy, literacy in English, acquired in a school setting, is associated with some types of decontextualization envisioned by Vygotsky. Scribner and Cole's most impressive finding is the tendency of English-literate subjects to formulate accurate, informative verbal accounts of task settings by relying on general, relatively decontextualized meanings. They assessed this result by examining the subjects' use of linguistic means, such as general class and attribute expressions, to provide well-structured, informative explanations and justifications of the principles employed to carry out a task. On this basis they concluded that "schooling affects verbal explanations over and above any influences it may exert on successful execution of the task itself" (ibid., p. 131).

Scribner and Cole did not find that their schooled, English-literate subjects consistently differed from other groups in their performance of the tasks themselves. They argued that this could be attributed to several causes, including the fact that many of their subjects had been out of school for a number of years. Hence they do not view their results as refuting the widely reported findings (for example, Rogoff, 1981) that increased schooling, when still ongoing or recently completed, is related to improved performance on categorization and abstract reasoning tasks. Their results do, however, call into question any claim that the effects of schooling are permanent. Following a line of argument similar to that of P. Tulviste (1978a), who has found that under certain circumstances schooling has only temporary effects on syllogistic reasoning, Scribner and Cole speculate that "even if we were to accept as a working proposition that school produces general changes in certain intellectual operations, we might have to qualify the conclusion to refer only to students, recent ex-students, or those continuing in schoolike occupations," (1981, p. 131).

A general claim about the impermanence of the effects of schooling and literacy is not necessarily inconsistent with Luria and Vygotsky's argument, since they never really addressed the issue. However, Scribner and Cole did not find *all* effects of schooled literacy to be impermanent. Rather, they found that their English-literate subjects did outperform other groups in providing informative verbal descriptions and justifications of their task activity. Superior task performance was also reported for the subgroup that had recently been in school. This combination of facts suggests that both task performance and verbal description of task performance may have improved as a result of schooled literacy, but that the former was relatively transient.

Vygotsky may have failed to recognize the difference between task performances and verbal description of task performance because he and Luria examined subjects who were in school or had recently been in school at the time of testing. When subjects are tested at this point, both verbal description and task performance are likely to be affected.

Hence the pattern of Luria and Vygotsky's empirical results was not conducive to their separating decontextualization of mediational means as reflected in subjects' explanations and higher mental functioning.

A second reason for their failure to recognize this distinction has to do with the empirical and analytic techniques used—specifically, with whether Luria and Vygotsky's experimental procedures measured the level of decontextualization, the level of higher mental functioning, or both. Vygotsky's approach encourages one to search for the relationships between such abilities rather than to isolate them. However, by using careful experimental and analytic procedures, Scribner and Cole were able to separate these two performance domains to some degree, and when they did so they were able to document differences in performance levels.

In summary, the research of Scribner and Cole calls into question Vygotsky's assumptions about the relationship between literacy and the decontextualization of mediational means on the one hand and between decontextualization and higher mental functioning on the other. Their findings indicate that it is not possible to draw a single dichotomy between people who are literate, schooled, capable of using decontextualized mediational means, and likely to use advanced higher mental functions on the one hand and people who cannot be characterized by any of these terms on the other. These relationships are more complex. It is possible to observe literacy in the absence of facility with decontextualized mediational means and advanced forms of higher mental functioning; it is possible to observe literacy with decontextualization but without a tendency to use advanced forms of higher mental functioning in actual task performance—and so on.

Given all these qualifications, Vygotsky's basic reasoning about change in the historical domain may seem no longer tenable. However, I would argue that his claims are ultimately based on the relationship between the decontextualization of mediational means and the emergence of advanced forms of higher mental functioning. While certain assumptions about the relationships among literacy, decontextualization, and higher mental functioning may not be accurate, decontextualization of mediational means as a general explanatory principle in the historical domain is not necessarily invalid.

A more serious challenge to Vygotsky's claims might appear to come from Scribner and Cole's argument about the effects of schooling above and beyond those of literacy. They suggest that "a practice account of literacy" may provide a more satisfactory approach than one based on literacy alone. Such an account concerns the general question of how "socially organized activities may come to have consequences for human thought" (1981, p. 235). However, Scribner and Cole's argument still rests fundamentally on issues of mediational means and their decontextualization, because schooling itself is inherently concerned with the manipulation of mediational means (natural language, mathematical symbols, and the like). Hence any statistically identifiable schooling effect still is tied directly to the mediational potential of signs.

In their conclusions on the effect of schooling, Scribner and Cole are still arguing for a practice account of literacy, that is, a practice account grounded in mediational means. Thus their findings demonstrate that the important point is not simply whether one is literate by some basic criterion, namely, that one can encode and decode graphic symbols; rather, it is how one *uses* such literacy that governs decontextualization and any consequences for higher mental functioning.

Clearly the facts and assumptions underlying Vygotsky's account of the sociohistorical domain are open to question in light of recent research. After reviewing some of the criticisms and proposed revisions, however, it seems to me that Vygotsky's basic line of reasoning remains intact: that is, phylogenesis and sociocultural history must be kept distinct because fundamentally different sets of explanatory principles apply to each. In Vygotsky's terms the very nature of development changes when one moves from one genetic domain to the other. Furthermore, the explanatory principle that Vygotsky saw as applying to the sociohistorical domain is concerned with mediation. Specifically, genetic change in this domain is attributed to the decontextualization of mediational means.

Ontogenesis

Vygotsky and his followers are best known in the USSR and in the West for their studies of ontogenesis. They conducted most of their theoretical and empirical research in this domain partly because it can be observed over its entirety and is thus more "accessible" than phylogenesis and social history. In addition, their focus was motivated by Soviet psychologists' desire to play an active role in the construction of a new socialist society, a task that required a better understanding of child development and education.

Vygotsky's approach cannot be understood by examining his account of ontogenesis in isolation. At several points he utilized information and modes of reasoning derived from his analysis of other genetic domains. This is not to say that he saw simple parallelisms between ontogenesis and other domains. Indeed he explicitly rejected arguments such as those in which ontogenesis is seen as recapitulating phylogenesis. His concern with multiple domains was not motivated simply by a desire to have several perspectives on one general process of development. Rather, he emphasized that the various domains involve different forms of development, each governed by its unique set of explanatory principles. This argument applies no less to ontogenesis than to phylogenesis and social history.

The main criterion that distinguishes ontogenesis from other domains for Vygotsky is the fact that ontogenesis involves the simultaneous, interrelated operation of more than one force of development. While this domain has the advantage of being observable in its entirety, it has the disadvantage of precluding the study of any developmental force in isolation. Unlike phylogenesis, for example, where one can study the operation of a single set of explanatory principles apart from those that govern other genetic domains, ontogenesis necessarily involves the simultaneous operation of more than one developmental force. Vygotsky saw it as involving both a "natural" and a "social" or "cultural" line of development:

> The cultural development of the child is characterized first by the fact that it transpires under conditions of dynamic organic changes. Cultural development is superimposed on the processes of growth, maturation, and the organic development of the child. It forms a single whole with these processes. It is only through abstraction that we can separate one set of processes from others.
>
> The growth of the normal child into civilization usually involves a fusion with the processes of organic maturation. Both planes of development—the natural and the cultural—coincide and mingle with one another. The two lines of change interpenetrate one another and essentially form a single line of sociobiological formation of the child's personality. (1960, p. 47)

This simultaneous operation of natural and cultural forces led Vygotsky to reject any claims about close parallels between ontogenesis and other genetic domains. For instance, he rejected the notion that ontogenesis recapitulates social history because social forces function in relative isolation in the latter. One member of the Vygotskian school, Tulviste (1978b), has formulated this point as follows: "In contrast to ontogenesis, the natural maturation of the brain does not play a role in the course of historical development (Vygotsky, 1960; Luria, 1971).

The natural course of the historical development of cognitive processes is the historical development of society" (p. 83). Such differences led Vygotsky to argue that a complete genetic analysis of human psychological processes calls upon the investigator to integrate facts from several domains. While ontogenetic studies form an essential part of this analysis, there are certain inherent limitations in such studies because more than one developmental force is always in operation. The way to deal with this problem is to supplement the findings from one genetic domain with those from others. For example, when investigating certain problems, one can utilize data from ontogenesis but one must also "turn to phylogenesis, where the two lines (the natural and the cultural) are not united and intermingled, in order to unravel the complex knot that we find in child psychology"(1960, p. 39).

Vygotsky's distinction between natural and cultural lines of development is closely linked to the distinction between elementary and higher mental functions. The natural line of development is generally associated with elementary mental functions, and the cultural line with higher mental functions. Furthermore, natural development is explained primarily on the basis of biological principles, whereas cultural development is attributed to principles that apply to mediational means, including the principle of decontextualization.

Vygotsky's claim about the intermingling of lines of development presents a major challenge for the investigator concerned with ontogenesis. While the two lines of development cannot be empirically separated, this domain is nonetheless regarded as properly conceptualized in terms of the interaction and mutual transformation of separate forces. The forces are not viewed as being additive or as simply supplanting each other in importance, as in the transition from phylogenetic to sociohistorical change. Instead, they operate in tandem to form a qualitatively unique explanatory framework.

Vygotsky's multidomain strategy avoids two fundamental forms of reductionism that often emerge in ontogenetic research. First, it avoids the pitfall of assuming that all aspects of cognitive development can be explained on the basis of principles devised to account for biological phenomena. With regard to contemporary theories, this is a point where Vygotsky's approach may be seen to differ from Piaget's. Rather than assuming that a single set of explanatory principles, such as adaptation and equilibration, can account for all aspects of cognitive development, Vygotsky argued that such principles need to be incorporated into a larger explanatory framework that deals with sociocultural phenomena as well.

The second form of reductionism that Vygotsky was striving to avoid might be termed "cultural reductionism," because it rests on the premise that human psychological processes can be explained solely on the basis of mastery and internalization of symbolic means or sociocultural practices. Such accounts often ignore biological forces and other constraints involved in ontogenesis. Vygotsky clearly rejected what I am calling cultural reductionism, a fact reflected most clearly in his critique of idealism and subjective psychology.

Vygotsky's explanation of the dynamics of ontogenesis rests on the assumption that the natural line of development may operate in relative isolation in early childhood but is soon integrated with the cultural line in a process of "emergent interactionism" (Kohlberg and Wertsch, in press). According to this position the explanatory principles that account for development must be *derived* from those that apply to the two separate forces of development, but they cannot be *reduced* to the principles that apply to either one in isolation.

Whereas Vygotsky's theoretical approach clearly led him to view ontogenesis in terms of interacting forces of development, his empirical psychological research often focused on only one of these forces as if it could be studied in isolation. Such inconsistencies have been noted by others. For example, V. V. Davydov and L. A. Radzikhovskii (1985) have argued that one must distinguish between "Vygotsky the methodologist"[3] and "Vygotsky the psychologist."

In his claims about the fusion of natural and cultural forces in ontogenesis, resulting in a "single line of sociobiological formation," Vygotsky's empirical procedures strayed from his theoretical dictates in several ways. The first inconsistency concerns what might be termed "direction of influence." Whereas Vygotsky's theoretical statements call for a "fusion" in which "both planes of development . . . coincide and mingle with one another" (1960, p. 47), in practice he focused almost exclusively on the ways in which cultural forces transform the natural line of development. That is, he tended to view the natural line as providing "raw materials" that are then transformed by cultural forces. He said virtually nothing about how changes in the natural line of development might affect cultural forces.

I would argue that his focus on only one of the two possible directions of influence is an echo of the relationship Vygotsky saw between the phylogenetic and sociocultural domains. Without falling into any full-fledged form of recapitualism, he did seem to see a parallel between the necessary but not sufficient conditions provided by phylogenesis on the one hand and the functioning of the natural line of development in ontogenesis on the other. That is, he assumed that natural forces cease to play an active role in ontogenetic change after an early period and that cultural forces thereafter take on the leading role. This is not to say that constraints from the natural line are no longer in effect. Just as in phylogenesis, the natural line in ontogenesis is viewed as proving necessary but not sufficient conditions for the operation of social forces. However, the natural line itself is seen as no longer providing a major independent source of change. Rather, it contributes a static framework within which cultural forces can operate. In contrast, Vygotsky claimed that cultural forces evolve and continue to play an active role in ontogenesis. Such a line of reasoning is reflected in his statement that "organic maturation plays the part of a *condition* rather than a motive power of the process of cultural development, since the structure of that process is defined by outward influences" (1929, p. 423).

This problem is closely tied to a second one, namely, the claim that during early phases of ontogenesis natural and cultural forces operate completely independently. Vygotsky made this statement at a time when little was known of the complex social and cognitive functioning of infants. Only in the years since his death have investigators such as J. Piaget (1952), T. G. R. Bower (1974), Bruner (1975a), and S. Sugarman (1983) made the major advances in infant research that inform present theoretical discussions. As a result, Vygotsky's claims about early phases of natural and cultural lines of development in ontogenesis are unsophisticated by today's standards. This has led to several critical comments on his idea that the two lines of development are completely separate during infancy. In a review of his theoretical approach Leont'ev and Luria point out that "after all, even in children at the very earliest ages mental processes are being formed under the influence of verbal social interaction with the adults who surround them. Consequently these mental processes are not 'natural'" (1960, p. 7). In the USSR M. I. Lisina (1974, 1978) and her colleagues (such as Vetrova, 1975; Elagina, 1977) conducted a series of studies in which they examined the early influence of social forces on memory and other mental processes. One implication of their studies is that the social and natural line of development are intertwined from the earliest phases of ontogenesis.

The two problems I have outlined in Vygotsky's account of ontogenesis are relatively minor, in that it would be possible to make appropriate revisions in his approach by incorporating updated theoretical and empirical findings. The third way in which Vygotsky failed to implement his theoretical dictates about the natural and cultural lines of development also derives largely from the fact that at the time he was writing, little was known about the complex and rapid psychological development of infants. In this case, however, the problem is more serious because it calls into question one of the basic terms in his argument: the natural line of development.

Vygotsky never was clear about what he had in mind when dealing with natural development. His treatment of this issue leaves many unanswered questions, largely because in his concrete research Vygotsky focused almost exclusively on social or cultural development. He tended to analyze the natural line only to the extent necessary to begin a discussion of sociocultural factors. For example, in a fifty-page paper on the development of attention in ontogenesis, Vygotsky (1981c) spent only two pages on a general discussion of the differences between natural and social development and devoted the rest to social development.

What Vygotsky did say about natural development was often simply borrowed from other researchers' findings. For example, he tried to incorporate results of phylogenetic research into his account of ontogenesis by using findings from research on higher apes' problem-solving activity (as in Köhler, 1921a, 1921b, 1925). His assumption was that apes' problem-solving activity approximates what elementary mental functioning would be in human ontogenesis if this functioning were not influenced by cultural development. It would remain only an approximation since Vygotsky saw a phylogenetic gap separating apes from humans. However, it supposedly could provide insight into "pure" elementary mental functioning in humans. Employing such findings from comparative psychology is a reasonable procedure for devising an account of elementary mental functioning, but it constitutes only the first step in understanding the natural line of development in human ontogenesis. The fact that Vygotsky stopped at this point in outlining elementary mental functioning is largely responsible for the weaknesses in this aspect of his approach.

Criticisms of Vygotsky's superficial treatment of natural development usually fall into one of two basic categories: (a) the very notion of "natural" is unclear in Vygotsky's writings; and (b) his extreme emphasis on social development results in an explanatory system in which principles from the natural line in reality play no role.

At first glance, in addressing the natural line of development Vygotsky seemed to be speaking of changes in organic, especially neurophysiological, mechanisms or processes. On some occasions, however, he seemed to be concerned with natural *behaviors* or *activities* rather than with neurophysiological mechanisms. This inconsistency is reflected in the fact that he used several constructs, some relating to neurophysiological phenomena and others to patterns of behavior. For example, in his writings he contrasted "elementary" and "higher functions" (1978, p. 39), "low and higher forms of behavior and thinking" (1960, p. 15), "organic development" and "cultural development" (ibid, p. 47). In some cases the first member of the dichotomy clearly referred to neurophysiological mechanisms or processes; in others, Vygotsky was concerned with patterns of behavior or forms of activity. The latter are presocial and hence are not mediated by sociohistorically evolved sign systems, but they are not necessarily reducible to neurophysiological principles.

Vygotsky's apparent confusion derives from the fact that he did not always clearly equate the development of natural or elementary processes with neurophysiological development. Yet at some points he seems to have done so. For example, when considering early phases in the development of attention, he wrote: "We call this entire period in the development of the child the period of natural or primitive development. This term is appropriate because the development of attention in this period is a function of the general organizational development of the child—above all, the structural and functional development of the central nervous system" (1981c, p. 193).

The trouble with his approach is that it fails to account for the development of natural processes that arise from the organism's experience with the external, physical world. Such development, which is based neither on neurophysiological maturation nor on social factors, has been the focus of much research over the past several decades. In particular, the research of Piaget (1952) on the ontogenesis of intelligence in humans has amply demonstrated that Vygotsky's notion of natural development must be revised to include factors other than organic maturation. The revision would not drastically alter Vygotsky's fundamental line of reasoning about the development of higher mental functions, but it would change some of his ideas about the early stages of this development. Specifically, it would mean that the natural line of development could not be explained solely on the basis of organic maturation. Instead, a larger set of explanatory principles would have to be employed, including those proposed by Piaget for the development of sensorimotor intelligence.

Of course the very notion of emergent interactionism precludes the possibility of reducing Vygotsky's approach to Piaget's. Even if one expands the notion of natural development to encompass Piaget's analysis of sensorimotor intelligence, the two approaches still differ because of Vygotsky's assumption that a fundamentally new set of explanatory principles is required when the child enters into certain levels of social life in a culture.

Besides the confusion in Vygotsky's discussion of natural development, critics argue that because he neglected this line of development so completely, he really viewed thinking as the product of social factors alone. For example, S. L. Rubinshtein (1946) asserted that Vygotsky's account of word meaning elevated the social processes involved in speech to the role of sole creator of thinking. Most investigators have not carried out analyses as detailed as Rubenshtein's, but implicit in many accounts of Vygotsky's ideas is the notion that social processes alone somehow create psychological processes.

At least in principle Vygotsky clearly rejected this interpretation. For example, in the course of a discussion of mental retardation he stated, "We shall begin with the basic tenet that we have managed to establish in the analysis of higher mental functions. We saw that this tenet consists of acknowledging the natural foundations for cultural forms of behavior. Culture creates nothing; it only alters natural data in conformity with human goals" (1960, p. 200). Even though such statements reflect Vygotsky's methodological position on ontogenesis, they are seldom evidenced in his empirical studies.

Although Vygotsky's account of natural development is a weak link in his overall line of reasoning, I would not suggest that the weakness can be rectified by abandoning this aspect of his approach. Indeed I would argue that his theoretical approach could not remain intact if his claims about emergent interactionism were dismissed. His overriding interest in mediation may have led him to underemphasize the role of natural forces in ontogenesis, but his methodological argument cannot be reduced to one in which cognitive growth can be explained solely in terms of the acquisition of psychological tools. Such a "modification" would result in an approach that either rejects the notion that natural forces play a role in ontogenesis or completely isolates natural from cultural forces of development. Either alternative would lead to an incomplete and fundamentally inaccurate account of human mental processes according to Vygotsky's theoretical dictates.

Vygotsky's account of the dynamics of the ontogenetic domain can be summarized as follows. Development is viewed in terms of the relationship between natural and cultural forces. Although Vygotsky's theoretical statements suggest that the two lines enter into a relationship of mutual transformation, his concrete proposals and empirical research consistently reveal another interpretation, one that assumes a unidirectional influence: specifically, the practical intelligence of the natural line of development is transformed as a result of coming into contact with aspects of the social line. Even if one were to devise such a unidirectional account of the dynamics between these two forces, one would have to specify what is transformed as well as what transforms it. Vygotsky's failure to do the former is perhaps the most serious weakness in his account of ontogenesis. Recognition of this problem, however, does not mean that his approach can be reduced to one involving a single line of development. Instead, it seems most reasonable to say that this is a point at which his empirical research failed to explore an issue that is an essential part of his methodological framework.

While Vygotsky himself failed to conduct empirical research on the natural line of development and its relationship to sociocultural forces, other investigators have conducted studies relevant to these issues. Examples include the studies of H. Ginsburg and his associates on the development of mathematical skills (Ginsburg, 1982; Ginsburg, Posner, and Russell, 1981; Ginsburg and Allardice, 1984). Indeed certain aspects of their research are explicitly motivated by Vygotsky's theory.

In their studies they distinguish among three cognitive systems of mathematical knowledge or functioning. First, they identify "System 1" functioning, which "does not involve counting or other specific information or techniques transmitted by culture" (Ginsburg, 1982, p. 191). Because it is not transmitted by culture, it is termed "natural," and because it emerges independently of formal schooling, it is termed "informal." In System 1 functioning Ginsburg includes such things as the perception of more as described by A. Binet (1969) and skills for making judgments about one-to-one correspondence, equivalence, and seriation as outlined by Piaget.

The description of System 1 functioning corresponds with Vygotsky's notion of the natural line of development and elementary mental functioning: performance is closely tied to the concrete context and involves no culturally developed mediational means. Indeed, Vygotsky wrote of "natural arithmetic" in the ontogenetic domain: "The first stage [in the child's arithmetic ability] is formed by the natural arithmetical endowment of the child, that is, the operation of quantities before the child knows how to count. We include here the immediate conception of quantity, the comparison of greater and smaller groups, the recognition of some quantitative group, the distribution into single objects where it is necessary to divide, and so on" (1929, p. 427).

The next level of mathematical skills is Ginsburg's approach involves "System 2" functioning, which is characterized as "informal" because it still emerges outside of formal instructional settings, but also "cultural" because it utilizes socioculturally evolved sign systems (that is, number systems). The fact that some sort of sociocultural sign system is now introduced means that System 2 mathematical functioning cannot be subsumed under Vygotsky's heading of elementary mental functions. Hence System 2 skills are part of higher mental functioning. However, when compared with "System 3" functioning, the level at which the sign system is utilized in System 2 skills is rudimentary. The minimal utilization of the sign system in mediating mental functioning is attributable to the fact that it is still being used in a context-bound way. Numbers are employed to count concrete objects rather than serving as abstract objects to be operated on in their own right; that is, decontextualization has occurred only to a minimal degree. Given this set of characteristics of System 2 mathematical skills, I would argue that they correspond to rudimentary higher mental functioning in Vygotsky's theoretical framework.

The final type of mathematical functioning identified by Ginsburg, System 3, is characterized as "formal" because it is taught systematically in formal schooling environs, and "cultural" because it involves socioculturally evolved sign systems and is "transmitted by social agents" (1972, p. 192).

Ginsburg's description of System 3 skills is very similar to Vygotsky's notion of advanced higher mental functions. Socioculturally evolved mediational means are involved and are used in relatively decontextualized ways. The tendency toward decontextualization is reflected in a comment by Ginsburg and Allardice about "explicitly stated mathematical principles" (ibid.). Such principles are typically formulated to apply across various contexts, that is, they are context independent.

Ginsburg and his associates have made ontogenetic, cultural, and subcultural comparisons in their investigation of the three types of mathematical skills. They begin with the assumption that "certain System 1 skills, particularly those studied by Piaget, are extremely widespread and may be found in members of diverse cultural groups" (Ginsburg, 1982, p. 192). On the basis of cross-cultural research such as that reported by P. Dasen (1977), Ginsburg speculates that "perhaps System 1 skills are an universal as basic language ability" (1982, p. 192)

In their empirical study of System 1 skills Ginsburg and his associates found no significant main effects for race, social class, or family type. They did, however, find significant main effects for age and type of problem. The effect for problem type reflected a difference between "misleading" problems on the one hand and "regular" and "random" problems on the other. The misleading problems could not be solved by using the concrete (that is, context-bound) perceptual mechanisms of elementary mental functioning. Rather, some experience with sign mediation was necessary to avoid being misled by information about length. A similar point has been made by Bruner and P. Greenfield (1966).

Perhaps the most important aspect of Ginsburg's findings for a Vygotskian account of elementary mental functioning is the performance difference attributable to age. Ginsburg's results indicate that this functioning continues to develop after infancy. He and his colleagues do not state whether they think this development is a result of organic maturation or of some other developmental mechanism. Whatever the mechanism, this finding provides another example of the weakness inherent in Vygotsky's account of elementary mental functioning. It indicates that such functioning develops in ways and in accordance with principles that he did not foresee.

The absence of performance differences in elementary mental functioning attributable to class, race, and family type is not surprising from a Vygotskian point of view. Even if Vygotsky's approach were expanded to include experience with the physical environment as well as organic maturation, there is no reason to expect sociocultural factors to influence this performance.

When they examined System 2 and System 3 skills, Ginsburg and his associates found some effects for schooling. In the System 2 skill of mental addition they also found that unschooled adults from the Ivory Coast had developed informal procedures that differed from those of schooled adults (both in the United States and on the Ivory Coast) but were just as efficient and accurate. In the System 3 skills involved in complex, written addition problems, Ginsburg and his associates observed cross-cultural differences for children during the early school years, but these differences disappeared with increased exposure to formal schooling. If one considers System 2 and System 3 skills to be rudimentary and advanced forms of higher mental functioning, respectively, this pattern of results is to be expected. In particular, the tendency toward decontextualization that is encouraged in schooling is reflected in the groups' progress on System 3 tasks.

Thus Ginsburg and his colleagues have managed to identify and measure forms of mental functioning associated with the natural and social lines of development. When it comes to the issue of how the two lines of development are *interrelated* in ontogenesis, however, the problems left unexamined by Vygotsky remain unresolved today. In particular, there is still no specification of the role of the natural line (System 1 in Ginsburg's framework) in the development of the cultural line. Ginsburg asserts that System 1 skills "might serve as a solid foundation for mathematical education" (that is, for the development of System 3 skills), but this connection is nowhere explicated or empirically examined. This does not constitute a criticism of Ginsburg's research, since his major concern was not to explain the interrelationships among forces of development, but it does reflect the fact that contemporary investigators of cognitive development still have not resolved the problem of integrating natural and sociocultural phenomena into an overarching theoretical framework.

During the past few years another group of researchers headed by G. Saxe (1981, 1982a, 1982b; Saxe and Posner, 1983) has independently conducted a series of studies on numeration and arithmetic reasoning that also bear on Vygotsky's ideas about the two lines of development and the decontextualization of mediational means. Like the research conducted by Ginsburg, these studies involve cross-cultural as well as ontogenetic comparisons. Much of the interest of Saxe's research stems from the fact that he studied the use of an unusual body-part numeration system. This system is employed by the Oksapmin, a remote and recently contacted group in Papua, New Guinea. Saxe (1982a) explains that "the standard Oksapmin numeration system differs markedly from the Western system . . . To count as Oksapmin do, one begins with the thumb of one hand and enumerates 27 places around the upper periphery of the body, ending on the little finger of the opposite hand" (pp. 159–160). Vygotsky cound not have known about this specific numeration system, since the Oksapmin were first contacted by Westerners in 1938. However, similar numeration systems exist elsewhere in New Guinea and were reviewed by Vygotsky in his account of the emegence of higher mental functioning in the sociocultural domain (Vygotsky and Luria, 1930).

A major concern in Saxe's research is the transition from "premediational" to "mediational" uses of number terms. This transition has been the topic of several ontogenetic studies. For example, R. Russac (1978) and Saxe (1977) have noted that when young children (three to four years of age) are asked to make quantitative comparisons of two sets of objects, they may count the sets but do not use the derived information to make their comparisons. Other investigators (such as B. Schaeffer, J. Eggleston, and J. Scott, 1974; R. Gelman and C. Gallistel, 1978) have shown that even though they have counted a set, young children may not use the last numeral to identify its sum. The studies have identified a general tendency among young children to manipulate the forms of sign systems but not to incorporate them appropriately into higher mental functioning. As Saxe (1982a) points out, such findings have important implications: "If this process of change from a phase in which number terms are used in a 'premediational' fashion to a phase in which they are used in a mediational fashion can be shown to be a general one, it would represent a way in which historical forms of knowledge become interwoven with the construction of concepts and problem-solving strategies during ontogenesis" (p. 162).

Saxe's investigation of ontogenetic change among the Oksapmin yielded results that were in many ways similar to those found among Westerners. Based on a series of observations, he reports that "young Oksapmin children counted, though often in response to a probe question, but typically did not base their comparisons of reproductions on the products of their counting, whereas older children did" (1982a, pp. 162–163). Saxe also notes that young children performed as well as older ones when the set size was quite small. This finding, however, reflects what Vygotsky termed elementary mental functioning or what

Ginsburg terms System 1 functioning and hence does not require the use of mediational means.

In Vygotsky's terminology these results indicate that certain aspects of a sociocultural sign system can emerge before becoming intertwined with the practical reasoning associated with the natural line of development. The findings accord with Vygotsky's claims about the independent growth of the two lines of development before they enter into emergent interaction. This set of claims raises the further issue of whether the sign system reflected in premediational functioning is really the same as that reflected in mediational functioning. Vygotsky's claims about the nature of decontextualization suggest that the sign systems at these two points may not be the same.

The developmental progression from premediational to mediational functioning is not the only point at which the issue of decontextualization arises in Saxe's research. It also appears in connection with the unique properties of the Oksapmin numeration system. Since this system employs body parts as sign forms, it uses concrete objects, which have an everyday significance of their own, in a system for manipulating potentially abstract mathematical means. This fact raises the possibility of confusion over the meanings of sign forms. In order to be employed consistently and appropriately in mathematical reasoning, the meanings of these forms must be separated or abstracted from their properties as concrete body parts.

Saxe has reported results from some studies on this issue. In one study he examined Oksapmin children's understanding of numeration systems that employ the same body parts as their own but that assign them different numerical values:

> Children were told that people in their own village count from the right to the left sides of their bodies . . . however, in a village over the mountains, people count from the left to the right side of their bodies . . . Children were then told a story about two men counting sweet potatoes, one from the child's hamlet and the other from a faraway hamlet over the mountains. The child was told that both men counted to the same body part, one beginning at the right thumb, the other beginning at the left thumb . . . The child was then asked whether the two men counted to the same number of sweet potatoes or whether they counted to a different number of sweet potatoes   (1982a, p. 163).

Saxe found that during the stage of premediational functioning young Oksapmin children "compared body parts with respect to their physical similarity rather than with respect to their values as summations" (1982, pp. 163–164). In contrast, older children considered the value of a body part in terms of its role in numeration, regardless of its physical properties. This observation reflects the process of decontextualization of mediational means: sign values are increasingly defined on the basis of their position in a context-free system of numerical values rather than their concrete properties and contexts.

As with Ginsburg's research, Saxe's studies are most informative about the decontextualization of mediational means. Of particular interest is the problem caused by the use of body parts as sign forms in the Oksapmin numeration system. Saxe's findings reveal a special type of difficulty that may be encountered in decontextualization. In addition, the studies of Saxe and others on the developmental progression from premediational to mediational functioning are relevant to Vygotsky's approach to higher mental functions, particularly his claim about the independent appearance and emergent interactionism of mediational means and the natural line of development.

The research studies reviewed here focus on mathematical skills, but the points I have made apply generally to the development of higher mental functioning, with its associated sociocultural mediational means. Ginsburg's studies reveal that progress has been made in identifying and assessing elementary mental functions as well as rudimentary and advanced forms of higher mental functions. However, in the end there has been little progress in answering the question of how the natural and cultural lines of development are interrelated in ontogenesis. The study of cognitive development remains at the stage of viewing the natural line of development as providing the necessary but not sufficient conditions for cultural development. Saxe's research makes it possible to extend the account of decontextualization by considering a case where sign forms are connected with concrete objects in a unique way.

Microgenesis

In addition to phylogenesis, sociocultural history, and ontogenesis, one other genetic domain—what I shall term "microgenesis"—occasionally played a role in Vygotsky's analysis. His understanding of microgenesis is most apparent in his comments on experimental procedures in psychology. He argued that when conducting laboratory studies, the investigator should at least be aware of the microgenetic processes involved in the formation and execution of a psychological process. Although he did not go into great detail on this issue, he seems to have recognized two basic types of microgenesis. As J. V. Wertsch and A. Stone (1978) have pointed out, the distinction he used is similar to the distinction H. Werner (1957, 1961) made between types of microgenetic experiments.

The first type of microgenesis identified by Vygotsky concerns the short-term formation of a psychological process. The study of this domain requires observations of subjects' repeated trials in a task setting. Thus one could think of it as a very short-term longitudinal study. In a chapter on methods in psychology, Vygotsky (1978) argued for the need to include this type of microgenetic analysis in psychological investigation. He pointed out that by ignoring this form of genetic transition, learning and experimental studies often fail to utilize what may be the most interesting data they generate. The data emerge when an investigator is trying to train a subject to criterion before beginning the "real observations":

> Uniformity was sought, so that it was never possible to grasp the process in flight; instead, researchers routinely discarded the critical time when a reaction appears and when its functional links are established and adjusted. Such practices lead us to characterize the responses as "fossilized." They reflect the fact that these psychologists were not interested in complex reactions as a process of development.   (1978, p. 68)

The second type of microgenesis is the unfolding of an individual perceptual or conceptual act, often for the course of milliseconds. As in the first case, Vygotsky probably derived his notion from Werner's writings in which two kinds of "genetic experiment" were proposed along these lines. In the final chapter of *Thinking and Speech* (1934) one can see Vygotsky utilizing this type of microgensis in his account of speech production. He was concerned with the transformations involved in the movement from thought to speech utterance. His argument on this issue has had an important influence on Soviet neurolinguists, such as Luria (1975a, 1981) and T. V. Akhutina (1975, 1978).

Vygotsky's genetic method may be summarized in a few fundamental tenets:

1. Human mental processes must be studied by using a genetic analysis that examines the origins of these processes and the transitions that lead up to their later form.

2. The genesis of human mental processes involves qualitative revolutionary changes as well as evolutionary changes.

3. Genetic progression and transitions are defined in terms of mediational means (tools and signs).

4. Several genetic domains (phylogenesis, sociocultural history, ontogenesis, and microgenesis) must be examined in order to produce a complete and accurate account of human mental processes.

5. Different forces of development, each with its own set of explanatory principles, operate in the different genetic domains.

Vygotsky posited Darwinian natural selection as the developmental force that operates in the phylogenetic domain. According to him, phylogenesis provides a necessary but not sufficient condition for the emergence of *Homo sapiens*. In addition to evolutionary changes in organic structure, especially the brain, the sociocultural phenomena of labor and communication are required to create human beings. The point at which these sociocultural phenomena begin to emerge and create human beings is the point at which the very nature of development changes, in that the explanatory principles which account for change are now sociocultural rather than biological.

Vygotsky's account of this transition must be revised in light of recent advances in primatology and physical anthropology. As researchers such as Geertz have pointed out, critical point theories that assume a sudden, sharp onset of sociocultural change are no longer tenable. Rather, it is now recognized that certain early forms of culture were developed while organic evolution was still under way. This fact raises the possibility that cultural practices exerted some influence on organic change, a possibility that holds particular interest for a Vygotskian approach with its emphasis on mediation and communication.

When one turns to the sociocultural domain, a different force of development with its unique set of explanatory principles is seen to be at work. The locus of change shifts from organic evolution governed by natural selection to the stage of mediational means. Mediational means (tools and signs) make possible the transmission of culture, but more important for Vygotsky's approach is the fact that they provide the mechanism for sociocultural change. Whereas the appearance of mediational means, especially tools, marks the emergence of sociohistorical forces of change, it is now the decontextualization of mediational means, primarily signs, that provides the possibility of sociocultural change. In Vygotsky's writings this decontextualization is linked to the transition from rudimentary to advanced forms of higher mental functioning.

Just as Vygotsky's account of phylogenesis and the emergence of sociohistorical change should be updated in light of recent advances in social science, his account of sociocultural change stands in need of revision. In this case the research of Scribner and Cole on the psychology of literacy is particularly useful. Specifically, the claims made by Vygotsky and Luria about the role of literacy in the decontextualization of mediational means need to be modified. Instead of viewing literacy as a single, undifferentiated phenomenon with a uniform impact on higher mental functioning, Scribner and Cole have shown that there are differing types of literacy with differing cognitive consequences. In particular, these results suggest that the real focus of Vygotsky's claims about literacy and decontextualization may be literacy as it emerges in formal schooling contexts.

Turning to Vygotsky's account of ontogenesis, one sees that he posited a fundamentally new kind of genetic dynamic. Unlike the first two, where a single developmental force served as the focus of Vygotsky's analysis, he conceptualized change in the ontogenetic domain in terms of two interacting forces of development: natural and sociocultural forces of change. Vygotsky argued that although these two lines cannot be empirically separated during most phases of ontogenesis, this domain can be properly understood only by analytically separating them in order to examine their mutually transformatory powers.

Vygotsky's concrete research on ontogenesis did not live up to the dictates of his methodological argument, hence the need to distinguish Vygotsky the methodologist from Vygotsky the psychologist. Vygotsky's account of natural development left much to be desired. He failed to provide a detailed account of the changes in this line of development and of how these changes influence cultural development. However, this issue is actually quite complex and has not been adequately addressed to this day in studies of cognitive development. Instead of focusing on the emergent interactionism suggested by his theoretical framework, Vygotsky's concrete investigations of ontogenesis focused on the unidirectional impact of cultural forces on the natural line of development, in particular, on how the decontextualization of mediational means produces ontogenetic change in higher mental functioning.

CHAPTER 3

The Social Origins of
Higher Mental Functions

O ne of the most fundamental assumptions that guided Vygotsky's attempt to reformulate psychology on Marxian foundations was that in order to understand the individual, one must first understand the social relations in which the individual exists. This assumption was outlined by Marx (1959) in his Sixth Thesis on Feuerbach and has been the focus of some current attempts to formulate a Marxist account of personality (compare Seve, 1978). The influence of Marx's claim on Vygotsky is manifested in the following statement: "To paraphrase a well-known position of Marx's, we could say that humans' psychological nature represents the aggregate of internalized social relations that have become functions for the individual and forms of the individual's structure. We do not want to say that this is the meaning of Marx's position, but we see in this position the fullest expression of that toward which the history of cultural development leads us" (Vygotsky, 1981b, p. 164).[1]

On the basis of this Marxian axiom Vygotsky argued that "the social dimension of consciousness is primary in time and in fact. The individual dimension of consciousness is derivative and secondary" (1979, p. 30). This concept in turn led him to identify what he considered a major weakness in the psychology that existed at the time he was writing:

Formerly, psychologists tried to derive social behavior from individual behavior. They investigated individual responses observed in the laboratory and then studied them in the collective. They studied how the individual's responses change in the collective setting. Posing the question in such a way is, of course, quite legitimate; but genetically speaking, it deals with the second level in behavioral development. The first problem is to show how the individual response emerges from the forms of collective life.   (1981b, pp. 164–165)

As Bruner (1962) has noted, Vygotsky bears an interesting resemblance to G. H. Mead (1924–25, 1934) in connection with this claim. There are important differences between the two theorists, but on this point they independently and simultaneously constructed similar ideas. The similarity can be seen by comparing Vygotsky's comments about the primacy of the social processes with Mead's claim that "the social act is a precondition of [consciousness]. The mechanism of the social act can be traced out without introducing into it the conception of consciousness as a separate element within that act; hence the social act, in its more elementary stages or forms, is possible without, or apart from, some form of consciousness" (1934, p. 18).

It is worthwhile considering Mead's point closely because in addition to reflecting the general parallel between his ideas and Vygotsky's, it explicitly raises an important issue inherent in Vygotsky's criticism of the individualistc bias in psychology: the claim that the principles that account for social processes are not reducible to those that account for psychological processes. In other words, both Vygotsky and Mead rejected individual psychological reductionism. In order to carry out such a critique, one must specify the nature of the social reality that is at issue. Mead did so primarily in his analysis of the social act, conversations of gestures, and the like. On the basis of his analysis of face-to-face social interaction, he devised a set of principles that apply to the interaction itself and that cannot be replaced by laws of individual psychology.

Vygotsky recognized social interaction of this type, but his commitment to Marxian theoretical foundations induced him to recognize another level of social phenomena as well, one that concerns processes typically studied by social theorists, sociologists, and economists. These processes are assumed to operate at the societal or social institutional level in accordance with a theory such as historical materialism. Like many other theorists, Vygotsky did not deny that individuals, guided by their own mental processes, participate in social life at this level. However, he clearly assumed that this fact alone cannot explain the nature of social processes. Rather, they operate according to sociological and economic principles, particularly the principles of exchange value and commodification as outlined by Marx (1977) and Marxists (for example, Lukacs, 1971). In these cases socioeconomic forces are understood to operate independently of individual human plan or volition. I shall term the principles that govern phenomena at this level "societal" or "social institutional" principles.

Vygotsky said very little about the principles that deal with social institutional phenomena. At first glance this seems ironic, given that such phenomena are the primary focus of Marx's writings and that Vygotsky wished to create a Marxist psychology. However, on further examination it becomes clear that other theories of social interaction and psychology had as much, if not more, of an impact on Vygotsky as Marx's writings did. Consequently, much that Vygotsky had to say about the social origins of human consciousness is not necessarily grounded in the ideas of Marx or of any other social theorist.

The type of social processes on which Vygotsky places primary emphasis is what I shall term "interpsychological."[2] In contrast to societal processes, interpsychological processes involve small groups (frequently dyads) of individuals engaged in concrete social interaction and are explainable in terms of small-group dynamics and communicative practices. Mead's notion of the social act is concerned with this level of social process. As with societal processes, interpsychological processes are not reducible to individual psychological processes, which would constitute a form of individualistic psychological reductionism. Furthermore, interpsychological processes cannot be equated with societal processes. To do so would be to engage in a form of sociological reductionism.

When dealing with the social origins of higher mental processes, Vygotsky was mainly concerned with interpsychological functioning, as reflected in his formulation of the "general genetic law of cultural development":

> Any function in the child's cultural development appears twice, or on two planes. First it appears on the social plane, and then on the psychological plane. First it appears between people as an interpsychological category, and then within the child as an in-

trapsychological category. This is equally true with regard to voluntary attention, logical memory, the formation of concepts, and the development of volition. We may consider this position as a law in the full sense of the word, but it goes without saying that internalization transforms the process itself and changes its structure and functions. Social relations or relations among people genetically underlie all higher functions and their relationships. (1981b, p. 163)

This law includes strong statements on two issues. First, it asserts that terms such as "voluntary attention," "logical memory," and "thinking" may be properly attributed to groups as well as to individuals. This unusual use of the terms is essential to Vygotsky's analysis. The second, related point concerns the linkage between interpsychological and intrapsychological functioning. Instead of merely claiming that individuals somehow learn by participating in interpsychological functioning, Vygotsky's formulation means that there is an inherent connection between the two planes of functioning. In certain instances he saw an isomorphism between the organization of processes on the two planes, and in all cases he argued that the form of interpsychological functioning has a powerful impact on the resulting form of intrapsychological functioning. The importance of the transition from interpsychological to intrapsychological functioning for Vygotsky is apparent in his statement that "we shall place this transition from a social influence outside the individual to a social influence within the individual at the center of our research and try to elucidate the most important moments from which it arises" (1960, p. 116).

Vygotsky's concern with the general genetic law of cultural development is manifested throughout his writings. I shall examine only two of the many phenomena he analyzed in this connection: internalization and the "zone of proximal development." When analyzing these and other phenomena, the underlying claim is always that in order to understand higher mental functioning on the intrapsychological plane, one must conduct a genetic analysis of its interpsychological precursors.

Internalization

Like other theorists, such as Piaget, Vygotsky viewed internalization as a process whereby certain aspects of patterns of activity that had been performed on an external plane come to be executed on an internal plane. Unlike many other theorists, however, he defined external activity in terms of semiotically mediated social processes and argued that the properties of these processes provide the key to understanding the emergence of internal functioning. The close relationship that Vygotsky saw between internalization and the social origins of individual psychological processes is evident in the following passage, where he argues that higher mental functions necessarily appear initially in an external form because they are social processes:

> It is necessary that everything internal in higher forms was external, that is, for others it was what it now is for oneself. Any higher mental function necessarily goes through an external stage in its development because it is initially a social function. This is the center of the whole problem of internal and external behavior . . . When we speak of a process, "external" means "social." Any higher mental function was external because it was social at some point before becoming an internal, truly mental function. (1981b, p. 162)

Vygotsky's focus on social processes induced him to examine the representational systems that are needed to participate in such processes—hence his emphasis on the internalization of *speech*. In contrast, Piaget's focus on the young child's interaction with physical reality led him to examine the representational systems required to manipulate objects. As a result he viewed internalization primarily in terms of schemata that reflect the regularities of an individual's physical action. Thus while both theorists addressed the issue of internalization, their different ideas about the origins of human mental processes led them to focus on quite different activities and representational means.

When contrasting the two positions on this issue, it is interesting to consider whether they are complementary or incompatible. I would argue here as I did earlier with regard to the natural and social lines of development that there is a degree of complementarity attributable to the relatively greater sophistication that Piaget brought to the study of very early stages of ontogenesis on the one hand and the relatively greater sophistication that Vygotsky brought to the study of sign-mediated higher mental functions on the other. Because Piaget carried out such detailed and insightful analyses of early sensorimotor intelligence, he was able to identify schemes that had been generalized, abstracted, and internalized by the final stages of the sensorimotor period. Of course he dealt with internalization associated with later ontogenetic stages as well, but the essential point here is that for Piaget internalization occurs in connection with what Vygotsky viewed as the natural line of development.

In contrast, for Vygotsky the notion of internalization applied only to the development of higher mental functions and hence the social or cultural line of development. In this account internalization is a process involved in the transformation of social phenomena into psychological phenomena. Consequently, Vygotsky saw social reality as playing a primary role in determining the nature of internal intrapsychological functioning.

On the basis of Vygotsky's claim about the close relationship between inter- and intrapsychological forms of higher mental functions, it might be tempting to assume that he was proposing a "transfer model of internalization," whereby properties of social processes are simply transferred from the external, interpsychological plane to the internal, intrapsychological plane. If one considers certain of Vygotsky's statements out of context, it would seem that this is indeed what he had in mind. A closer examination of his writings, however, reveals that he clearly did not view internalized higher mental processes as simple copies of external, interpsychological processes. In formulating his general genetic law of cultural development, he stated that, "it goes without saying that internalization transforms the process itself and changes its structure and functions" (1981a, p. 163).

Zinchenko (1985) has noted that Vygotsky's approach rejects both the assumption that the structures of external and internal activity are identical and the assumption that they are unrelated. The first position makes the notion of internalization uninteresting and trivial, whereas the second makes it unresolvable. Instead of taking either position, Vygotsky argued that there is an inherent relationship between external and internal activity, but it is a *genetic* relationship in which the major issue is how internal mental processes are *created* as a result of the child's exposure to what Vygotsky called "mature cultural forms of behavior" (1981b, p. 151).

Leont'ev (1981) has examined this process in relation to the broader issue of consciousness:

Earlier approaches in psychology viewed consciousness as some sort of metapsychological plane of movement of mental processes. But consciousness is not given from the beginning and is not produced by nature: consciousness is a product of society: it is *produced*. Therefore consciousness is not a postulate and is not a condition of psychology; rather, it is a problem for psychology—an object of concrete investigation.

Thus the process of internalization is not the *transferral* of an external activity to a preexisting, internal "plane of consciousness": it is the process in which this internal plane is *formed*.   (pp. 56–57)

There are important differences between Leont'ev's and Vygotsky's general theoretical frameworks, especially with regard to the emphasis given to semiotic mediation (compare Wertsch, 1981b; Kozulin, 1984). As Wertsch and Stone (1985) have noted, however, Leont'ev's approach to internalization provides a means for extending and clarifying Vygotsky's comments. Consider the latter's analysis of the origins and development of nonverbal pointing:

> At first the indicatory gesture is simply an unsuccessful grasping movement directed at an object and designating a forthcoming action. The child tries to grasp an object that is too far away. The child's hands, reaching toward the object, stop and hover in midair . . . Here we have a child's movements that do nothing more than objectively indicate an object.
>
> When the mother comes to the aid of the child and comprehends the movement as an indicator, the situation changes in an essential way. The indicatory gesture becomes a gesture for others. In response to the child's unsuccessful grasping movement, a response emerges not on the part of the object, but on the part of another human. Thus, other people introduce the primary sense into this unsuccessful grasping movement. And only afterward, owing to the fact they already have connected the unsuccessful grasping movement with the whole objective situation, do children themselves begin to use the movement as an indication. The functions of the movement itself have undergone a change here: from a movement directed toward an object it has become a movement directed toward another human being. The grasping is converted into an indication . . . this movement does not become a gesture for oneself except by first being an indication, that is, functioning objectively as an indication and gesture for others, being comprehended and understood by surrounding people as an indicator. Thus the child is the last to become conscious of the gesture.   (1981b, pp. 160–161)

In this case the communicative significance of the behavior does not exist until it is created in adult–child interaction. The *combination* of the child's behavior and the adult's response transforms a noncommunicative behavior into a sign on the interpsychological plane. The sign form is transformed from a general reaching and grasping movement to an indicatory gesture. Later, the child gains voluntary control on the intrapsychological plane over what had formerly existed only in social interaction.

Wertsch and Stone (1985) have argued that the emergence of this voluntary control is the general process involved in Vygotsky's approach to internalization. More specifically, we have argued that internalization is the process of gaining control over external sign forms. In the example just outlined, the sign form is converted from a general reaching and grasping movement to a true indicatory gesture. Correspondingly, the object involved is transformed for the child from something that is represented as part of a nonsocial, noncommunicative setting to something indicated or requested in a social context.

Hence when one asks what it means to gain voluntary control over signs on the intrapsychological plane, one is asking about internalization as defined by Vygotsky and Leont'ev. According to Vygotsky, in the "most important type of internalization" children "master the rules in accordance with which external signs must be used" (1981b, pp. 184–185).

Thus when a child begins to master a sign form such as pointing in order to direct an adult's attention to an object, the child has begun to develop an aspect of the internal plane of consciousness. This accomplishment is still very primitive and indeed is only the beginning in the formation of an aspect of internal, intrapsychological functioning. However, the fact that pointing begins to exist for the child as for the adult means that the child's intrapsychological functioning has changed. Furthermore, subsequent progress on the interpsychological plane reflects additional development on the intrapsychological plane. In this way changes in interpsychological functioning are inherently linked to changes in intrapsychological functioning.

Although the veracity of Vygotsky's account of the origins of pointing is open to question (compare Bates, 1976), it illustrates a general line of reasoning that is clearly valid for several other phenomena in his analysis. Wertsch and Stone (1985) have argued that in a Vygotskian approach structural properties of interpsychological functioning, such as its dialogical, question–answer organization, are part of the resulting internal, intrapsychological plane of functioning. This touches on a broader claim of Vygotsky's about external and internal functioning, namely, that because the external processes from which internal ones derive are necessarily social, internal processes reflect certain aspects of social structuring:

> The very mechanism underlying higher mental functions is a copy from social interaction; all higher mental functions are internalized social relationships . . . Their composition, genetic structure, and means of action [forms of mediation]—in a word, their whole nature—is social. Even when we turn to mental [internal] processes, their nature remains quasi-social. In their own private sphere, human beings retain the functions of social interaction. (1981b, p. 164)

During the past few decades in the USSR, one of Vygotsky's followers by way of Khar'kov, P. Ya. Gal'perin, has produced several major works on internalization (for example, 1959, 1960, 1965, 1966, 1969, 1977). His approach does not correspond in all respects with Vygotsky's, especially with regard to the nature of the semiotic phenomena involved, but in several ways it represents an extension of the latter's ideas. Gal'perin's claims about the stages involved in the internalization process are particularly valuable. The stages include (1) making an external action maximally explicit; (2) transferring its representation to audible speech, first on the interpsychological plane and then on the intrapsychological plane; and (3) transferring it to inner speech.

Like Vygotsky and Leont'ev, Gal'perin has been interested in the changes an action undergoes as it advances through these stages—in particular, in how such actions become condensed or abbreviated. He has argued that "the abbreviation of an operation and its transfer to the position of a 'provisionally performed' operation does not mean the transition of this operation to the mental plane. On the mental plane the abbreviated operations are only presumed, not executed" (1969, p. 257). As I have noted (Wertsch, 1981b) this comment is consistent with the general point that the relationship between external and internal functioning is one involving genetic transformation rather than an identical replica.

The specifics of Vygotsky's account of internalization cannot be fully explicated until one goes into detail on his semiotic analysis. However, it should be clear by now that this account is grounded in four major points: (1) Internalization is not a process of copying external reality on a preexisting internal plane; rather, it is a process wherein an internal plane of consciousness is formed. (2) The external reality at issue is a social interactional one. (3) The specific mechanism at issue is the mastery of external sign forms. And (4) the internal plane of consciousness takes on a "quasi-social" nature because of its origins.

The Zone of Proximal Development

It was in connection with the "zone of proximal development"[3] that Vygotsky outlined some of his most concrete ideas about the relationship between interpsychological and intrapsychological functioning.

Vygotsky (1934a, 1978) introduced the notion of the zone of proximal development in an effort to deal with two practical problems in educational psychology: the assessment of children's intellectual abilities and the evaluation of instructional practices. With respect to the former, he believed that existing techniques of psychological testing focused too heavily on intrapsychological accomplishments and failed to address the issue of predicting future growth, a major concern to Soviet psychology even today. Indeed it has been identified by some members of the Vygotskian school as a point that distinguishes Soviet from American research. As Leont'ev noted in a discussion with U. Bronfenbrenner (1977) many years after Vygotsky's death, "American researchers are constantly seeking to discover how the child came to be what he is; we in the USSR are striving to discover not how the child came to be what he is, but how he can become what he not yet is" (p. 528).

Interest in the problem of how a child can become "what he not yet is" can be traced, in part, to Vygotsky's analysis of the zone of proximal development. One of his chief reasons for introducing this construct was that it allowed him to examine "those functions that have not yet matured but are in the process of maturation, functions that will mature tomorrow but are currently in an embryonic state. These functions could be termed the 'buds' or 'flowers' of development rather than the 'fruits' of development" (1978, p. 86). Not surprisingly, Vygotsky saw the "buds of development" in interpsychological functioning. Thus the zone of proximal development is a special case of his general concern with the genetic law of cultural development. It is the dynamic region of sensitivity in which the transition from interpsychological to intrapsychological functioning can be made.

Vygotsky defined the zone of proximal development as the distance between a child's *"actual developmental level as determined by independent problem solving"* and the higher level of *"potential development as deter-*

mined through problem solving under adult guidance or in collaboration with more capable peers" (ibid.) He argued that it is just as crucial, if not more so, to measure the level of potential development as it is to measure the level of actual development. In his view, however, existing practices were such that "in determining the mental age of a child with the help of tests we almost always are concerned with the actual level of development" (1956, p. 446).

In assessing a child's mental age, the importance of conducting a separate analysis of the potential level of development derives from the fact that it may vary independently of the actual level. Vygotsky illustrated this point as follows:

> Imagine that we have examined two children and have determined that the mental age of both is seven years. This means that both children solve tasks accessible to seven-year-olds. However, when we attempt to push these children further in carrying out the tests, there turns out to be an essential difference between them. With the help of leading questions, examples, and demonstrations, one of them easily solves test items taken from two years above the child's level of [actual] development. The other solves test items that are only a half-year above, his or her level of [actual] development.   (1956, pp. 446–447)

Given this set of circumstances Vygotsky proceeded to ask, "Is the mental development of these two children the same?" (ibid., p. 447). He argued that in an important sense they are not:

> From the point of view of their independent activity they are equivalent, but from the point of view of their immediate potential development they are sharply different. That which the child turns out to be able to do with the help of an adult points us toward the zone of the child's proximal development. This means that with the help of this method, we can take stock not only of today's completed process of development, not only the cycles that are already concluded and done, not only the processes of maturation that are completed; we can also take stock of processes that are now in the state of coming into being, that are only ripening, or only developing.   (Ibid., pp. 447–448)

Concern with assessing both the actual and the potential levels of development has characterized the work of several researchers in the Soviet Union (for example, T. A. Vlasova and M. S. Pevzner, 1971; Vlasova, 1972; T. V. Egorova, 1973), and it has begun to have an impact on U.S. investigators concerned with assessment. A. Brown and her colleagues (Brown and French, 1979; Brown and Ferrara, 1985; Campione, Brown, Ferrara, and Bryant, 1984) have carried out several concrete analyses of the relationship between children's actual and potential levels of development.

In these studies adult experimenters provided standardized prompts to assess a child's potential level on some task after the actual level had been measured. For example, in one study Brown and R. Ferrara (1985) presented third and fifth graders with the task of identifying and continuing sequential patterns of letters, which involved several different types of sequences and levels of difficulty. Performance was assessed both on the interpsychological and the intrapsychological planes of functioning.

On the basis of the interpsychological functioning they devised an "index of speed of learning" for each child, based on the total number of standardized prompts required to reach a criterion of original learning of the letter sequences. While the experimenters found that grade level and IQ were significantly correlated with the index of speed of learning, much of the variance in this latter measure was left unexplained. Indeed, "a good third of the children had learning speeds not predictable from their IQ scores" (Brown and Ferrara, 1985, p. 228). That is, by using a measure based on interpsychological functioning, Brown and Ferrara identified an aspect of performance that could not be accounted for on the basis of a standard assessment of the subjects' intrapsychological functioning.

Brown and Ferrara reinstated an interpsychological procedure of providing standardized prompts after each child had spent an intermediate period working independently (that is, on the intrapsychological plane). During this third stage of the study subjects were asked to solve new sets of letter series completion tasks designed to assess their level of maintenance and transfer of learning. The children were divided into low and high transfer groups according to the number of prompts needed at this time. IQ was found to be significantly correlated with the performance measure—in this case the level of transfer—for over two-thirds of the children. However, the "static" intrapsychological measure of IQ once again failed to account for a significant amount of the variance in the performance of the interpsychological tasks; many of the children fit neither of the expected profiles of average IQ and poor transfer or high IQ and good transfer.

From their findings Brown and Ferrara conclude that measures of interpsychological performance (basically, susceptibility to adults' prompts) provide a great deal of information about students' cognitive level that cannot be obtained from traditional intrapsychological measures:

> Overall, the IQ of almost 50 percent of the children did not predict learning speed and/or degree of transfer. Thus, from this fairly wide range of "normal"-ability children (IQ range 88–150) a number of different learning profiles have emerged, including (1) slow learners, narrow transferrers, low IQ (*slow*); (2) fast learners, wide tranferrers, high IQ (*fast*); (3) fast learners, narrow tranferrers (*context-bound*); (4) slow learners, wide transferrers (*reflective*); and (5) fast learners, wide transferrers, low IQ (somewhat analogous to Budoff's *high scorers*). All of these profiles are hidden when one considers only the child's initial unaided performance. (1985, p. 293)

Studies like this are motivated by Vygotsky's claims about the usefulness of the zone of proximal development when analyzing intelligence testing procedures. The studies typically involve some assessment of individual children on the basis of a standard instrument such as an IQ test. This measure of intrapsychological functioning is then compared with the level of interpsychological functioning created when an adult experimenter provides a standard script of hints and other forms of assistance to the child. In several studies (for example, Ferrara, Brown, and Campione, 1983; Campione, Brown, Ferrara, and Bryant, 1984) Vygotsky's claims about the independence of the actual and potential levels of development have been borne out.

A second way in which Vygotsky argued that the zone of proximal development is a useful construct concerns processes of instruction. Here again, the general genetic law of cultural development underlies his discussion, but in addition he saw a specific relationship between development and instruction.[4] In his view "instruction and development do not directly coincide, but represent two processes that exist in very complex interrelationships" (1934a, p. 222). On the one hand, "instruction creates the zone of proximal development" (ibid., p. 450). But to say that a child can do more when collaborating with an adult does not mean that the level of potential development may be arbitrarily high. Rather, Vygotsky argued, the child can operate "only within certain limits that are strictly fixed by the state of the child's development and intellectual possibilities" (1934a, p. 219). Hence the zone of proximal development is jointly determined by the child's level of development and the form of instruction involved; it is a property neither of the child nor of interpsychological functioning alone.

According to Vygotsky, instruction in the zone of proximal development "calls to life in the child, awakens and puts in motion an entire series of internal processes of development. These processes are at the time possible only in the sphere of interaction with those surrounding the child and in collaboration with companions, but in the internal course of development they eventually become the internal property of the child. (1956, p. 450)

When considering specific forms of instruction, Vygotsky focused on how interpsychological functioning can be structured such that it will maximize the growth of intrapsychological functioning: "*Instruction is good only when it proceeds ahead of development*. Then it *awakens and rouses to life an entire set of functions which are in the stage of maturing, which lie in the zone of proximal development*. It is in this way that instruction plays an extremely important role in development" (1934a, p. 222). In the West, research such as that of Olson (1970) and I. Sigel (1970, 1979, 1982; also Sigel and Cocking, 1977; Sigel and Saunders, 1979; Sigel and McGillicuddy-DeLisi, 1984) is motivated by similar claims.

The kind of instruction Vygotsky had in mind was not concerned with "specialized, technical skills such as typing or bicycle riding, that is, skills that have no essential impact on development" (1934, p. 222), but rather had as its goal "all-round development," such as instruction in formal, academic disciplines, each of which has a sphere "in which the impact of instruction on development is accomplished and fulfilled" (ibid.).

These and other comments by Vygotsky on the relationship between instruction and development concern school-age children. He recognized, however, that the same general dynamic occurs in other planes of development as well: "instruction and development do not meet for the first time at school age; rather, they are in fact connected with each other from the very first day of a child's life" (1956, p. 445). His approach to analyzing this interrelationship assumed that "we must understand, first, *the relationship that exists between instruction and development in general,* and then we must understand *the specific properties of this relationship during the school-age years*" (ibid., p. 446).

Regardless of the child's age, Vygotsky emphasized that instruction is involved in the development "not of natural, but of historical characteristics of humans" (ibid., p. 450). He viewed instruction as an aspect of the social rather than the natural line of development and as giving rise to higher rather than elementary mental functioning.

Vygotsky's account of the zone of proximal development has spawned research both in the USSR (for example, Rubtsov, 1981) and in the West (for example, Rogoff and Wertsch, 1984). However, its formulation is wanting in several respects. Three problems must be addressed if the notion of the zone of proximal development is to be robust enough to continue generating useful research hypotheses.

The first problem is Vygotsky's concept of development. In formulating his argument on the relationship between instruction and development he briefly examined and rejected three views: (1) that the process of development is independent of instruction ("development or maturation is viewed as a precondition of learning but never the result of it" [1978, p. 80]); (2) that the process of learning in instruction[5] *is* development; and (3) that approaches such as Koffka's to overcome the extremes of the first two by combining aspects of both are valid. Of the first two views, Vygotsky wrote:

> There is a major difference in their assumptions about the temporal relationship between learning[6] and developmental processes. Theorists who hold the first view assert that developmental cycles precede learning cycles; maturation precedes learning and instruction must lag behind mental growth. For the second group of theorists, both processes occur simultaneously; learning and development coincide at all points in the same way that identical geometrical figures coincide when superimposed.   (1978, p. 81)

When speaking of the first group of theorists, Vygotsky primarily had Piaget in mind; when speaking of the second, E. Thorndike.

In contrast to these two approaches (as well as Koffka's unsatisfactory compromise), Vygotsky argued that a more complex relationship exists between development and instruction: "Instruction . . . is not development, although properly organized instruction of the child pulls mental development behind it and rouses to life a whole series of developmental processes that outside instruction is an internally necessary and universal moment in the process of a child's development" (1956, p. 450). He recognized that "periods of sensitivity," such as those identified by Montessori, exist for various aspects of development. During these periods, Vygotsky was concerned with the "higher psychological functions that emerge from the cultural development of the child, having their origins in collaboration and instruction"(1934a, p. 223).

These comments leave unanswered the question of what exactly Vygotsky considered to be development. In his discussion of the relationship between development and instruction, he argued that development cannot be reduced to learning in instruction, yet that is precisely the interpretation that seems most compatible with his comments about the emergence of intrapsychological from interpsychological functioning.

The apparent inconsistency arises from the fact that "Vygotsky the methodologist" (Davydov and Radzikhovskii, 1985) called for an approach in which development proceeds at least partially in accord with its own internal dynamic. Vygotsky the psychologist, however, outlined an approach in which it is not clear that development is anything more than the product of learning in instruction.

This problem is perhaps most evident in Vygotsky's comments about the upper limit of a child's potential level of development. Although he argued that this limit is partially set by the child's actual development, he gave no account of why this development could not be reduced to past learning in instruction. If it could be so reduced, then it would seem that more extensive instruction at any level of development could by itself produce arbitrarily high levels of actual and potential development. This, however, is widely understood not to be the case, for reasons that Vygotsky recognized in principle but not in the actual practice of his research: namely, that development occurs in part as a result of its own internal dynamic. Hence the nature of development and its relationship to instruction is not fully clarified in a Vygotskian approach.

This weakness is related to another in Vygotsky's account of the natural line of development. There he also needed to invoke some internal developmental dynamic but failed to do so. Only when an adequate account of development is formulated in a Vygotskian approach will it be able to avoid reducing development to learning in instruction.

My second comment on Vygotsky's account of the zone of proximal development concerns his views on the early period of ontogenesis. Vygotsky said very little about this period, largely because of the general lack of knowledge about infancy at the time he was writing. During the past few decades, however, this situation has changed drastically, and it is now possible to examine the zone of proximal development at earlier ages than Vygotsky ever attempted to do.

Studies such as those conducted by Bruner (1975a, 1975b, 1981), K. Kaye and R. Charney (1980), and Kaye (1982) have identified some of the complex processes of social and cognitive development that characterize the very early period of ontogenesis. In many respects the findings they report may be viewed as bearing more on the precursors of the zone of proximal development than on the zone itself, but a complete genetic analysis would strive to incorporate them.

Recently investigators such as J. Valsiner (1984) and B. Rogoff, C. Malkin, and K. Gilbride (1984) have examined adult–infant interaction specifically from the perspective of the zone of proximal development. For example, Rogoff and her colleagues observed such interaction involved in operating a jack-in-the-box and reported that "the focus of interaction shifted from attempting to maintain joint attention (four months), to managing joint use of the jack-in-the-box (five-and-one-half to twelve months), to managing the social relationship in the joint activity through persistent symbolic communication (twelve to seventeen months)" (1984, p. 43). These findings deal with crucial processes of entering into interpsychological functioning. In a Vygotskian genetic analysis, facts about these processes would have to be viewed as essential for understanding later functioning in the zone of proximal development. Only recently, however, have they begun to be incorporated into this research. As such findings are reported, it will be possible to understand the fundamental social interactional processes that give rise to increasingly complex zones of proximal development.

My third comment on Vygotsky's formulation of the zone of proximal development concerns the two types of social phenomena I outlined earlier in this chapter. Most of Vygotsky's discussion of this zone involves interpsychological processes. In certain respects, however, his comments bear on social institutional phenomena as well. For example, he argued that the "process of instruction that takes place before school age is essentially different from the process of school instruction" (1956, p. 445). Here he apparently viewed certain social institutional contexts as bearing on interpsychological processes. The influence in this case grows from the decontextualization of mediational means. Vygotsky's general point was that sociohistorical processes at the social institutional level influence interpsychological functioning in the zone of proximal development.

This point has recently been elaborated by researchers such as Saxe,

M. Gearhart, and S. Guberman (1984) and P. Griffin and Cole (1984). Saxe and his colleagues have emphasized that most tasks carried out in the zone of proximal development are socioculturally specific. For example, in their analysis of the "cultural task context" (p. 28) of solving simple number problems, the adult's representation of the "goal structure" of the task is grounded in a sociohistorically specific semiotic system, namely, arithmetic. Saxe (1977, 1981) has demonstrated that the arithmetic system and its uses are not natural or universal but instead depend on sociohistorical context. Hence Saxe and his colleagues assume that a full understanding of the zone of proximal development is possible only if the historically specific context is taken into account.

Griffin and Cole (1984) have approached the role of social institutional phenomena in the zone of proximal development somewhat differently. Following D. B. El'konin (1972; see also Wertsch, 1981b), Griffin and Cole have argued that in order to understand interaction in the zone of proximal development, one must identify the "leading activities" that characterize various phases of ontogenesis: "as an alternative to internal, individual stage approaches to the study of development, leading activities provide for a notion of societally provided progressions, the sort of context-selection mechanisms that we have considered important for understanding development" (1984, p. 51). The types of leading activity that Griffin and Cole have in mind are play, formal learning, and work. As children engage in these and other institutionally defined contexts, the nature of interaction and the zones of proximal development in which they participate may be expected to change.

For Saxe and his colleagues as well as for Griffin and Cole, the general point is that the interpsychological functioning found in zones of proximal development may vary widely depending on the social institutional contexts in which this functioning occurs. Since such contexts may be expected to change with sociohistorical settings, the zone of proximal development provides a point where the ontogenetic and sociohistorical domains may be examined in interaction (compare Cole, 1985).

Vygotsky's comments about internalization and the zone of proximal development are part of a larger concern with the social origins of higher mental functioning in the individual. In outlining this argument, I have emphasized some of its weaknesses as well as its strength. The weaknesses are many, but his insight about the relationship between social and individual processes still constitutes a major contribution today. Again, this contribution is largely attributable to the fact that Vygotsky did not operate within the boundaries of a single social science or humanities discipline. His breadth of knowledge is at least partially responsible for his success in avoiding the kind of individual reductionism that so often characterizes contemporary psychology.

CHAPTER 4

Vygotsky's Semiotic Analysis

During the last decade of his life Vygotsky's account of the mediation of higher mental processes was constantly evolving. The sources of his ideas were varied, but at the most general level the writings of Marx and Engels played a central role. In their view labor activity is crucial in the creation of human consciousness. Indeed, they argued that we *become* human by engaging in the process of labor. As Radzikhovskii (1979) has pointed out, Vygotsky accepted this claim about how humans evolve, but he placed special emphasis on the role of tools in the process, a concept he derived from Engels. According to Vygotsky, "To assume that labor, which fundamentally changes the character of humans' adaptation to nature, is not connected with a change in the type of human behavior is impossible if, together with Engels, we accept the notion that 'the tool signifies specifically human activity, a transformation of nature by humans—production'" (1960, p. 80).

Vygotsky extended Engels's notion of instrumental mediation by applying it to "psychological tools" as well as to the "technical tools" of production. He invoked the analogy between psychological tools, or what he termed "signs," and technical tools, or simply "tools," at several places in his writing. While recognizing a general similarity between signs and tools, Vygotsky also noted that "this analogy, like any analogy, has its limits and cannot be extended to a full comparison of all the features of both concepts" (1981a, p. 136). He was quite clear about the fundamental differences between technical tools and psychological tools, or signs. Drawing on Marx (1977), he stated that "a tool . . . serves as a conductor of humans' influence on the object of their activity. It is directed toward the external world; it must stimulate some changes in the object; it is a means of humans' external activity, directed toward the subjugation of nature" (1960, p. 125). In contrast to this external object orientation of a technical tool, Vygotsky argued that "a sign [that is, a psychological tool] changes nothing in the object of a psychological operation. A sign is a means for psychologically influencing behavior—either the behavior of another or one's own behavior; it is a means of internal activity, directed toward the mastery of humans themselves. A sign is inwardly directed" (ibid.).

Vygotsky's notion of a psychological tool evolved over the course of his research, as manifested by the variety of terms he used when discussing psychological tools; examples include "stimulus-means," "instruments" (hence the "instrumental method"), and "signs." In general, however, he steadily moved toward placing greater and greater emphasis on the meaningful and communicative nature of signs.

Since my primary focus is the issue of mediation by meaningful signs, I shall not go into detail on the early versions of Vygotsky's account of psychological tools. A single example, recounted by Luria and Leont'ev (as reported in Radzikhovskii, 1979), will suffice for the purpose of contrast. While investigating patients with Parkinson's disease, Vygotsky asked them to perform certain physical actions. In one case when a patient was requested to walk, his only response was an increase in tremors. Pieces of white paper were then arranged on the floor to indicate the locations of a sequence of steps, and the patient was again requested to walk. Luria and Leont'ev reported that the patient's tremors decreased at this point, and he was able to walk by treading sequentially on the pieces of paper. This effect recurred in some cases with other patients.

As Radzikhovskii points out, Vygotsky's explanation began with the fact that *two* sets of stimuli were involved: first, the verbal commands, stimuli that alone were incapable of eliciting the appropriate behavior from the patient; second, the pieces of white paper, which served to *mediate* the patient's response to the first set. Because they served to control the behavior, Vygotsky labeled them "stimuli means."

In this instance there is no reason to invoke the notions of meaning and communication as used by Vygotsky in his later writings. No claims about generalization, reference, or linguistic meaning are needed to account for the efficacy of the psychological tools or stimulus-means in helping the patients to walk. As Radzikhovskii points out, this noncommunicative interpretation of psychological tools was evident in Vygotsky's ideas until the late 1920s.

By 1930 Vygotsky had shifted to a much more semiotically oriented account of psychological tools. In a report presented that year he stated, "the following can serve as examples of psychological tools and their complex systems: language; various systems for counting; mnemonic techniques; algebraic symbol systems; works of art; writing; schemes, diagrams, maps, and mechanical drawings; all sorts of conventional signs; and so on" (1981a, p. 137). The items on this list can be understood only if some concept of meaning is invoked.

As Radzikhovskii (1979) has noted, this more semiotically oriented interpretation of psychological tools can be traced to Vygotsky's early concern with literary and philological studies. This emphasis became increasingly more pronounced in Vygotsky's later years, a fact reflected in a statement made in his personal notebooks in 1932: the analysis of sign meaning (*semicheskii analiz*) is "the only adequate method for analyzing human consciousness" (1977, p. 94). This semiotic interpretation clearly guided his investigation of word meaning, inner speech, and other psychological tools.

A few criterial properties of psychological tools must be taken into account when trying to understand Vygotsky's explanation of human mental processes. The first major feature of psychological tools is that "by being included in the process of behavior, the psychological tool alters the entire flow and structure of mental functions. It does this by determining the structure of a new instrumental act, just as a technical tool alters the process of a natural adaptation by determining the form of labor operations" (Vygotsky, 1981a, p. 137). In other words, Vygotsky viewed the introduction of a psychological tool (language, for example) into a mental function (such as memory) as causing a fundamental transformation of that function. In his approach psychological tools are not viewed as auxiliary means that simply facilitate an existing mental function while leaving it qualitatively unaltered. Rather, the emphasis is on their capacity to transform mental functioning.

This feature of psychological tools is central to Vygotsky's genetic analysis of mental processes. He viewed development not as a steady stream of quantitative increments but in terms of fundamental qualitative transformations or "revolutions" associated with changes in the psychological tools.

To state that forms of mediation define levels of development is to make a point that is certainly not unique to Vygotsky's approach. Indeed many contemporary theories of cognitive development rest on the general assumption that increasingly sophisticated forms of mediation (or more generally, representation) allow the developing human to perform more complex operations on objects from an increasing spatial and temporal distance. However, as soon as one examines the specific properties of the mediational means Vygotsky considered, the uniqueness of his approach comes into focus.

The second criterial property of his account of mediation is that "by their nature [psychological tools] are social, not organic or individual" (ibid.). There are two senses in which Vygotsky considered psychological tools to be social. First, he considered psychological tools such as "language; various systems for counting; mnemonic techniques; algebraic symbol systems; etc." to be social in the sense that they are the products of sociocultural evolution. Psychological tools are neither invented by each individual nor discovered in the individual's independent interaction with nature. Furthermore, they are not inherited in the form of instincts or unconditional[1] reflexes. Instead, individuals have access to psychological tools by virtue of being part of a sociocultural milieu—that is, individuals "appropriate" (a term later used by Leont'ev [1959]) such mediational means:

> The word "social" when applied to our subject has great significance. Above all, in the widest sense of the word, it means that everything that is cultural is social. Culture is the product of social life and human social activity. That is why just by raising the question of the cultural development of behavior we are directly introducing the social plane of development.   (1981, p. 164b)

The second sense in which Vygotsky viewed psychological tools as social concerns the more "localized" social phenomena of face-to-face communication and social interaction. Instead of examining forces that operate on a general sociocultural level, the focus here was on the dynamics that characterize individual communicative events. Of course the two types of phenomena are not unrelated. However, they are governed by different explanatory principles and therefore require separate analyses.

This second sense in which psychological tools are social was central to Vygotsky's understanding of signs, a fact reflected in statements such as, "A sign is always originally a means used for social purposes, a means of influencing others, and only later becomes a means of influencing oneself" (1981b, p. 157). In a similar vein he said of language, the most important psychological tool in his approach, that "the primary function of speech, both for the adult and for the child, is the function of communication, social contact, influencing surrounding individuals" (1934a, p. 45).

The claim that psychological tools are social in this sense has important implications for Vygotsky's theory of human mental processes. For example, if the primary function of psychological tools such as language is to communicate, it is reasonable to expect these mediational means to be formed in accordance with the demands of communication. If these means also play an important role in shaping individuals' mental processes, we can expect such processes to be indirectly shaped by forces that originate in the dynamics of communication.

The Influence of Soviet Semiotics and Poetics

No other aspect of Vygotsky's work has been as consistently ignored or misinterpreted by psychologists as his semiotic analysis and the intellectual forces that gave rise to it. This criticism applies to most secondary treatments of Vygotsky's work as well as to most of his students' attempts to reformulate and extend his approach. For example, in otherwise excellent accounts of Vygotsky's ideas neither L. Rahmani (1968) nor E. Berg (1970) broached the issue of how his semiotic analysis influenced his understanding of higher mental functions, and neither took into consideration schools such as the Russian Formalists or individuals such as L. P. Yakubinskii in their review of the forces that influenced Vygotsky's thinking.

While everyone who has examined Vygotsky's work recognizes that semiotic mediation was a central concept for him, the treatment of this issue usually is limited either to asserting that it was important or to showing how his analysis was concerned with Pavlov's notion of a second signal system. While I do not wish to underestimate Pavlov's influence, I reject the notion that Vygotsky's idea of mediation was based entirely or even primarily on Pavlov's account of the second signal system. To understand the origins and nature of Vygotsky's ideas on this topic, one must look elsewhere—in particular, to the figures in semiotics, linguistics, and poetics that influenced him.

Recall that before making his appearance on the scene of Soviet psychology, Vygotsky had been engaged in the study of problems in art and literary criticism. In 1915 he wrote the first version of a major work on *Hamlet;* during the next several years he wrote other related articles; and in 1925 he published *The Psychology of Art*. Although these works have had little lasting influence on research in literary criticism, aesthetics, literary history, or the psychology of art, it is impossible to ignore them when trying to analyze Vygotsky's approach to issues in psychology between 1925 and 1934, particularly his ideas about the role of signs in mediating human activity. As V. V. Ivanov (1971) points out in his commentary on *The Psychology of Art,* "A direct continuation of the aesthetic theory presented in this volume is [Vygotsky's] investigation of the role of signs in controlling human behavior, a topic to which [he] devoted a series of theoretical and experimental psychological works" (p. 266).

The dominant force in literary criticism and linguistics in the USSR at the time Vygotsky was writing *The Psychology of Art* was Russian formalism. This school dates from 1914, when V.B. Shklovskii published his brochure *The Resurrection of the Word*. The Formalists insisted that the study of literature must begin with the identification of its own object. As B. M. Eikhenbaum (1965) later put it, "In principle the question for the Formalist is not how to study literature, but what the subject matter of literary study actually is" (p. 102). Like the New Critics in the West, the Formalists rejected existing eclectic approaches that borrowed from a variety of disciplines but failed to create their own unique object of study.

R. O. Jakobson provided the classic definition of what this object of study must be: "The object of the science of literature is not literature, but literariness—that is, that which makes a given work a work of literature" (Eikhenbaum, 1965). The Formalists argued that in order to study "literariness," one must identify and examine the linguistic devices and principles that characterize it. They were concerned with the objective study of how linguistic forms are utilized in poetry, fables, and novels. As Jakobson said, "If the study of literature wants to become a science, it must recognize the device as its only hero" (from Medvedev/Bakhtin, 1978, p. 117).

Given the Formalists' position on this issue and their impact on literary studies at the time, it is not surprising that Vygotsky focused on objective semiotic devices in *The Psychology of Art*. One cannot be completely certain about the course of events and the direction of influence, but one can at least say that the Formalists' insistence on studying objective linguistic facts was consistent with Vygotsky's desire to outline an objective science of human mental functioning. Like the Formalists, Vygotsky's arguments partly evolved from a criticism of the Symbolists, especially A. A. Potebnya (1913). Instead of relying on methods such as introspective reports about the impressions and images elicited by a text, he argued that one must begin with concrete facts about the text itself:

> The work of art, rather than its creator or its audience, should be taken as the basis for analysis . . . For the psychologist any work of art is a system of stimuli, consciously and intentionally organized in such a way as to excite an aesthetic reaction. By analyzing the structure of the stimuli we reconstruct the structure of the reaction . . . This method guarantees a sufficient objectivity of results and of investigation, since it proceeds every time from the study of solid, objectively existing, accountable facts. Here is the formula of this method: from the form of the work of art, via the functional analysis of its elements and structure, recreate the aesthetic reaction and establish its general laws. (1971, pp. 23–24)

This statement already reflects two major ideas that were to guide much of Vygotsky's later thinking: (1) it calls for an objective analysis of psychological phenomena and (2) it proposes that ideas from linguistics and literary analysis can provide one of the points of entry into this objective analysis.

While Vygotsky's claim that objective analysis must begin with an understanding of semiotic devices parallels the fundamental working assumption of the Formalists, important differences separated him from this school. The Formalists' ultimate goal was to catalogue and analyze the semiotic devices used in literature. For Vygotsky, such an analysis was only a means for investigating the psychological effects of art rather than a final goal. He believed that analyses such as those carried out by the Formalists were essential, but they addressed only the first of two questions he viewed as central. Thus in his introduction to *The Psychology of Art* Leont'ev (1971) wrote that the book "should be read on two levels: as the psychology of *art* and as the *psychology* of art" (p. vi).

If the first tenet in the Formalists' approach was that objective semiotic fact must form the basic object of study, the second tenet was that it is possible to isolate distinct languages or semiotic codes. In particular, since their object of study was "literariness," they wanted to identify the literary or poetic language that existed alongside "everyday language." These two linguistic systems were hypothesized to have unique sets of devices and organizational principles at each of several analytic levels (phonemic, lexical, and the like). Of course poetic language was not viewed by the Formalists as having no connection with other forms of language. Rather, it was viewed as a type of dialect that, like other dialects, had its own units and laws.

In addition to the formal differences that distinguished the two codes, the Formalists argued that they could be distinguished on the basis of *language function*. Yakubinskii and Jakobson were largely responsible for developing this argument during its early stages. Yakubinskii (1916) argued that practical language can be distinguished from other types of language on the basis of the speaker's purpose. His basic claim was that the function of poetic language is to force the listener or reader to focus on the code itself. Unlike the automatic processing of practical language, perception is "deautomatized" and foregrounded in poetic language. This notion was formulated in slightly different ways by other members of the Formalist school. However, a basic tenet for all was the distinction between practical language, in which the meaning of the communication is essential and formal devices are unnoticed, and poetic language, in which the expression itself becomes the end and content is only the means.

In short, the Formalists were concerned with the formal properties that characterize functionally differentiated codes or languages. Although they limited their analysis to the distinction between practical and poetic language, more general debates about the form–function relationship in language occupied a major role in the discussions on linguistics and poetics during the formative years of Vygotsky's career. This issue was also to become a major concern for Vygotsky in his later formulations about thinking and speech. An outline of his views can be found in his reaction to the Formalists in *The Psychology of Art*.

Vygotsky's position toward the early proposals advanced by the Formalists was that they, like Potebnya, had erred, but in the opposite direction. In Vygotsky's opinion, Potebnya had failed to examine the concrete semiotic devices used in artistic texts. He had focused too narrowly on the image and general psychological impact of texts instead of trying to understand the relationship between concrete semiotic devices and psychological phenomena. Conversely, Vygotsky viewed the Formalists as being overconcerned with the devices used in text, thereby ignoring important aspects of content and meaning.

The influence of linguists and semioticians such as Potebnya and members of the Formalist school is seen more readily in *The Psychology of Art* than in any of Vygotsky's other works. However, it would be a mistake to assume that this influence ceased after Vygotsky's interests shifted somewhat from the psychology of art to issues in general psychology. One of the points where this becomes most evident is in Vygotsky's account of language functions.

The problem of distinguishing various functions of language was a principal concern of the Formalists. Vygotsky went beyond the Formalists' treatment, however, and examined the proposals of other figures, especially Humboldt. Thus in the final chapter of *Thinking and Speech* Vygotsky wrote:

> In recent times the problem of the functional diversity of speech has emerged as one of the major issues in linguistics. It turns out that even from the point of view of the linguist, language is not a single form of speech activity, but an aggregate of diverse speech functions. . . . The functional diversity of speech had already been clearly recognized by Humboldt in connection with the languages of poetry and of prose, which are distinguished from one another in their orientation and means . . . Thus Humboldt's idea was that each of the various forms of speech, distinguished by functional assignment, has its own special lexicon, its own grammar, and its own syntax. This is an extremely important idea. (1934a, p. 297)

Like other critics of the Formalist school, such as Medvedev/Bakhtin (1978), Vygotsky viewed the simple dichotomy between poetic and prosaic speech as insufficient:

> Neither Humboldt nor Potebnya, who adopted and developed his idea, appreciated the full significance of this idea [of the functional diversity of the language]. They did not go beyond distinguishing poetry and prose. Furthermore, within prose they did not distinguish between sophisticated conversation that is filled with thoughts and everyday or conversational idle gossip that simply communicates about matters without introducing ideas or generalizations. (1934a, p. 297)

In making this criticism as well as in developing a proposal for overcoming the problems it identified, Vygotsky was heavily influenced by the ideas outlined by Yakubinskii in his monograph *On Dialogic Speech* (1923). As Medvedev/Bakhtin (1978) point out, this monograph represents a sociological orientation that contrasts with Yakubinskii's earlier work in which he formulated some of the most well known Formalist claims about sound patterns in poetic and practical language.

Yakubinskii argued that in order to develop a viable account of language functions, one must distinguish between monologic and dialogic speech. This line of reasoning had an obvious impact on Vygotsky, as reflected in the following statements from the last chapter of *Thinking and Speech:*

> As Yakubinskii says, even posing the problem [of language function] is alien to linguistics . . . The psychology of speech as well as linguistics, each proceeding along its own path, brings us to the problem of distinguishing the functional diversity of speech. The fundamental distinction between dialogic and monologic forms of speech takes on an overriding significance for linguistics and especially for the psychology of speech.   (1934a, p. 297)

In his second chapter ("Forms of Verbal Expression") Yakubinskii defines dialogue and monologue in the following terms:

> Corresponding to a *direct ("face-to-face") form of human interaction,* we have *direct forms of verbal interaction* that are characterized by direct visual and auditory perception of the interlocutor. Corresponding to mediated or indirect interaction, we have in the area of speech, for example, a written form of expression.
>
> Corresponding to alternating forms of interaction that involve a relatively rapid succession of actions and reactions by the interlocutors, we have a *dialogic form* of verbal social interaction; corresponding to *protracted* or *drawn out* forms of influence in social interaction, we have a *monologic form* of verbal expression.   (p. 117)

Thus for Yakubinskii the criterion that distinguishes monologic from dialogic forms of speech is not the number of individuals involved; in all cases it was assumed that a speaker or writer addresses a listener or reader. Rather, what distinguishes the two speech forms is the degree to which both parties participate in a concrete speech setting to create a text. He also noted that such facts as the availability of kinetic cues distinguish dialogic from monologic interaction.

Yakubinskii argued that dialogue is a genetically prior, "natural" form of verbal interaction, whereas monologue is a later, "artificial" form. His argument about the naturalness and priority of dialogue and the artificiality of monologue clearly influenced Vygotsky's account of these speech forms and their relationship to spoken and written speech.

This influence is reflected in Vygotsky's statement that "monologue is a higher, more complicated form of speech, and of later historical development than dialogue" (ibid., p. 299).

After developing his argument, Yakubinskii (1923) proceeded to examine some of the characteristics that distinguish dialogue from monologue. He argued that a phenomenon "rooted in the very essence of dialogue" is that it often relies less on explicit verbal mention or representation of a message than does monologue. Monologue in written form contrasts even more with dialogue than does monologue in spoken form. The need for maximally explicit linguistic formulation in written monologue arises not only because of the absence of verbal interchange that makes possible abbreviation of the sort mentioned above, but also because of the absence of a communicative context shared by the reader.

Yakubinskii pointed out that in some cases the knowledge or "apperceptual mass" shared by a speaker and listener can be so great that there is very little need to rely on external linguistic stimuli to convey a message: "The more our apperceptual mass has in common with the apperceptual mass of our interlocutor, the easier we comprehend and perceive his or her speech in conversation. In this connection our interlocutor's speech may be incomplete; it may abound in hints" (p. 156). This notion of communicating through hints was borrowed from Polivanov, who argued that it is the rule rather than the exception: "If everything that we wished to express were enclosed in the formal meanings of the words we used, we would have to use many more words than we in reality use in order to express any thought. We speak only through the use of necessary hints" (Yakubinskii, 1923, p. 161).

As an example of how interlocutors may rely on common apperceptual mass and hints rather than on explicit linguistic expression, Yakubinskii cited Tolstoy's account in *Anna Karenina* of how Kitty and Levin were able to use only the beginning letters of words to convey messages to one another. On the basis of such examples and Polivanov's claim about communicating through hints, Yakubinskii argued that such communication involves a "unique syntactic form." Vygotsky used the same example to make the same general point in *Thinking and Speech*.

Yakubinskii's formulation of the relationship between explicit linguistic expression and interlocutors' shared assumptions played an important role in shaping several of Vygotsky's ideas. The extent of Vygotsky's indebtedness is reflected in his use of several of Yakubinskii's examples and much of his general line of reasoning, as well as in statements such as the following:

> The comprehension of speech requires an understanding of what is being talked about . . . Yakubinskii is quite correct in arguing that in cases of such abbreviation [that is, the use of hints à la Polivanov] we are dealing with a unique syntactic system of speech. We are dealing with an objective simplification as opposed to the form found in more discursive speaking. Simplified syntax, syntactic condensation, the expression of a thought in condensed form, significantly fewer words—all of these facts characterize a tendency toward predicativity as it is manifested in external speech in certain situations.   (1934a, p. 295)[2]

To summarize, certain schools of Soviet poetics and semiotics helped determine the problems Vygotsky investigated and the methods he used to investigate them. Of overriding importance was the impact of Russian formalism. Again, my claim is not that Vygotsky accepted the tenets of this school; in certain respects just the opposite was the case. Rather, the point is that by conducting semiotic studies at a time when Russian formalism set the tone and course of discussion, Vygotsky was led to focus on issues that might not be considered in another time or place. He joined the Formalists in their insistence that linguistic and poetic research must begin with an objective analysis of concrete semiotic phenomena. However, he opposed the Formalists' tendency to identify only two language functions (the poetic and the practical), and he disagreed with the early Formalist doctrine of focusing on language form in isolation from its meaning. In developing his ideas about language functions, Vygotsky was heavily influenced by Yakubinskii's arguments about the differences between monologue and dialogue. In particular, he was influenced by Yakubinskii's notions about the forms of abbreviation and other formal characteristics that separate dialogic from monologic speech.

The Notion of Function

Vygotsky's list of speech functions is somewhat of a mixed bag, but by reviewing and interrelating the items, one can touch on most of the constructs that influenced his reasoning about the semiotic mediation of human mental processes. At various points in his writings Vygotsky mentioned the following types of speech function: the signaling function (1934a, p. 70), the significative function (ibid., p. 90), the social function (1960, p. 194), the individual function (ibid., p. 194), the communicative function (1934a, pp. 11–13), the intellectual function (ibid.), the nominative function (1934a, p. 98), the indicative function[3] (ibid., p. 160; 1981c, p. 219), and the symbolic function 1934a, (p. 89). He also spoke of the "functional diversity" of speech (ibid., p. 297).

The speech functions in Vygotsky's account can be categorized in terms of a set of oppositional pairs:

Signaling function versus significative function

Social function versus individual function

Communicative function versus intellectual function

Indicative function versus symbolic function

These oppositions do not all play equally important roles in Vygotsky's semiotic analysis. Rather, they can be divided into two categories. The first three oppositions deal with the mediation of social and psychological processes at a fairly general level of analysis and have little to say about the specifics of the signs involved. In contrast, the indicative and symbolic functions are defined in terms of specific relationships that exist between signs and extralinguistic reality and between signs and other signs. My review of speech functions will be based on this division of the oppositions. I shall provide relatively brief accounts of the first three oppositions, whereas the last one will serve as the basis for a detailed account of several additional aspects of Vygotsky's semiotic analysis.

Vygotsky's distinction between signaling and signification is based on Pavlov's distinction between the first and second signal system. Vygotsky went beyond Pavlov's original formulation of this distinction, however, by integrating it into the broader set of problems raised in a theory of consciousness. Nevertheless, the basic ideas about the neurophysiological mechanisms involved were generally borrowed intact from Pavlov's original statements.

As Joravsky (in preparation) has noted, Pavlov began using the notions of the first and second signal systems as early as 1927. Perhaps the clearest formulation of them can be found in a volume published by Pavlov in 1935:

To an animal, reality is signalled almost exclusively merely by the stimulations . . . which converge directly to the special cells of the visual, auditory, and other receptors of the organism. This is what we likewise possess in the form of impressions, sensations, and conceptions of the environment . . . This first system of signalling reality is the same in our case as in the case of animals. But words have built up a second signal system of signalling reality, which is peculiar to us, being a signal of the primary signals. The numerous stimulations by word have, on the one hand, removed us from reality, a fact we should constantly remember so as not to misinterpret our attitude towards reality. On the other hand, it is nothing other than words which has made us human. However it is beyond a doubt that the essential laws governing the work of the first system of signalling necessarily regulate the second system as well, because it is work done by the same nervous tissue.   (1941, p. 179)

The influence of Pavlov's position on this issue can be seen at many points in Vygotsky's writings on sign mediation. In particular, the notion that language has "removed us from reality" and the claim that the same physiological laws are involved in both the first and the second signal systems are clearly present in Vygotsky's (1981b) writings.

However, when outlining the distinction between signalization and signification, Vygotsky extended Pavlov's points in some crucial ways, as reflected in the following passage by Vygotsky:

The most general foundation of behavior, both in animals and in humans, is *signalization*. As Pavlov says, "Thus the fundamental and most general activity of the cerebral hemisphere is signal activity, involving an untold number of signals and the transmission of signals." As is known, this is the broadest formulation of the whole idea of the conditional reflexes that lies at the basis of the physiology of higher nervous activity.

But the behavior of humans is unique because they create artificial signal stimuli—above all, the grandiose signalistics of speech. Through these, humans master the signal activity of the cerebral hemispheres. If the fundamental and most general activity of the cerebral hemispheres of animals and humans is signalization, then the basic and most general activity of humans, the activity that above all distinguishes humans from animals from the psychological point of view, is *signification* . . . Signification is the creation and use of signs, that is, artificial signals . . . Humans' active adaptation to the environment, their changing of nature, cannot be based on signalization, the passive reflection of natural connections of various kinds of agents. It requires the active establishment of such connections that are impossible with a purely natural type of behavior (that is, one based on a natural combination of agents). Humans introduce artificial stimuli; they signify behavior and with the help of signs create new connections in the brain that constitute external influence.   (1960, pp. III–II2)

In this passage it is clear that Vygotsky accepted Pavlov's basic formulation, but he also raised other questions that are part of a broader theoretical framework. For example, his concern with the "creation and use of signs" touches on semiotic questions not raised by Pavlov, and his interest in the issue of how humans change nature is a reflection of the Marxist issue of how in changing nature people change themselves.

Vygotsky continued his formulation of signalization and signification by arguing that the emergence of the latter is associated with "a new regulative principle of behavior." The fact that humans can create stimuli to regulate their behavior rather than being controlled solely by stimuli existing in the environment is of crucial importance in Vygotsky's definition of higher mental processes.

Vygotsky readily recognized that formulating the notion of signification as he had begs the question of what is responsible for the "external influence" involved. The fact that he chose to address this issue and the line of argumentation he used to deal with it provide further reasons for distinguishing his approach from Pavlov's. Obviously, if one tries to account for the external influence by invoking other psychological processes, one is making a claim that raises the possibility of infinite regression. Vygotsky dealt with this problem by treating the issue of external influence as an issue of the relationship between social and individual processes:

> [What] explains the possibility of the emergence of the new regulative principle of behavior is the social life and interaction of people. In the process of social life humans have created and developed extremely complex systems of psychological ties without which labor activity and all of social life would be impossible. These means of psychological connection are by their very nature and their function signs, that is, artificially created stimuli, the purpose of which is to influence behavior, to form new conditional connections in the human brain . . . Social life creates the necessity of subordinating the individual's behavior to social demands and in addition creates complex signalization systems—the means

of connection that direct and regulate the formation of conditional connections in the brains of individual humans. (1960, pp. 113–114)

This passage reflects the intimate connection Vygotsky saw between social life and signs. As Dobrogaev (1947) has pointed out, Pavlov did not understand, or at least did not emphasize, the inherently social nature of signs. Thus, although Vygotsky was influenced by Pavlov's distinction between first and second signal systems, his account of signalization and signification cannot be equated with Pavlov's formulation.

A more extended formulation of Vygotsky's position on the social aspects of signs can be seen in his comparison of the *social* and *individual functions* of speech. In developing his ideas about these functions, he drew extensively from the work of the French psychiatrist P. Janet.

> The history of signs . . . brings us to a much more general law governing the development of behavior. Janet calls it the fundamental law of psychology. The essence of this law is that in the process of development, children begin to use the same forms of behavior in relation to themselves that others initially used in relation to them . . . With regard to our area of interest, we could say that the validity of this law is nowhere more obvious than in the use of the sign. A sign is always originally a means used for social purposes, a means of influencing others, and only later becomes a means of influencing oneself . . . the mental function of the word, as Janet demonstrated, cannot be explained except through a system extending beyond individual humans. The word's first function is its social function; and if we want to trace how it functions in the behavior of an individual, we must consider how it used to function in social behavior. (1981b, pp. 157–158)

In general, Vygotsky's distinction between the social and individual functions of speech is a distinction between mediational means for interpsychological and intrapsychological functions, respectively. Thus in order to understand the role of verbal mediation in volitional, intrapsychological functioning, he argued that one must examine speech on the interpsychological plane. In particular, one must view such phenomena as the use of directives or commands by adults to regulate children.

Vygotsky argued that the origins of the social function of speech could be found in very early stages of ontogenesis. He made a further distinction between two functions of speech that appear during the first year of life: *emotional release* and *social contact*. With regard to the latter he wrote:

> In the first year of the child's life (that is, during the preintellectual stage of development in speech) we find rich development in the social function of speech.
> The relatively complex and rich social contact of the child leads to a very early development of a "means of contact." There is no doubt that one can establish identical specific reactions to the human voice in the child as early as the third week of life (presocial reactions) and the first social reaction to the human voice during the second month. Similarly, during the first months of a child's life laughter, babbling, behavioral displays, and gestures emerge as a means of social contact.   (1934a, p. 88)

Vygotsky borrowed from the work of others, especially Charlotte Buhler (1927), in outlining this notion of the social contact function of speech. His ideas on this topic are similar to those proposed by B. Malinowski (1960) in connection with the "phatic function" of language, as reflected in Malinowski's statement that the "phatic communion" is a form of interaction that "serves to establish bonds of personal union between people brought together by the mere need of companionship and does not serve any purpose of communicating ideas." As with most aspects of Vygotsky's account of early development, he provided little detail about the social contact and emotional release functions of speech; instead he borrowed from existing accounts and outlined them only to the degree necessary to launch into a discussion of the issue that most interested him—sociocultural development.

If the emotional release and social contact functions of speech play a role in the first stages of ontogenesis, Vygotsky argued that with further development, especially with the advent of the influence of sociocultural forces, new functions begin to emerge. It was in this connection that he introduced the notions of the *communicative (kommunikativnaya)* and *intellectual (intellektual'naya)* functions of speech (1934a, p. 11). From his discussions it is clear that these two functions represent a further specification of his notions of the social and individual functions. The main difference is a shift in focus from the general distinction between the social and individual use of language to the nature of the semiotic processes on the interpsychological and intrapsychological planes.

A major concern for Vygotsky when analyzing the communicative and intellectual functions of speech was that their inherent and necessary interconnection be recognized. He criticized other approaches for failing to recognize this essential point:

> The initial function of speech is the communicative function. Speech is first and foremost a means of social interaction, a means of pronouncement and understanding. This function of speech, which is usually analyzed in terms of isolated units, has been separated from the intellectual function of speech. Both functions are ascribed to speech as if they were parallel to or independent of one another. Speech, as it were, combines within itself both the function of social interaction and the function of thinking, but what the relationship is between these two functions, what brings about the presence of the two functions of speech, how they develop, and how they are structurally intertwined are questions that have remained uninvestigated.   (Ibid.)

Vygotsky made this point repeatedly in his writings. In his view it was only through understanding the inextricable ties as well as the genetic transitions between interpsychological and intrapsychological functioning that we can hope to build an adequate account of higher mental functioning.

My comments on the first three pairs of speech functions can be summarized as follows. Vygotsky borrowed from Pavlov's distinction between first and second signal systems in order to contrast signalization with signification. One of the most important ways in which Vygotsky extended Pavlov's formulation to arrive at the notion of signification was to argue that social factors must be taken into account, thus raising the general issue of social and individual functions of speech. Then, in an attempt to specify the origins of the social function as called for in a genetic analysis, Vygotsky introduced the notions of the emotional release and social contact functions of speech. Vygotsky's reason for dealing with them was that they provided insight into the origins of the sociocultural line of development in ontogenesis. Finally, Vygotsky introduced the notions of the communicative and intellectual functions of speech and argued for their inherent interconnection. The three pairs of speech functions mentioned so far do not specify the concrete properties that give signs their mediational power. For this reason, they should be viewed as doing no more than setting the stage for Vygotsky's semiotic analysis.

Concrete Semiotic Mechanism in Mediation

Vygotsky's account of the linguistic means used in semiotic mediation is based on two opposing tendencies that he recognized in the organization of human languages. On the one hand, language has the potential to be used in abstract, decontextualized reflection. This premise underlies his analysis of concept development, categorization, and syllogistic and scientific reasoning. In carrying out this aspect of his research he focused on the potential for decontextualization in language, especially the decontextualization of "meaning" (*znachenie*). On the other hand, there is a side of linguistic organization that is rooted in contextualization. In this connection Vygotsky introduced the indicative function of speech, and he studied the ways in which the structure and interpretation of linguistic signs depend on their relationships with the context in which they appear. This aspect of his semiotic analysis provides the foundation for his account of inner speech and relies on his notion of "sense" (*smysl*).

At first glance it may appear that the two aspects of Vygotsky's semiotic analysis are based on contradictory assumptions about the nature of language. Decontextualization, after all, is the opposite of contextualization. The point is, however, that while these two tendencies are in opposition, they operate simultaneously in determining the structure and interpretation of speech. The organization of specific utterances can be dominated by one of these forces, but the other is almost always reflected as well.

Vygotsky's account of decontextualized semiotic means and the symbolic function of speech is grounded in a claim made by E. Sapir (1921). As B. Lee (1984) has noted, there are in fact several points of contact between Vygotsky's and Sapir's ideas. In this case, the issue is the inherent link between generalized categorization and human communication. Following Sapir, Vygotsky wrote:

> In order to transmit some experience or content of consciousness to another person, there is no other way than to ascribe the content to a known class, to a known group of phenomena, and as we know this necessarily involves generalization. Thus it turns out that social interaction necessarily presupposes generalization and the development of word meaning, that is, generalization becomes possible in the presence of the development of social interaction. Thus higher, uniquely human forms of psychological social in-

teraction are possible only because human thinking reflects reality
in a generalized way. (1934a, pp. 11–12)

Hence Vygotsky viewed genuine, or "psychological," social interaction as necessarily involving the use of generalized sign meaning.
Signs that simply indicate the presence of an uncategorized object or
state of affairs do not meet this criterion in his view:

We know that social interaction such as that found in the animal
world that is not mediated by speech or any other system of signs
or means is social interaction of only the most primitive or limited
type. In essence, such social interaction that uses expressive movements does not even merit the name social interaction; it should
instead be called *contagion*. The frightened gander that recognizes
danger and spreads alarm to the whole flock is not really communicating to it what it saw but is rather contaminating the flock
with fear. (Ibid., p. 11)

As a corollary to the claim that genuine social interaction rests on
generalization, Vygotsky argued that stages in the development of
generalization are directly linked to stages in the development of social
interaction: "the levels of generalization in a child correspond strictly
to the levels of development in social interaction. Any new level in the
child's generalization signifies a new level in the possibility for social
interaction" (ibid., p. 432).

Vygotsky introduced the notions of the *indicative* (*indikativnaya* or
ukazatel'naya) and *symbolic* (*simvolicheskaya*) functions of speech as part
of his genetic analysis of generalization. The role of these speech functions is crucial in his line of reasoning, since without them the investigator is left with an account of ontogenesis in which generalization
suddenly and mysteriously appears. Indeed Vygotsky specifically criticized C. and W. Stern (1928) and others for their failure to recognize
this problem. Vygotsky's general claim was that early levels of generalization and corresponding levels of development in social interaction
are based on the indicative function of speech, whereas more advanced
levels are possible because of the symbolic function of speech. Furthermore, it is because Vygotsky recognized the two opposing tendencies in human language that he could identify and relate these two
functions.

Vygotsky's most complete treatment of the notion of the indicative
function of speech can be found in his analysis of the regulation of
attention. He argued that during very early phases in the development

of attention an adult's words do not function to categorize objects or abstract particular features of these objects. Rather, words function solely to direct a child's attention to an object. At some of the points where he discussed the indicative function of speech he tied it to the notion of an orienting response in Pavlovian approaches. In his discussions of speech functions he argued that the pure indicative function is the first to appear:

> Our initial words have indicatory meaning for the child. In this, it seems to us that we have identified the *original function of speech,* which has not been appreciated by other researchers. The original function of speech is not that the word has meaning for the child; it is not that a corresponding new connection is created with the help of the word. Rather, the *word is initially an indicator.* The word as an indicator is the primary function in the development of speech, from which all others may be derived. (1981c, p. 219)

In contrast, the symbolic function of speech involves the classification of events and objects in terms of generalized categories and eventually the formation of relationships among these categories.

In order to explicate the complex relationship Vygotsky envisioned between the indicative and symbolic functions, one must examine some of the properties of Vygotsky's account of the linguistic sign, especially the word. The analysis of word meaning was central for Vygotsky in this respect. The analysis rests squarely on the distinction between *meaning (znachenie)* and *reference (predmetnaya otnesennost').*[4] Borrowing from E. Husserl (1900) he pointed out that "it is necessary to distinguish . . . the meaning of a word or expression from its referent, that is, the objects indicated by the word or expression. There may be one meaning and different objects or, conversely, different meanings and one object. Whether we say 'the victor at Jena' or 'the loser at Waterloo,' we indicate the same person (Napoleon). The meaning of the two expressions [however] is different" (1934a, p. 142). For Vygotsky this distinction had great significance for understanding the development of human consciousness; it "provides the key to the correct analysis of the development of early stages of children's thinking" (ibid., p. 143). The importance of the distinction derives from the fact that it allowed Vygotsky to deal with the function of referring, or picking out particular objects in terms of meaning categories. That is, the indicative function of the word is a purely referential function.

Vygotsky's account of the indicative function of words reveals that he had in mind a type of sign similar to what C. S. Peirce (1931–1935) called an *index*. In some cases even the terminology coincides. For example, Vygotsky (1934a) commented that in many languages the term for the primary instrument of pointing derives from its function—hence, "index finger" in English.

Scholars such as A. Burks (1949), T. Goudge (1965), C. Morris (1971), and M. Silverstein (1976) have identified several properties of Peirce's index that are of particular relevance in understanding Vygotsky's indicative function of speech. First, "an index has a direct physical connection with its object" (Goudge, 1965, p. 53). In Peirce's analysis this "existential" connection can be one of several types, but of primary interest here is the fact that when using an index in communication, the sign vehicle and its object must be spatially and temporally copresent. Thus in the case of an indexical sign such as pointing, the sign is context bound in that the relationship between the sign vehicle and the object is dependent on spatiotemporal contiguity. The criterion of spatiotemporal copresence between sign vehicle and object entails a second fact, namely, that unique utterance events are involved. In Peirce's terminology this means that one is dealing with sign "tokens" rather than sign "types." A third property of an index is that in using it to identify an object, the object is characterized in only a minimal way. As Goudge (1965) states, an index is "a nonassertive sign. It *says* nothing but only *shows* what it refers to" (p. 65). Although Vygotsky never differentiated these three properties of the index in his account of the indicative function of speech, his comments demonstrate that he had an intuitive grasp of them. Recently Silverstein (1985), M. Hickmann (1985), and other researchers have begun to examine these connections in more detail.

If the original function of speech in Vygotsky's account is the indicative (that is, indexical) function, how is it related to the symbolic function? This is part of the larger question of how the decontextualization of mediational means occurs. On the one hand, one finds sign functioning that reflects the context-bound aspect of linguistic organization; it is concerned with the relationship between sign vehicles and the contexts in which they occur. On the other hand, one finds sign functioning that reflects the decontextualized aspect of linguistic organization; it is concerned with the notion that certain aspects of language organization can operate independently of the context in which sign vehicles occur. Both aspects are latent potentials in human language. The task of genetic analysis is to account for the transition from a level where semiotic functioning is always contextualized to a level where decontextualized functioning is also possible. In terms of the issues currently under consideration, this means that genetic analysis must account for the transition from a level where the indicative function of speech alone is used to a level where the symbolic function appears as well. Vygotsky approached this issue from the perspective of the development of word meanings, or concepts.

The Development of Word Meaning

One of the factors that motivated Vygotsky's genetic analysis of word meaning was the claim by Stern and Stern (1928) and others that children discover the nature of word meaning rather than go through a sequence of stages culminating in the mature form of categorization and generalization. The essence of this criticism is that word meaning continues to develop long after the point when new words (that is, sign vehicles or sign forms) first appear in children's speech. He argued that although it is tempting to attribute a complete understanding of word meaning to children when they begin to use word forms in what seem to be appropriate ways, the appearance of new words marks the beginning rather than the end point in the development of meaning. Vygotsky warned:

> The outward similarity between the thinking of the three-year-old and the adult, the practical coincidence in the child's and adult's word meaning that makes verbal social interaction possible, the mutual understanding of adult and child, the functional equivalence of the complex and concepts—all these things have led investigators to the false conclusion that the three-year-old's thinking is already present. True, they assumed that this thinking is undeveloped, but they nonetheless assume that it has the full set of forms found in adult intellectual activity. Consequently, it is assumed that during the transitional period there is no fundamental change, no essential new step in the mastery of concepts. The origins of this mistake are very easy to understand. At a very early age children acquire many words whose meanings for them coincide with those of adults. Because of the possibility of understanding, the impression has been created that *the end point of development in word meaning coincides with the beginning point,* that a ready-made concept is given from the very beginning, and consequently that there is no room for development. Those investigators (such as Ach) who equate the concept with the initial

meaning of the word thereby inevitably arrive at false conclusions, based on an illusion. (1934a, p. 132)

In making a proposal for how to avoid such problems, Vygotsky (1934a) outlined an ontogenetic progression from "unorganized heaps" to "complexes" and then to "concepts" on the basis of a block-sorting and classification task. In collaboration with L. S. Sakharov (1930), Yu. V. Kotelova, and E. I. Pashkovskaya he used this task in a series of studies on concept formation. The studies involved more than 300 subjects, including normal children, adolescents, and adults, as well as "individuals suffering from pathological disturbances of intellectual and speech activity" (1934a, p. 113). His experimental setting was the following:

> Several figures differing in color, form, height, and size were placed in front of the subject on a board. They were arranged randomly with respect to the various dimensions . . . One of the figures was turned over to show the subject the nonsense word written on the bottom.
> The subject was asked to set aside all of the figures on which he or she predicted the same word would be written. After each set of selections by the subject, the experimenter provided feedback by turning over a figure that had not been selected. This new figure either had the same word written on it as the one revealed at the beginning of the task and was different from it in some features and similar in others, or it was a figure with a different sign that was similar in some respects and different in others from the one turned over earlier. (Ibid., p. 113)

Vygotsky's data from this experiment were in the form of subjects' patterns or sequences of selecting blocks. If the experimenter began a session by showing the subject that the nonsense word *mur* was written on the bottom of a small, tall, yellow, triangular figure, the subject might make a prediction by selecting a sequence of yellow blocks, a sequence of small blocks, a sequence of small tall blocks, and so on, or the subject might select one yellow block that happens to be a cylinder, then select a cylinder that happens to be blue, then select a blue block that happens to be triangular, and so on.

Vygotsky's main finding from analyzing sequences of block selections was that the criteria and operations used in making these selections change during ontogenesis. It is only at later stages that children use stable categories in carrying out this task. Thus it is only then that one could expect subjects to select a series of blocks on the basis of a single stable criterion such as yellowness, tallness, largeness, yellowness and tallness, and the like.

One of Vygotsky's major contributions to this line of research was to demonstrate that development does not simply consist of switching from random selection to selection based on stable criteria. Instead, he proposed a genetic account that identifies the stages leading up to the stable functioning found in adults' performance. He identified three basic levels in this development. First, he spoke of the use of "unorganized heaps" in young children. At this level it is very difficult for an adult observer to discern any criteria that guide the child's selection. In describing children's performance at this stage, Vygotsky spoke of the diffuse, unstable, syncretic image that unites the objects. The criteria used for selecting objects are often subjective and hence not obvious to an outside observer. However, some objective criteria may also be in evidence at this early stage. Thus a child may group a tall, small, black cylinder with a short, large, yellow cube because the two are seen as a chimney and a building. Then the child may add a yellow block that matches the yellow one already selected, then a red cube because it is pretty, and so on.

The second level in Vygotsky's account of concept development is "thinking in complexes." Vygotsky (1934a) wrote that "the generalizations created with the help of this mode of thinking are complexes of various concrete objects or things that are no longer related on the basis of the child's subjective ties or impressions, but on the basis of objective connections that actually exist among the objects" (p. 121). Vygotsky outlined several types of complexes on the basis of the criteria that guided subjects' selection of blocks. Although he noted important differences among the forms of thinking in complexes, he emphasized that they are united by the fact that they are tied to the concrete context in which the subject carries out the task.

An examination of what he called a "chain complex" illustrates this point:

> A chain complex is constructed in accordance with the principle of a dynamic, temporary combination of various links into a single chain and the transmission of meaning through the individual links of this chain . . .
>
> For example, when given a yellow triangle as the original block, the child may select several angular blocks and then, if the last of

these is blue, the child may add other blue figures, say semicircles and circles. This in turn is sufficient to change to a new feature again and make subsequent selections on the basis of being round. During the process of forming a complex, the subject constantly switches from one feature to another.   (1934a, p. 126)

From this example it is obvious that rather than being governed by a single stable category throughout the task, the subject is influenced by properties of the concrete objects in the task setting, specifically, the indexical iconic relationships (compare Silverstein, 1976, 1985) among these objects. Thus some feature or features of the external, concrete objects themselves have taken on the role of the sign that regulates the subject's activity. Rather than the subject's using signs (specifically, symbols) to structure the context, signs (indexical icons) in the context are structuring the subject's activity.

During the past few decades investigators such as Bruner, Greenfield, and R. Olver (1966) have reported findings that indicate a tendency of children to group objects on the basis of principles other than possession of a common attribute. Furthermore, L. Bloom (1973) and M. Bowerman (1976, 1978, 1980) have documented phenomena in young children's use of words during language acquisition that indicate the use of "complexive categories" (Bowerman, 1980). This does not mean, however, that these and other investigators concerned with language development agree in all respects with Vygotsky's account of concept development. As Bowerman (1980) notes, some children seem to acquire terms by mapping them onto a preexisting nonlinguistic category that emerges during early stages of ontogenesis (for example, Sugarman, 1983). Hence Bowerman's comments indicate the need to supplement Vygotsky's claims about the emergence of word meaning by providing a more sophisticated analysis of the natural line of development.

The third period in Vygotsky's schema of conceptual development is when "genuine concepts" appear. Vygotsky argued that experience in educational activity is an important force that guides the development of genuine concepts, hence his distinction between the genuine or "scientific" concepts learned as a result of schooling and the "everyday" or "spontaneous" concepts learned by the child elsewhere. In addition to schooling, Vygotsky used another criterion to distinguish scientific from everyday concepts. He argued that the "first and most decisive distinction between spontaneous and nonspontaneous, especially scientific, concepts is the absence of a system in the former"

(1934a, p. 194). In the case of spontaneous concepts, the child's attention "is always centered on the object being represented and not on the act of thought that grasps it" (ibid.). In contrast, "scientific concepts, with their quite different relationship to an object, are mediated through other concepts with their internal, hierarchical system of interrelationships" (ibid.).

By making this claim about systematicity, Vygotsky was taking an important step in his argument about generalization, semiotic mechanisms, and word meaning. Whereas the statements about generalization that I have analyzed up to this point involve a relationship between signs and the nonlinguistic context in which they appear, his claim about systems of concepts goes into the issue of how signs relate to other signs. Vygotsky believed that at higher levels of development, *both* relationships must be considered in order to provide an adequate account of word meaning. Thus when speaking of the most advanced form of generalization, that found in scientific concepts, Vygotsky argued that the concept involves "simultaneously a relationship to an object and a relationship to another concept, that is, the initial elements of a system of concepts" (ibid., p. 196). With the development of scientific concepts, a child not only can use words such as "table," "chair," and "furniture" appropriately in connection with the objects to which they refer, but the child also can operate on statements of logical equivalence, nonequivalence, entailment, and the like, such as "All tables are furniture." Hence the emphasis has shifted away from those aspects of linguistic organization that involve contextualization to the capacity of linguistic signs to enter into decontextualized relationships, that is, relationships which are constant across contexts of use.

For Vygotsky, a further criterion that distinguishes scientific from everyday concepts is the fact that the former are learned in a formal schooling setting whereas the latter emerge on the basis of children's experience in the everyday world. He argued that schooling's emphasis on using language to talk about language (that is, on decontextualized, metalinguistic reflection), as opposed to talking about nonlinguistic reality, is an important force in the emergence of scientific concepts.

According to Vygotsky, the development of scientific concepts has great significance for the evolution of higher mental processes because these concepts necessarily involve conscious realization and hence voluntary control. In contrast to earlier, context-bound forms of functioning supported by spontaneous concepts, the decontextualization inherent in scientific concepts makes possible these properties of higher mental processes:

> We could say that the power of scientific concepts is evident in the sphere that generally defines the higher mastery of concepts—conscious realization and voluntariness. At the same time it is in this sphere that one can observe the weakness of the child's everyday concepts, concepts that are strong in the sphere of spontaneous, situationally specific, concrete application, in the sphere of experience and empiricism.   (1934a, p. 232)

Vygotsky claimed that this was a natural consequence of the systematicity of scientific concepts that derives from the decontextualized relations into which they enter and from the nature of their presentation and mastery in instruction:

> Thus the generalization of genuine mental processes that leads to their mastery lies at the foundation of conscious realization. Above all else instruction plays a decisive role in this process. Scientific concepts [as opposed to everyday concepts], with their unique relationship to objects, with their mediation through other concepts, with their internal hierarchical system of interrelationships among themselves are the area in which the conscious realization of concepts, that is, their generalization and mastery, emerges first and foremost. Once the new structure of generalization emerges in one sphere of thought, it is transferred, as any structure is, as a well-know principle of activity, without any training to any other area of thought and concepts. Thus, conscious realization enters through the gates of scientific concepts.   (Ibid., pp. 193–194)

In Vygotsky's account of higher mental functions, scientific concepts are what make it possible for humans to carry out mental activity in a way that is maximally independent of the concrete context. That is, they represent the end point in the decontextualization of mediational means. This does not mean that such mental activity is somehow purer or less bound by constraints. After all, the structure of sign systems themselves are crucial in this respect. It does mean, however, that sociohistorically evolved semiotic mechanisms come to play an increasingly important role in mental functioning while concrete context plays a decreasing role. This trade-off in the sources of control of mental activity is the topic of Vygotsky's research on complexes and concepts.

The ability to deal with word meanings makes it possible to use words in terms of one set of their relationships—their relationships to other words—independently of the relationship between sign vehicle tokens and their context. It was in his genetic analysis of the emergence of these two types of relationship that Vygotsky developed the notion of a *pseudoconcept*. A pseudoconcept is the transitional construct between complexes and concepts. It is transitional because the relationship between sign and nonlinguistic reality is similar to that in genuine concepts, but the relationship between sign and other signs is different. In the case of the pseudoconcept:

> the generalization in the child's thinking reminds us in its external form of the concept used by the adult in intellectual activity, but in its essence, in its psychological nature, it is something quite different from a concept in the true sense of the word.
>
> If we examine carefully this last level in the development of thinking in complexes, we find a collection of concrete objects that phenotypically (that is, in its external form, its aggregate of external properties) corresponds completely with the concept. However, in its genetic nature, in the conditions of its emergence and development, in the causal dynamic connections that lie at its foundation, it is by no means a concept. From its external perspective a concept stands before us; from its internal perspective, a complex. Therefore, we call this a pseudoconcept.   (Ibid., p. 129)

In terms of the blocks task used by Vygotsky and his colleagues, the level of pseudoconceptual thinking is manifested by certain types of behaviors that initially appear to reflect the use of genuine concepts but upon further analysis fail to live up to this standard. Pseudoconceptual performance is most readily seen in connection with the subject's reply to the experimenter's feedback. E. Hanfmann and J. Kasanin (1937) report such instances as follows:

> In many cases the group or groups created by the subject have quite the same appearance as in a consistent classification, and the lack of a true conceptual foundation is not revealed until the subject is required to put in operation the ideas that underlie this grouping. This happens at the moment of correction when the examiner turns one of the wrongly selected blocks and shows that the word written on it is different from the one on the sample block, e.g., that it is not *mur*. This is one of the critical points of the experiment . . .
>
> Subjects who have approached the task as a classification prob-

lem [that is, with genuine conceptual thinking] respond to correction immediately in a perfectly specific way. This response is adequately expressed in the statement: "Aha! Then it is not color" (or shape, etc.) . . . The subject removes all the blocks he had placed with the sample one, and starts looking for another possible classification.

On the other hand, the outward behavior of the subject at the beginning of the experiment may have been that of attempting a classification. He may have placed all red blocks with the sample, proceeding quite consistently . . . and declared that he thinks those red blocks are *murs*. Now the examiner turns up one of the chosen blocks and shows that it has a different name . . . The subject sees it removed or even obediently removes it himself, but that is all he does: he makes no attempt to remove the other red blocks from the sample *mur*. To the experimenter's question if he still thinks that those blocks belong together, and are *mur*, he answers definitely, "Yes, they still belong together because they are red." This striking reply betrays an attitude totally incompatible with a true classification [that is, truly conceptual] approach and proves that the groups he had formed were actually pseudoclasses [pseudoconcepts]. (pp. 30–31)

This passage reveals several important facts about pseudoconcepts. First, unlike earlier forms of thinking in complexes in this task, the pattern and end product of selection are not what distinguish pseudoconceptual from conceptual thinking. The set of objects selected is the same as what could be selected when operating with a concept. What *is* different is the reasoning that lies behind this selection. In the case of pseudoconcepts this reasoning is still at least partially determined by the concrete environment in which it is carried out. The locus of control or regulation has moved somewhat from the objects and the iconic relationships that exist among them to the active individual. However, a response to experimenter feedback such as the one reported by Hanfmann and Kasanin indicates that the source of control has not entirely shifted to the subject.

To say that the source of regulation is located entirely within the subject in this experimental setting means that the subject is able to operate on word meanings and the systemic relationships among them independently of the relationship of sign tokens to their context. That is, one must be dealing with completely decontextualized mediational means. It is precisely when children are capable of operating with decontextualized word meanings alone without being distracted by the nonlinguistic context that one can speak of the movement from thinking in complexes and pseudoconcepts to thinking in genuine, especially scientific, concepts.

Thus Vygotsky's distinction between meaning and reference provides the key to interpreting his claims about the development leading to genuine concepts. In the case of pre-pseudoconceptual thinking in complexes, subjects' selections in the blocks task correspond neither in meaning nor in reference with conceptually based selections; in the case of pseudoconceptual thinking the sets of objects selected correspond with those produced by conceptual thinking, but responses to experimenter feedback reveal that these referential sets are not based on the same kind of meanings and interrelationships among meanings; and finally in the case of conceptual thinking the relations between signs and nonlinguistic objects reflect stable, decontextualized relations between signs and other signs.

Vygotsky saw social interaction as providing the motivating force for the transition from the level of thinking in complexes and pseudoconcepts to thinking in concepts. This view simply is one example of his claim about the close relationship between levels of generalization and levels of social interaction in ontogenesis:

> We have seen that the speech of adults surrounding children, with its constant, determinant meanings, determines the paths of the development of children's generalizations, the circle of formations of complexes. Children do not select the meaning for a word. It is given to them in the process of verbal social interaction with adults. Children do not construct their own complexes freely. They find them already constructed in the process of understanding others' speech. They do not freely select various concrete elements and include them in one or another complex. They receive a group of concrete objects in an already prepared form of generalization provided by a word . . . In general, children do not create their own speech; they master the existing speech of surrounding adults. (1934a, p. 133)

Clearly Vygotsky's claim was that by interacting with adults, children induce or infer the structure of concepts and word meanings that lies behind adults' speech and that this process is motivated by the need to define and redefine word meanings as a result of words being used in various referential contexts.

Thus Vygotsky's analysis of the development of concepts is based on his semiotic analysis. Specifically, it is based on one of the organizing principles of human language, the capacity of words to enter into decontextualized relationships with other words. He traced the origins of concept development to contextualized signs, or the indicative function of speech, which involves relations between sign tokens and their contexts, and identified ways in which semiotic functioning eventually reaches a point where decontextualized sign–sign relationships provide the basis for regulating the child's activity. This aspect of development is defined in terms of the degree to which semiotically mediated functioning uses what Sapir (1921) termed "the highest latent or potential content of speech, the content that is obtained by interpreting each of the elements in the flow of language as possessed of its very fullest conceptual value" (pp. 14–15).

Social, Egocentric, and Inner Speech

Vygotsky's account of conceptual development is based on decontextualized linguistic organization, that is, on the potential of language to serve in abstract reflection. In contrast, the development of egocentric and inner speech is characterized by increasing contextualization of a certain sort. In this case development relies on the second, contextualized aspect of linguistic organization outlined earlier.

At first glance, the tendency toward increased contextualization appears to contradict Vygotsky's general claim that development in sociogenesis and ontogenesis occurs through the decontextualization of mediational means. In order to see why this is not so, one must distinguish between two types of context. First there is what may be termed *extralinguistic context*. I have invoked this notion at several points in my argument. In my account of the indicative function of speech, for instance, I spoke of the relationship between the sign vehicle and the context. In these cases I was concerned with the extralinguistic context composed of nonlinguistic objects, actions, events, and the like, which are spatiotemporally copresent with a sign token. For example, certain aspects of interpreting the utterance "What is that over there?" (with or without an accompanying nonverbal point) depend on the existence of a nonlinguistic object; namely, in order to compute the reference value of "that over there," a nonlinguistic object must be present in the speech event.

In contrast to the extralinguistic context, the *intralinguistic,* or simply *linguistic, context* also must often be taken into consideration in order to explain the organization and interpretation of utterances. Language often serves as its own context, as in the sign–sign relationships that underlie Vygotsky's account of genuine concepts. This, however, would seem to be an inappropriate way to use the term "context." After all, I have stressed throughout that the relationships involved here are constant across contexts and hence are decontextualized in an important sense. Hence I have not used the term "linguistic context" when dealing with these issues.

It is true that the use of decontextualized meaning, as in the block-sorting task, makes possible a shift in the locus of control of an activity from the extralinguistic context to a semiotic level. However, the notion of linguistic context need not be invoked in order to describe this shift. Instead, I shall reserve the notion of linguistic context for another use: as in the case of extralinguistic context, I shall be concerned with the relationship between a sign token (for example, a unique verbal utterance) and its context. In this instance, however, the context will be linguistic in nature. Since I am dealing with speech events or sign tokens, which have a unique spatiotemporal location, I am referring to a context that is constantly changing. Unlike the sign–sign relations involved in reflective conceptual reasoning, the linguistic context of an utterance does not remain constant across contexts.

As a simple example of linguistic context, consider the sentence "I saw a man walking down the street" uttered by a speaker to a listener in the absence of anyone else. If this utterance is followed by "He was very tall," one can see that part of the interpretation of "He" in the second utterance is dependent on linguistic context provided by the first. In this case there is no copresent extralinguistic object that is the referent of "He." Rather, the identity and existence of the referent must be determined from prior discourse. Furthermore, it is easy to see that this aspect of the interpretation of "He" will change, depending on the linguistic context in which it appears (for example, compare the context provided by the utterance "I saw a clown at the circus yesterday").

The type of decontextualized relations I examined in conceptual development and the kind of relations provided by linguistic context are similar in that they both make possible mental processes that are not directly dependent on the extralinguistic context. They both fall under the heading of semiotic mediation, which plays a central role in Vygotsky's account of higher, uniquely human mental functioning. Furthermore, they both involve sign–sign relationships. However, they differ in that the sign–sign relationships found in genuine concepts remain constant across speech utterances, whereas the sign–sign relationships involved in ongoing speech are unique to specific utterances. These similarities and differences are reflected in Table 1.

The studies Vygotsky and Luria conducted in Central Asia focused on the decontextualization of mediational means as an explanatory principle for social history. The question thus arises as to whether the emergence of intralinguistic contextualization as evidenced in inner speech also can serve as an explanation in this genetic domain. Vygotsky made some general claims to this effect, but he never developed them in detail. To see how the process of linguistic contextualization in inner speech can play a role in social history, it would be necessary to introduce several semiotic constructs that he did not utilize (see chapter 8).

For my present purposes, it is important to note that Vygotsky did rely heavily on the notion of increasing linguistic contextualization in his account of ontogenesis. Indeed this is at the foundation of his analysis of how egocentric and inner speech develop in the child. For this reason the decontextualization of mediational means (as I have defined it) cannot stand alone as an explanatory principle of ontogenesis. Instead, the issue is the more general process of emerging sign–sign relations both contextualized and decontextualized. This process reflects the shift in the locus of control of higher mental functioning from external, unmediated reality to semiotic systems.

Vygotsky claimed that inner speech enables humans to plan and

Table 1   The forms of sign use in Vygotsky's account of semiotic mediation

Contextualized	Decontextualized
Extralinguistic context (relations between signs and nonsemiotic objects as in the indicative function of speech; relations depend on unique utterance events)	Sign–sign relations in reflective, conceptual reasoning; relations are constant across utterance events
Intralinguistic context (sign–sign relations in egocentric and inner speech; relations depend on unique utterance events)	

regulate their activity and derives from previous participation in verbal social interaction. Egocentric speech is "a [speech] form found in the transition from external to inner speech" (1934a, p. 46). It is because egocentric speech provides insight into the development, and therefore the very nature, of inner speech that it has "such enormous theoretical interest" (ibid.). The appearance of egocentric speech, roughly at the age of three, reflects the emergence of a new self-regulative function similar to that of inner speech. Its external form reflects the fact that the child has not fully differentiated this new speech function from the function of social contact and social interaction. Thus Vygotsky described egocentric speech as "inner speech in its psychological function and external speech physiologically" (ibid.).

At about the age of seven, egocentric speech disappears, a fact that Vygotsky attributed to its "going underground" to form inner speech. The close genetic relationship he saw among the forms and functions of social, egocentric, and inner speech is described in the following passages from chapter 2 of *Thinking and Speech*:

> The first thing that links the inner speech of the adult with the egocentric speech of the preschooler is similarity of function: both are speech for oneself as opposed to social speech, which carries out the task of communication and social relation with surrounding people . . .
> The second thing that links the inner speech of the adult with the egocentric speech of the child is their structural properties . . . the structural changes [in egocentric speech] tend toward the structure of inner speech, namely, abbreviation . . . According to this hypothesis egocentric speech grows out of its social foundations by means of transferring social, collaborative forms of behavior to the sphere of the individual's psychological functioning . . . Thus the overall scheme takes on the following form: social speech—egocentric speech—inner speech. (1934a, pp. 41–46)

During the earlier phases of ontogenesis the issue of the verbal regulation of action translates into the issue of how the speech of adults redirects and transforms action deriving from the child's natural line of development. Vygotsky's claim that the emergence of speech transforms the child's practical actions is illustrated in his analysis of labeling, a use of speech somewhat more sophisticated than the pure indicatory function but not as developed as the stable categorization found in the mature communicative function. Vygotsky argued that labeling, which appears first in the service of social interaction, is instrumental in reshaping children's perception:

> Labeling enables the child to choose a specific object, to single it out from the entire situation he is perceiving . . . By means of words children single out separate elements, thereby overcoming the natural structure of the sensory field and forming new (artificially introduced and dynamic) structural centers. The child begins to perceive the world not only through his eyes but also through his speech. As a result, the immediacy of "natural" perception is supplanted by a complex mediated process; as such, speech becomes an essential part of the child's cognitive development. (1978, p. 32)

Vygotsky emphasized that the form of perception that results from the impact of speech on practical action must not be viewed as reducible or even similar to the natural perception that existed earlier. The new form of mental function that emerges is a product of the inherent properties of the semiotic code involved. Among these properties are linearization and sequential processing of discrete units, leading to the transformation of "integral" into "analytic" perception.

A further semiotic property of verbal regulation on the intrapsychological plane that derives from requirements placed on speech in social interaction is its dialogic organization. Scholars such as Ivanov (1977), C. Emerson (1983), and V. S. Bibler (1975, 1981, 1983–84) have argued that inner speech is inherently dialogic. Vygotsky recognized this point in his claim that "egocentric speech . . . grows out of its social foundations by means of transferring social, collaborative forms of behavior to the sphere of the individual's psychological functioning" (1934a, p. 45). He expanded on this general comment in his analysis of Piaget's early work on collaboration among young children:

> The tendency of children to put into practice in relation to themselves the same forms of behavior that were earlier social forms of behavior is well known to Piaget and is used well by him . . . in his explanation of the emergence of reflection from argumentation. Piaget showed how children's reflection emerges after the emergence in the child collective of argumentation in the strict sense of the word. It is in argumentation, in discussion, that the

functional moments appear that will give rise to the development of reflection.

In our opinion something similar happens when the child begins to converse with himself exactly as he had earlier conversed with others, when he begins to think aloud by conversing with himself when the situation calls for it.   (1934a, p. 45)

On the basis of such passages one would expect that the regulative speech found on the intrapsychological plane should reflect the inherent dialogicality of that found on the interpsychological plane (compare Wertsch, 1980b). A concrete indication that Vygotsky understood this point can be seen in his use of the notion of abbreviation.

Abbreviation is one of the properties of dialogue identified by Vygotsky. Like Yakubinskii, he viewed abbreviation as being possible because of the "apperceptual mass" shared by interlocutors in dialogue. In terms of the analysis summarized in Table 1, one can say that the possibility of a common apperceptual mass, and hence abbreviation, derives from contextualized sign use. Of particular importance in this respect is linguistic context, since in dialogue previous discourse (both of the speaker and of the interlocutor) provides much of the context in which subsequent utterances are interpreted and can be abbreviated.

Yakubinskii used the notions of apperceptual mass and abbreviation primarily in order to deal with communicative settings in which more than one interlocutor is involved. In contrast, the main use Vygotsky made of these notions was in characterizing egocentric and inner speech, which allowed him to show how semiotic mediation on the intrapsychological plane reflects the structures and processes of such mediation in interpsychological functioning. Vygotsky's most complete treatment of egocentric speech can be found in a fifty-four-page introductory essay he wrote for the Russian translation of Piaget's (1923) book *Le langage et la pensée chez l'enfant*. This translation was published in 1932, and Vygotsky's essay later became the second chapter in his volume *Thinking and Speech* (1934a). While Piaget's account of egocentric speech clearly influenced Vygotsky's thinking, Vygotsky did not agree with all aspects of this account. Quite the contrary. However, Piaget was the first investigator to identify and examine the speech form that was to play such an important role in Vygotsky's theoretical and empirical investigation of verbal regulation.

In his review of Piaget's account of egocentric speech, Vygotsky noted that Piaget separated children's speech into two functionally defined categories: egocentric speech and socialized speech. Vygotsky summarized Piaget's views as follows:

> "This speech is egocentric," says Piaget, "above all because the child speaks only about herself, and mainly because she does not attempt to place herself at the point of view of the listener" (Piaget, 1932, p. 72). The child is not interested in whether others listen, she does not expect an answer, she does not wish to influence her neighbors or in fact communicate anything to them. This is a monologue . . . the essence of which can be expressed in a single formula: "The child talks to herself as though she were thinking aloud. She does not address anyone" (ibid.). When she is doing lessons the child accompanies her action with various utterances. Piaget names this verbal accompaniment to the child's activity egocentric speech and distinguishes it from the child's socialized speech, the function of which is quite different. In this case the child actually exchanges thoughts with others. She requests, orders, threatens, communicates, criticizes, questions. (1934a, p. 34)

Before turning to Vygotsky's criticism of Piaget's conception of egocentric speech, it is worthwhile to focus briefly on his comments about Piaget's notion of socialized speech. These comments provide some important insights into how these two scholars disagreed, not only about the role of speech in development but also about the development of human cognition in general. In contrast to his own approach, which argues for the priority of social forces, Vygotsky held that Piaget's approach argued for the priority of individual functioning. He wrote that for Piaget "the social lies at the end of development, even social speech does not precede egocentric speech but follows it in the history of development" (ibid., p. 44). Vygotsky contrasted this with his own claim:

> The initial function of speech is the function of communication, social contact, influencing others (children influencing adults as well as being influenced by them). Thus the initial speech of the child is purely social. To call it socialized would be incorrect since this word is tied to the presupposition of something that is initially nonsocial, something that becomes social only in the process of its change and development. (Ibid., p. 45)

In truth, Vygotsky was either engaging in a bit of polemics here or did not recognize an important difference in his use of "social" and

Piaget's use of "socialized." It is not really a simple matter of what comes first—social (or socialized) or individual. Rather, it is a matter of what is meant by "social" and "socialized" and how these terms fit into a general theoretical framework.

The term "socialized" as employed by Piaget properly belongs to the realm of the psychological characterization of the individual. It is a notion that is in fact consistent with Vygotsky's analysis of the ontogenesis of higher mental functions. For example, in his account of the development of generalization and word meaning it would have been appropriate to use the term "socialized speech" to refer to individuals' speech behavior that reflects social norms, that is, speech behavior that reflects socialization into the speech community. In this sense it is clear that Vygotsky's analysis dealt with socialized, as opposed to unsocialized, speech.

In contrast, the term "social speech" as used by Vygotsky refers to a phenomenon that is not analyzable within the realm of the psychology of the individual. He was reaching outside the realm of individual psychology into the realm of social interaction or interpsychological functioning when he wrote of social speech. The fundamental assumption that one must go outside psychology if one wishes to carry out a complete genetic analysis of the psychology of the individual is a crucial issue over which Vygotsky's and Piaget's approaches disagree. Hence the confusion, intentional or real, over Piaget's claim that "the social lies at the end of development." The socialized individual lies at the end of development in both Vygotsky's and Piaget's account. The difference between the two theorists is that Vygotsky searched for the beginning of development in social life in a way that Piaget did not.

When one compares Vygotsky's and Piaget's accounts of egocentric speech, one finds even more important differences. While recognizing the "indisputable and enormous credit" that was due Piaget for outlining the phenomenon of egocentric speech, Vygotsky disputed his interpretation of its function and fate. Piaget's assumption that egocentric speech "fulfills no objectively useful or necessary function in the child's behavior" (1934a, p. 37) would lead to the conclusion that it simply disappears or dies away with progressive socialization. In contrast, Vygotsky argued that egocentric speech plays an important role in the regulation of action and continues to be a part of the child's psychological functioning, eventually on the internal plane.

The Function and Fate of Egocentric Speech

Vygotsky's claims about egocentric speech were based on a series of studies that he and his students (Leont'ev, R. E. Levina, and Luria) conducted in the late 1920s and early 1930s, in which they examined children's use of egocentric speech in various settings. By altering these settings in certain ways they hoped to identify the cognitive and social factors that influence the use of egocentric speech. The studies can be divided into two groups, corresponding to two main issues over which Vygotsky disagreed with Piaget's interpretation of egocentric speech: the *function* and the *fate* (or more broadly the origin and fate) of egocentric speech.

Vygotsky's contention that the function of egocentric speech is to plan and regulate human action led him to argue that for children an increase in the cognitive difficulty of a task should result in an increase in the incidence of egocentric speech. To test this hypothesis he used a technique in which an experimenter surreptitiously introduced an impediment into the flow of a child's action in order to observe the effect this would have on the child's use of egocentric speech. Vygotsky reported, "Our research showed that the coefficient of a child's egocentric speech, calculated only for those points of increased difficulty, rose quickly to almost twice the normal coefficient established by Piaget and the coefficient calculated for these same children in situations devoid of difficulties" (1934a, p. 38). This finding was corroborated by L. Kohlberg, J. Yaeger, and E. Hjertholm (1968), who compared the amount of overt self-regulative speech that children (4,6–5,0) used in four task settings and reported a statistically significant increase in the mean number of egocentric comments with an increase in task difficulty.

On the basis of his findings on the relationship between task difficulty and incidence of egocentric speech, Vygotsky concluded that "egocentric speech very early . . . becomes a means of the child's realistic thinking" (1934a, p. 42). He argued that his data clearly refuted Piaget's claim that egocentric speech reflects egocentric thinking (and hence serves no useful function) and supported his own claim about its role in planning and regulating action: "the child's egocentric speech not only may not be an expression of egocentric thinking; it fulfills a function that is diametrically opposed to egocentric thinking, the function of realistic thinking. This thinking does not approximate the logic of daydreaming and dreaming; rather, it approximates the logic of intelligent, purposeful action and thinking" (ibid., p. 43).

If Vygotsky's first criticism of Piaget's account of egocentric speech concerned the function of this speech form, his second criticism focused on the related issue of its origin and fate. In a second set of studies, Vygotsky reasoned that if egocentric speech is "a transitional form from external to internal speech" (1934a, p. 464a), one should be able first of all to document a close relationship between social speech and early forms of egocentric speech. Then, with the development of ego-centric speech one should be able to document an increasing divergence between it and social speech and an increasing approximation to inner speech. These hypotheses about the origin and fate of egocentric speech contrasted sharply with those generated by Piaget's position, since according to Piaget egocentric speech reflects egocentric thinking and should therefore lose its egocentric quality and disappear with pro-gressive socialization.

The specific semiotic mechanism that Vygotsky posited as giving rise to egocentric speech was the differentiation of speech functions: "in the process of growth the child's social speech, which is multi-functional, develops in accordance with the principle of the differen-tiation of separate functions, and at a certain age it is quite sharply differentiated into egocentric and communicative speech" (ibid., p. 45). On the basis of this claim about the differentiation of speech functions, Vygotsky outlined the development of egocentric speech in the fol-lowing terms:

> The structural and functional properties of egocentric speech grow with the child's development. At three years of age the distinction between this speech and the child's communicative speech is al-most zero. At seven years of age we see a form of speech that is fully 100 percent different from the social speech of the three-year-old in almost all its functional and structural properties. It is in this fact that we find the expression of the progressive dif-ferentiation of two speech functions and the separation of speech for oneself and speech for others out of a general, undifferentiated speech function, which, during the early years of ontogenesis, fulfills both assignments with virtually identical means. (Ibid., p. 284)

This understanding of functional differentiation during the period when egocentric speech is used provided the foundation for specific empirical hypotheses. The first issue Vygotsky addressed concerned the relationship that one should find between social and egocentric speech. He reasoned that one should find a lack of differentiation or even a thorough confusion between social and egocentric speech in young children's verbal behavior. Accordingly Vygotsky carried out three "critical experiments" that were designed to determine the degree to which children's use of egocentric speech is influenced by phenomena that affect the use of social speech (for example, the presence or absence of an interlocutor). His argument was that if the use of egocentric speech is sensitive to the same factors that affect the use of social speech, it is not egocentric in the sense that Piaget had in mind. Furthermore, such a sensitivity would reflect a close connection between egocentric speech and what Vygotsky saw as its genetic precursor, social speech.

Each of the three studies conducted by Vygotsky focused on conditions required for egocentric speech that reflect its lack of differentiation from social speech: the illusion of understanding by others, the presence of potential listeners, and vocalization. In all cases the procedure relied on creating a relatively high incidence of egocentric speech in children and then changing the context so that one of the conditions for such speech was no longer present.

In the first study Vygotsky placed children whose coefficient of egocentric speech had already been established in a situation where the illusion of being understood by others was no longer tenable. He did this by putting individual subjects in a group of deaf-mute children or in a group of children who spoke a language foreign to the subject. In all other respects the child collective and the activity remained the same as it had been in the setting where the baseline of egocentric speech had been established. Vygotsky reported that when the illusion of understanding by others was removed, the coefficient of egocentric speech fell drastically. In the majority of cases egocentric speech disappeared altogether, and in the remaining cases its mean coefficient was only one-eighth what it had been under normal conditions.

In his second critical experiment Vygotsky examined the effect of removing potential listeners on the incidence of egocentric speech. After having established a baseline coefficient of egocentric speech for each subject in a collective monologue, he removed the subject from the setting that included the potential listeners. He did this either by placing the subject in a group of children with whom the subject was not acquainted and with whom the subject did not converse before, during, or after the study, or he excluded the possibility of collective monologue altogether by placing the child alone at a table isolated from others or in a separate room. He reported that, as it had in the first study, the coefficient of egocentric speech fell in the experimental condition. The decrease was not as drastic as in the first study, but it still was striking, falling to one-sixth the level it had been in the control condition.

In the third study Vygotsky varied conditions so that the requirement of vocalization in egocentric speech could not be met. After establishing a baseline level of egocentric speech in his subjects, Vygotsky placed them in a setting where vocalization was difficult or impossible. For example, he placed them in a room where the noise level was so high that subjects could not hear their own speech or the speech of others around the table at which they were sitting. (In one case this involved an orchestra playing behind a wall of the laboratory where the study was being conducted). In another case all the children in the collective were forbidden to speak loudly and had to converse in whispers. As in the first two studies, Vygotsky found that the coefficient of egocentric speech in the experimental condition was much lower (5.4 times lower) than in the control condition. Thus the difference was somewhat less (but still striking) than in either of the first two studies.

Vygotsky summarized the results of these three experiments as follows:

> In all three studies we were pursuing the same goal. We took as our basis of research the three phenomena that appear with almost all egocentric speech by the child: the illusion of understanding, collective monologue, and vocalization. All three phenomena are common to egocentric and social speech. We experimentally compared situations in which these phenomena were present with situations in which they were absent and found that the exclusion of these moments . . . inevitably results in the dying out of egocentric speech. On the basis of these findings we can legitimately conclude that although the child's egocentric speech is already becoming distinguished in function and structure, it is not definitely separated from social speech, in whose depths it is all the while developing and maturing.   (1934a, p. 291)

Recently P. Goudena (1982, 1983; Goudena and Leenders, 1980) conducted a series of studies that extend and refine Vygotsky's claim about the confusion of social and self-regulative functions in egocentric speech. Unlike Vygotsky, who examined children's egocentric speech in the presence of peers, Goudena examined it in the presence of adults.

Furthermore, instead of posing the question of whether the simple presence or absence of potential interlocutors influences the level of egocentric speech, he examined how the presence of particular types of potential interlocutors may influence it. Specifically, he distinguished between adults who were viewed by children (preschoolers and primary school pupils) as being willing and able to help solve a task and adults who were not. In the presence of the former, Goudena reasoned that children would use more egocentric speech than in the presence of the latter, because in the case of the former, children would consider the adult to be a potential interlocutor in that setting, whereas in the case of the latter, they would not.

Goudena's results supported his predictions. His findings indicated that a child was more likely to use egocentric speech in the presence of an adult who was perceived as willing to assist in the problem-solving effort than in the presence of an adult who was not. This represents a further specification of Vygotsky's claims about the child's temporary confusion of the social and self-regulative functions of speech.

A second major aspect of Vygotsky's analysis of the origin and fate of egocentric speech concerns the way in which this speech form increasingly diverges from social speech as it develops toward inner speech. Vygotsky did not disagree with Piaget that the quantity of egocentric speech decreases with age.[5] However, he argued that the quality of egocentric speech changes in a way that supports his interpretation and not Piaget's. Specifically, he argued that if the development of egocentric speech represents the progressive differentiation of speech for oneself from speech for others, it should become less intelligible to others with age. Such a prediction contradicts the one that would be generated by Piaget's interpretation of egocentric speech. On the basis of Piaget's contention that egocentric speech is a manifestation of egocentric thinking, one would expect its intelligibility to increase with age. This inference follows from the fact that progressive socialization should result in the child's being more likely to take others' perspectives into account, therefore producing egocentric speech (and speech in general) that is more intelligible to others.

Vygotsky found that his analysis of egocentric speech supported his prediction and not Piaget's:

> One of the most important and decisive factual results from our research is that we established that the structural characteristics of egocentric speech which distinguish it from social speech and

make it incomprehensible to others do not decrease, but increase with age. These characteristics are at a minimum at the age of three and are at a maximum at the age of seven. Thus they do not die away but evolve; their development is inversely related to the coefficient of egocentric speech. (1934a, p. 283)

The research of Kohlberg, Yaeger, and Hjertholm (1968) again supports Vygotsky's claim on this point. These researchers reported that with an increase in age there is an increase in the proportion of egocentric speech that is unintelligible. The proportion of all egocentric speech that fell in the category of "inaudible muttering" (statements uttered in such a low voice that they are indecipherable to an auditor close by") rose from about 0.24 to about 0.50 between the ages of five and nine. This increase in the proportion of unintelligible egocentric speech contrasts with the egocentric speech that falls in other categories such as "describing own activity," categories made up of speech that could be understood by others.

Structural and Functional Properties of Egocentric and Inner Speech

Motivated by his interest in semiotic issues, Vygotsky carried his analysis of speech forms a step beyond, arguing that the function, origin, and fate of egocentric speech indicate that it culminates in inner speech. In addition, he argued that the study of the specific properties of social and egocentric speech can provide insight into such properties in inner speech.

Vygotsky's concern for creating an objective, scientific psychology led him to reject the use of introspective reports and other subjective techniques for analyzing inner speech. Instead, he insisted that the objective properties and developmental tendencies of egocentric speech must serve as the main source of information. For him "the study of egocentric speech and the emergence in it of dynamic tendencies toward the emergence of certain structural and functional properties and the weakening of others is the key to the investigation of the psychological nature of inner speech" (1934a, p. 292).

In reviewing Vygotsky's conclusions about the characteristics of inner speech, it should be pointed out that he provided virtually no concrete examples of how the characteristics he mentioned are manifested in egocentric speech. Instead, he described the characteristics of inner speech by drawing from theoretical literature in semiotics and poetics and by using illustrations from everyday and artistic texts. Therefore, in reviewing his account I do not have access to the specific egocentric speech data on which he based his claims.

Vygotsky divided the characteristics of inner speech into two broad categories: "syntactic" and "semantic." He stated that the "first and most important" (ibid.) property of inner speech is its unique abbreviated syntax. One can gain insight into the "fragmentary, abbreviated nature of inner speech as compared to external speech" (ibid.) by examining egocentric speech. Vygotsky's analysis of egocentric speech led him to conclude that abbreviation takes a specific form, which he described in terms of *predicativity* (*predikativnost'*):

> As it develops, egocentric speech does not manifest a simple tendency toward abbreviation and the omission of words; it does not manifest a simple transition toward a telegraphic style. Rather, it shows a quite unique tendency toward abbreviating phrases and sentences by preserving the predicate and associated parts of the sentence at the expense of deleting the subject and other words associated with it. (Ibid., p. 293)

As noted elsewhere (Wertsch, 1979b), Vygotsky's notions of subject and predicate here are concerned with a level of analysis that focuses on utterances in context rather than the formal analysis of sentence types. Although these levels of analysis were not clearly elaborated at the time Vygotsky was writing, he apparently understood this distinction, as evidenced by some of his comments about the difference between the "phasic" and "semantic" aspects of speech. He wrote of the difference between the *grammatical subject* and *predicate* on the one hand and the *psychological subject and predicate* on the other. The psychological subject (*psikhologicheskoe podlezhashchee*) is "what is being talked about in [a given] phrase" or what is "in the consciousness of the listener first" (1934a, p. 272), whereas the psychological predicate (*psikhologicheskoe skazuemoe*) is "what is new, what is said about the subject" (ibid.). The fact that Vygotsky saw the independence of the level of analysis concerned with contextualized utterances is reflected in his statement that "any member of the sentence can become the psychological predicate, in which case it carries the logical emphasis" (ibid.).

Vygotsky developed his account of the predicative syntax of inner speech by tracing it back to its precursors in egocentric and social speech. In all cases his analysis focused on how the structure and interpretation of speech utterances are governed by the context in

which they appear. Hence he was interested in the processes of contextualization in social, egocentric, and inner speech. Borrowing heavily
from Yakubinskii (1923), Vygotsky noted that in social speech the
tendency toward predicativity occurs primarily in two types of situations. In the first, the topic of conversation is equally well known to
all interlocutors. He provided the following example:

> Suppose that several people are waiting for the "B" tram at a
> tramway stop in order to go in a certain direction. Upon seeing
> the tram approaching, no one in such a situation would ever say
> in expanded form, "The 'B' tram for which we are waiting to go
> to a certain point is coming." Rather, the expression would always
> be abbreviated to the predicate alone: "It's coming," or "The
> 'B.'" (1934a, p. 294)

In this case the extralinguistic context of the utterance is at issue.

The second type of situation in which predicativity occurs in external
social speech is in response to a question. Vygotsky pointed out that
"in response to the question of whether you want a cup of tea, no one
answers with the expanded phrase: 'No, I do not want a cup of tea.'
The answer will be purely predicative: 'No.' It will consist solely of
the predicate" (ibid., p. 293). In this instance the relevant context of
the utterance is provided by another utterance. Hence linguistic context
provides the basis for abbreviation.

Vygotsky's concrete examples of abbreviation that are grounded in
linguistic context usually involve cases of dialogue between two interlocutors. However, sign–sign relationships between an utterance and
its linguistic context also exist among utterances by a single speaker
(as in "I saw a man walking down the street yesterday. He . . ."). Hence
while abbreviation based on the linguistic context may appear first on
the interpsychological plane (see Bernstein, 1979), it also can play a
role on the intrapsychological plane in egocentric and inner speech.

In developing his account of the factors that contribute to predicativity, Vygotsky argued that the end points of a continuum that
extends from minimal to maximal predicativity are represented by written language and inner speech, respectively. The nature of the dialogue
and the level of apperceptual mass à la Yakubinskii guided Vygotsky's
argument throughout this discussion.

Thus, according to Vygotsky the first general characteristic of inner
speech that makes possible its abbreviation is the (functional) syntactic
fact of predicativity. The second general characteristic is "semantic" in

nature. For the semantic characterization of inner speech he identified three interrelated properties: the predominance of "sense" over "meaning," the tendency toward "agglutination," and the "infusion of sense into a word." The key to understanding all these properties is Vygotsky's distinction between meaning (*znachenie*) and sense (*smysl*). Up to this point, especially in my review of generalization and word meaning, I have focused on meaning. Vygotsky outlined this distinction as follows:

> The sense of a word, as Paulhan has demonstrated, is the aggregate of all the psychological facts emerging in our consiousness because of this word. Therefore, the sense of a word always turns out to be a dynamic, flowing, complex formation which has several zones of differential stability. Meaning is only one of the zones of the sense that a word acquires in the context of speaking. Furthermore, it is the most stable, unified, and precise zone. As we know, a word readily changes its sense in various contexts. Conversely, its meaning is that fixed, unchanging point which remains stable during all the changes of sense in various contexts. This change in a word's sense is a basic fact to be accounted for in the semantic analysis of speech. The real meaning[6] of a word is not constant. In one operation a word emerges in one meaning and in another it takes on another meaning. This dynamism of meaning leads us to Paulhan's problem, the problem of the relationship of meaning and sense. The word considered in isolation and in the lexicon has only one meaning. But this meaning is nothing more than a potential that is realized in living speech. In living speech this meaning is only a stone in the edifice of sense. (1934a, p. 305)

The issue of sense for Vygotsky is not a matter of lexical ambiguity, or meaning distinctions that remain constant across speech contexts. Instead, the notion of sense is concerned with contextualized aspects of signification and linguistic organization. Hence it reflects his concern with how the semiotic mediation of higher mental functions can utilize the potential of the contextualized aspect of linguistic organization and interpretation.

With this general point in mind, I turn to what Vygotsky called the "semantic" properties of inner speech. The "first and most fundamental" of these properties is the "predominance of a word's sense over its meaning." Thus Vygotsky saw the context-specific, indexical aspects of signification as predominating over the cross-contextual, stable aspects; the signification of the word is more a function of the stream of consciousness and the intralinguistic context in which it appears than it is a function of a stable, cross-contextual meaning system. This differs from the situation in most interpsychological communication, since for Vygotsky social interaction is necessarily linked to stable generalized meanings. Hence the communicative function of speech relies more heavily on stable aspects of linguistic organization than does the self-regulative function.

Of course this is not to say that the emergence of inner speech destroys the capacity for using conceptual thinking as employed in communication and epitomized in scientific concepts. Vygotsky's claim was simply that different aspects of signification predominate in different types of semiotic functioning:

> In spoken language as a rule we go from the most stable and permanent element of sense, from its most constant zone, that is, the meaning of the word, to its more fluctuating zones, to its sense in general. In contrast, in inner speech this predominance of sense over meaning that we observe in spoken language in certain cases as a more or less weakly expressed tendency approaches its mathematical limit and occurs in an absolute form. Here the prevalence of sense over meaning, of the phrase over the word, and of the entire context over the phrase is not the exception but the general rule.   (1934a, pp. 306–307)

Vygotsky (1934a) and his followers (for example, Akhutina, 1975, 1978; Luria, 1975a, 1981) have elaborated on this account of the relationship between sense and meaning in their analysis of speech production. A major point has been that inner speech plays a role in the microgenesis of speech production. It is viewed as occupying a relatively early position in the series of steps that results in external speech. That several steps are required to convert inner speech to external speech indicates these investigators' understanding of the relative predominance of sense and meaning in the two speech forms.

Vygotsky's claim that the predominance of sense over meaning is the most important and fundamental semantic property of inner speech is reflected in the fact that he viewed the two remaining properties as following from it. Both properties involve the ways in which word signification operates in an intralinguistic context. The first one is "agglutination." Vygotsky's comments reveal that for him this semantic property was no more than an analogy to the notion of agglutination as used in studies of language typology. Thus he cited K. Bühler's observations about Amerindian languages, such as Delaware, that have a tendency toward agglutination. He noted that two features of agglutination are of particular interest: "first, in entering into the composition of a complex word, separate words often undergo abbreviation in sound such that only part of them becomes part of the complex word; second, the resulting complex word that expresses an extremely complex concept emerges as a structurally and functionally unified word, not as a combination of independent words" (1934a, p. 307). Vygotsky argued that features analogous to those of agglutinative languages characterize inner speech and begin to make their appearance in egocentric speech:

> We have observed something analogous in the child's egocentric speech. To the degree that this speech form approximates inner speech, agglutination as a means for forming unified complex words for the expression of complex concepts emerges more and more frequently and more and more distinctly. In egocentric speech utterances the child increasingly displays a tendency toward an asyntactic combination of words that parallels the decrease in the coefficient of egocentric speech. (ibid.)

The third semantic property of inner speech is what Vygotsky termed the "infusion of sense." He argued that because it is more dynamic than word meaning, word sense follows different laws of combination. The basic difference between the two, a difference that reflects the relative predominance of either decontextualized or contextualized aspects of signification, is that a word's sense is influenced and changed as a function of its entering into an intralinguistic context, whereas a word's meaning is not. Vygotsky turned to artistic texts to illustrate and develop this point:

> By passing through an artistic work, a word absorbs all the diversity contained in its sense units and becomes, as it were, equivalent to the entire work. This is especially clear in the case of titles of artistic works. In artistic literature the title stands in a different relation to the work than, for example, in painting or music. To a much greater degree it expresses and crowns the entire sense content of the work than, say, the title of a picture. Words such as Don Quixote and Hamlet, Eugene Onegin and Anna Karenina reflect this law of the infusion of sense in the purest form. The sense content of the entire work is really contained in one word. The title of Gogol's *Dead Souls* is a particularly clear example of the law of the infusion of sense . . . in passing like a red seam

throughout the entire fabric of this work these two words take on a completely new, immeasurably richer sense; as sponges absorb moisture, they absorb the deep sense message of the various parts and images of the work, and they turn out to be fully saturated by the sense only toward the very end. At this point these words signify something quite unlike their initial meaning . . .

We observe something analogous—in inner speech. In inner speech the word, as it were, absorbs the sense of preceding and subsequent words, thereby extending almost without limit the boundaries of its meaning.   (Ibid., p. 308)

In summary, Vygotsky's account of social, egocentric, and inner speech includes several implicit and explicit claims. First, egocentric and inner speech function to control and regulate human activity. Second, a genetic analysis of semiotic regulation must begin with social speech. It cannot begin with intrapsychological forms of verbal regulation, that is, egocentric and inner speech. Third, intrapsychological forms of verbal regulation reflect the structural and functional properties (such as dialogicality) of their interpsychological precursor. Fourth, *contra* Piaget, egocentric speech does not simply reflect egocentric thinking; rather, it plays an important role in the planning and regulation of action. Fifth, *contra* Piaget, the origins of egocentric speech are to be found in social speech (through the differentiation of speech functions), and the fate of egocentric speech is inner speech. Sixth, it is possible to identify specific structural and functional characteristics of inner speech through the study of egocentric speech. These include the functional syntactic characteristic of predicativity and semantic characteristics deriving from the relatively greater importance of sense as compared to meaning in inner speech.

Vygotsky's ideas about semiotic mediation evolved in an intellectual milieu quite different from today's. In particular, the discussions of the Russian Formalists played an important role in focusing attention on issues such as the differentiation of speech functions and the corresponding, functionally specific formal properties of language. This led Vygotsky to formulate his questions about the semiotic mediation of higher mental functions in terms of speech functions. He identified several pairs of speech functions, the distinction between the indicative and symbolic functions being particularly important in understanding his approach.

Underlying Vygotsky's account of semiotic mediation is the distinction between decontextualized and contextualized aspects of linguistic organization. Both tendencies are coordinated and manifested simultaneously in language, but different types of semiotic mediation rely primarily on the potential of one or the other. Conceptual development proceeds in accordance with the potential of decontextualized linguistic organization, and the development of egocentric and inner speech proceeds on the basis of increasing contextualization. In the latter case linguistic context replaces extralinguistic context in determining the syntactic and semantic properties of mediational means.

CHAPTER 5

Extending Vygotsky's Semiotic Analysis: Propositional and Discourse Referentiality

Vygotsky's semiotic analysis can be clarified and extended in light of ideas from semiotics, linguistics, and the philosophy of language. Although some of the ideas at issue were not available at the time Vygotsky was writing, others were, at least in an early form, but he failed to recognize their implications for his approach.

Much of what I have to say concerns the notion of reference as outlined by W. V. O. Quine (1960, 1973) and extended by Silverstein (1978, 1980a, 1980b). As Quine puts it, reference is concerned with an "apparatus for speaking of objects" (1973, p. 81).[1] This use of language contrasts with others, such as indicating deference and status. However, it is the most relevant one when examining and extending Vygotsky's analysis of categorization and the self-regulative function of speech.

Silverstein has distinguished two types of referentiality that must be taken into account when examining language:

> (a) discourse-reference, or "pragmatic" reference; and (b) prop-ositional-reference, or "semantic" reference. These are distin-guished as *extensional* and *intensional* reference-values of language signs, and must be seen as being separable on the basis of whether or not the rules for the underlying linguistic units necessarily involve or do not necessarily involve, computing the referential value of the sign with relation to the situation of speaking (the

context, including the prior language context in discourse) in which the instance of the sign occurs. Such elements of language as the pronouns or the deictics are essentially pragmatic referring forms of language; such elements of language as common nouns are not, so that their actual pragmatic reference depends both on their semantic value as underlying lexical elements *and* their instantiation (occurrence of a token or instance) in a specific context. (1980b, p. 1)

Part of Silverstein's claim is that attempts to analyze human communication on the basis of propositional referentiality alone overlook essential aspects of the linguistic phenomena involved. In a comprehensive analysis, both types of referentiality must be recognized. For example, consider an utterance of the sentence "The dog helped that man." Its interpretation requires that both discourse and propositional referentiality be considered. Discourse referentiality is involved at several points: information from the linguistic context (the preceding utterances) or the extralinguistic context (the presence of a dog and an adult male human in the context of speaking) is required to identify the referents of "the dog" and "that man." The referents of such expressions may change in different contexts of speaking. Propositional referentiality is also involved, because in addition to identifying the referents, the utterance relays specific information about their relationship as defined by the verb "help." Thus even if the referents of the expressions "the dog" and "that man" are clearly identified in a speech setting, the interpretation is quite different depending on whether we say, "The dog helped that man" or "That man helped the dog." One of the issues of propositional referentiality is the number and arrangement of arguments in a predicate, which in linguistics is often considered in terms of case roles and case markings.

Propositional Referentiality

Propositional referentiality has been at the heart of developments in symbolic logic and formal grammatical analysis over the past half-century. The developments can be traced to the work of figures such as G. Frege, B. Russell, and members of the Vienna circle on the one hand and to F. Saussure, F. Boas, Sapir, L. Bloomfield, and N. Chomsky on the other. Silverstein has argued that the ideas of these scholars and their successors represent "the result of the last great refinement of the folk view of language as the overt expression par excellence of the rational faculties" (1980a, p. 1). He goes on to state:

> The central problem here is the way in which different languages have formal arrangements of units in overt signals that express the systematicity of propositions, as to both the devices of reference (identifiable with the quantification of logical variables) and those of predication (identifiable with the specification of logical predicates). Viewed in this way, the proper domain of analysis of language becomes the form that can minimally be identified with the quantified proposition, that is, the sentence. (p. 1)

In terms familiar to contemporary discussions in linguistics, the issue of propositional referentiality consists of how case relations are signaled by case markings (inflections, word order). As Silverstein points out, the notion of case marking here is defined as:

> the totality of formal means for indicating what predicational role (or propositional role) is played by the entity referred to by any given noun phrase in its immediately relevant proposition, that is, what is coded by a sentence or clause. Hence case marking has implicit value at the *propositional referential* level of analysis . . .
> A typical example of the case-marking phenomenon is the indication of the referential values "Agent" and "Patient," in propositional terms. Part of giving a propositional analysis of speech is determining some consistent schema showing the difference between "The man hit the boy" versus "The boy hit the man" . . .
> In other words, we need a consistent schema for specifying (1) how many entities there are in a referential (propositional) schema coded by noun phrases in speech and (2) the principle of ordering them in a referential schema again coded by certain formal characteristics of speech. (1977, p. 3)

A fundamental assumption of theories that focus on the study of propositional referentiality or "referential function$_2$" is that linguistic analysis is concerned with sign types. The emphasis is on the relationship of linguistic form and linguistic meaning independently of any variation in actual use. Proponents of such approaches have argued that questions of use are problems for a model of performance, whereas the primary issue for the linguist and cognitive psychologist is the examination of linguistic competence. As Silverstein notes:

For purposes of this theory of language, we are not interested in the particular occasions on which exemplars of linguistic forms have been used, correctly or incorrectly, to refer and to predicate, but rather in the system of grammar that, independent of occasion, defines the position of each formal expression by its differential capacity with respect to a system of reference-and-predication, and inversely. We wind up with a description of formal arrangements of units, in the familiar metalanguage of *constituency* (hierarchical linear combinations of structural units), and a description of their referential-and-predicational potential, in the familiar metalanguage of logical sense (implication, synonymy, antonymy, taxonomy, and so on).   (1980a, p. 2)

The most influential recent model of this type is the transformational generative model as outlined by Chomsky (1957, 1965, 1981). His approach has been extensively modified in linguistics (Fillmore, 1968; McCawley, 1968; compare Cook, 1979; Longacre, 1983), but most of these modifications do not alter the fundamental assumptions. The generative model has had a major impact on the study of the psychology of language. Research in this domain has shifted from issues traditionally raised by psychological theories to the issue of how decontextualized propositional and grammatical relationships are represented in the human mind.

If Vygotsky had incorporated the ideas of modern theories of propositional referentiality into his approach, how would his semiotic analysis have been different? He assumed that the basic unit of semiotic analysis is the word, whereas for most modern theories of grammar it is the proposition or its linguistically encoded representation, the sentence. Hence Vygotsky did not recognize many of the issues that have interested contemporary linguistic researchers.

There are several ways in which Vygotsky's approach can be extended—but not replaced—in light of modern analysis of propositional referentiality. Although several theorists went beyond Vygotsky in their treatment of certain semiotic issues, many of their ideas are entirely compatible with his. They can be interpreted as an extension of his framework rather than as a rejection or even a fundamental revision. Moreover, Vygotsky's semiotic analysis was ultimately concerned with the mediation and regulation of human action. His concern with how semiotic analysis can be combined with an account of human action distinguishes his overall approach from ones that focus on propositional referentiality alone. Vygotsky's examination of the role of unique speech events (sign tokens) in the regulation of ongoing action led him to consider several semiotic issues not usually addressed by grammatical theoreticians. Thus even if one were to revise his semiotic analysis in light of contemporary grammatical theory, many of his basic insights about the regulation of human action would continue to distinguish his theory from others.

Two issues raised by grammatical theory that have direct implications for Vygotsky's theory of semiotic mediation are (a) the relationship between the natural and cultural lines of development and (b) the definition of word meaning. These issues are likely to be recognized only if the investigator begins with the sentence rather than the word as the unit of analysis.

The first issue concerns the aspects of language that are most likely to come into contact with and take advantage of the products of the natural line of development. Recent research in developmental psycholinguistics has investigated the question of how prelinguistic cognitive categories are related to early linguistic categories.

Much of the research has been motivated by the claim that early vocabulary and grammatical development reflects prelinguistic cognitive development. In summarizing such reasoning E. Clark has argued:

> Children clearly learn a good deal about different objects, actions, and relations before they ever begin to talk. They learn to identify objects that can move on their own and make other things move— a primitive class of "movers" that probably includes people, particularly adult caretakers familiar to the child, and vehicles like cars and trains. They also identify objects that can easily be moved by themselves or by other people, "moveables" such as items of clothing (shoes, socks, gloves) or toys (balls, rattles, teddy bears). They identify possible recipients . . . places . . . instruments . . . In fact, one can plausibly argue that children have already organized much of their knowledge about particular categories of objects, actions, and relations before they start on language at all. While it is important to keep such conceptual development distinct from language development, it clearly provides a critical foundation for language to build on. (1979, p. 149)

The conceptual categories Clark had identified are at least partly the result of the infant's sensorimotor experience and activity. As Bruner (1975) has pointed out, prelinguistic social interaction (a form of "direct" social interaction, in Vygotsky's terms) may also influence the emergence of these categories. Certain routines and games carried out by mothers and young children are instrumental in helping the child structure experience in accordance with languagelike categories, such as agent and patient.

Greenfield and J. Smith (1976) have argued that children's early one-word utterances can be understood only by taking into account grammatical (propositional case) role as well as reference. They view these early utterances as identifying the particular role that an object plays in an event as well as the object itself. For example, utterances may identify movers, which are usually the instigators of an action, as in "Dada" uttered as someone opens the door, or "Mama" said as the mother puts on the child's shoes. Early one-word utterances may also name "movables," objects affected by an action, as in "spoon" said as the child drops a spoon, or they may name recipients, usually people, and places. Children may also use one-word utterances to talk about states that result from actions, as in "down" said after sitting down or "off" after turning off a light (compare Farwell, 1977).

Research indicates that certain cognitive categories or roles may be more important than others at certain stages of development. For example, the children studied by K. Nelson (1973) seemed to name movers (people, vehicles, animals), movables (food, clothing, toys), and, less frequently, recipients (people). They mentioned places and instruments hardly at all. Greenfield and Smith (1976) pushed this argument a step further by proposing a sequence in which these different roles are acquired: the sequence begins with movers or agents, followed by movables or objects affected by an action, and finally by places or locations, and possessors or recipients.

This line of reasoning in modern developmental psycholinguistics highlights some important questions that Vygotsky never addressed. He took the word as his basic unit of semiotic analysis and thus overlooked an essential way in which young children's speech may "hook up" with certain aspects of prespeech practical action. Such a notion is missing in his proposal for how the natural and cultural lines of development come into contact and transform one another in emergent interactionism.

The second issue raised by grammatical theory with implications for Vygotsky's approach is concerned with categorization based on word meaning. Vygotsky's focus on words as isolated units prevented him from recognizing certain crucial aspects of word meaning itself and the mechanisms that contribute to its development. In this case, his semiotic analysis can be extended on the basis of grammatical theory.

Because of its focus on isolated words, Vygotsky's account of meaning development had to rest solely on sign–object relationships and the inferences children can draw from them. His emphasis on the fact that adults and children can agree on reference while failing to agree on meaning suggests that he viewed referential mismatches as the main impetus for development. The assumption is that children make preliminary hypotheses about word meanings and change them as a result of adults' using words in unexpected ways (that is, to refer to unexpected objects) or failing to use words in expected ways. This is the main developmental mechanism posited by Vygotsky, at least up to the point where scientific concepts begin to be used.

The fact that Vygotsky did not consider the issues raised by a theory of grammar prevented him from recognizing that by mastering a word's privileges of occurence as defined by a grammar, children come to master certain important aspects of what he would call its meaning. In discussing the research of Greenfield and Smith (1976), I noted that when children begin to use a word, they recognize more than its relation to nonlinguistic objects; they also recognize its propositional role. This fact is of no small consequence for word meaning since lexical content and propositional role are related in essential ways. For example, nouns with certain lexical content (+ animate, + human) make good "natural agents," nouns with other lexical content (− animate, − human) make good "natural patients," and so on. Silverstein (1977) has formulated this notion in terms of markedness theory. He has argued for the existence of a universal hierarchy of noun phrase types and has proposed that every language treats noun phrases above a certain point in this hierarchy (as defined by feature specification of referential content) as natural agents and treats noun phrases below a certain point as natural patients. The criterion for determining how noun phrases are treated in a particular language is whether they are marked or unmarked for specificity of reference. In other words, there is a close relationship between the lexical content of a noun phrase and how it occupies certain propositional roles (as reflected in surface structure case markings).

Because Silverstein's argument is about a universal hierarchy, it may at first appear that it could reflect some kind of underlying cognitive factors and that semiotic factors simply encode or map onto these preexisting factors. Such an interpretation is untenable for at least two reasons. First, Silverstein's argument is based on the assumption that an analysis of noun phrase types and the features that specify referential content must begin with the speech situation. The origins of this assumption can be found in the analysis of the communicative situation proposed by Jakobson (1960). Thus the hierarchy extends from noun phrases used to denote speaker and hearer, speaker, true pronominals, indexicals of speech, indexicals of speech event, and so on to noun phrases whose referential content is specified by features such as + discrete and + quality. That is, it is defined in terms of the degree to which factors in the speech situation are involved. Thus any attempt to argue that it simply reflects some kind of nonsemiotic, cognitive factors would be misguided. The hierarchy may be universal, but it is universal because of limitations on how it is possible to organize speech events.

The second point has to do with how languages differ in their utilization of the noun phrase hierarchy. Silverstein (1977) argues that while the hierarchy itself is universal, different languages "choose" different points in it to distinguish agentlike noun phrases from non-agentlike noun phrases. In mastering the grammatical systems of different languages, children master different systems of what Vygotsky would call word meaning. What counts as a good agent in one language may not count as a good agent in another language. Such differences highlight the fact that grammatical distinctions do not simply map onto nonsemiotic cognitive categories.

As Silverstein (1977) points out, the argument about this hierarchy is supported by findings in psycholinguistic research. For example, Dubois and Irigaray (1970) conducted a study in which subjects were asked to form sentences (written in French) from triplets of words. They found that the order of presentation of the nouns in the triplets had some effect on the assignment of items to a position in the sentences, but the lexical content had an even more important role: "It is apparent that the animate/inanimate correlation always exerts more influence than the inertia of the presentation [the order of items in the triplets] . . . when the respondent is given an animate and an inanimate noun, he always makes the animate noun the subject, and the inanimate noun the object or indirect object (pp. 218, 220). On the basis of such findings Dubois and Irigaray argue:

> Grammatical function [in the response sentences] is not then unrelated to the nature of the noun (animate/inanimate, concrete inanimate/abstract inanimate, contained inanimate/containing animate, and so on). If two nouns of a different nature are offered

to the respondent, the grammatical functions which he assigns them in the produced sentence depend on the nature of the nouns and their potential for interrelation based on their lexemic class membership.   (p. 220)

Silverstein (1977) notes that other psycholinguistic studies such as those conducted by H. H. Clark and J. Begun (1971) and C. James (1972) also support the claim that there is an essential relationship between a word's lexical content and its privileges of occurrence as defined by grammar.

This claim reveals that in coming to master a word's grammatical privileges of occurrence, a child is provided important hints about its lexical content. This supplies a major missing link in Vygotsky's account—an account that otherwise must rely solely on referential mismatches to explain the development of word meaning until the child is introduced to scientific concepts. More generally, a theory of grammar reveals that Vygotsky's account of word meaning is essentially incomplete as long as it does not address the issue of propositional role. By starting with the isolated word rather than with the sentence, he was limited in the extent to which he could see this question.

In addition to case role, other grammatical relations that determine privilege of occurrence are fundamentally involved in the meaning of words. For example, sets of lexical items within a general form class (such as nouns) may be selected on the basis of their combinatory properties or privileges of occurrence as defined by the grammar of the language.

An example is the distinction between "count" and "mass" nouns, which has been examined by researchers such as B. L. Whorf (1956) and J. Lucy (1981, 1984). English implicitly assigns every noun to one of two classes on the basis of whether or not it takes a plural form (for example, "tables," but not "sugars"). If a noun can take the plural form, it is termed a "count" noun and can be enumerated in a straightforward way (two tables, three tables, and so on). If a noun does not take a plural form, it is termed a "mass" noun and can be enumerated only with the use of further lexical material (two pieces, teaspoons, or lumps of sugar). In notional terms, the referents of mass nouns are viewed as having no intrinsic divisions in form, and so they require the specification of a unit (such as "piece of") in order to produce a countable whole. In contrast, the referents of count nouns are viewed as "predetermined units" and therefore require no such specification.

Whorf (1956) argued that the notion of formless substance inherent in mass nouns in English has led to a folk theory that separates substance from form. In the theory count nouns are felt to be inherently duplex in that they represent formless substance (tableness) and substanceless form (table form). According to Whorf, this grammatical distinction lies at the foundation of Western philosophical systems concerning form and substance. The fact that the distinction is not used in certain other languages, such as Hopi, means that these categories may not guide the habitual patterns of mental functioning of speakers of those languages.

Lucy (1981) compared the performance of English-speaking subjects with subjects who speak Yucatec Mayan on a task involving attention and perceptual memory. The subjects were asked to examine a picture and then, in its absence, judge whether any of five other pictures were exactly like it. All pictures were line drawings of a scene from everyday Yucatec household and village life. Each of the five test items was identical to the original except for the addition or deletion of a critical object (for example, there was more grain on the ground in one of the test item pictures than in the original). Lucy predicted that the Mayan subjects would be more likely than the English-speaking subjects to recognize differences in unstructured (masslike) objects, whereas the English-speaking subjects would be more likely than the Mayans to identify changes in the intrinsically structured (countlike) objects. This prediction was based on the fact that English treats many objects as forms and has extensive rules for pluralization (that is, of count nouns), whereas in Yucatec Mayan almost all nouns are mass nouns and hence almost all objects are treated as formless substances. As Lucy notes, in Mayan "plurality tends to be restricted to animates and even so is not obligatory; all nouns require the insertion of additional morphological material to indicate 'form' of the substance for the purposes of numerical enumeration" (1981, p. 3).

Lucy's predictions about the different relative advantages of the English and Yucatec Mayan speakers were borne out at a statistically significant level, thus supporting Whorf's claims about the influence of linguistic patterns on human mental processes. Such findings have direct implications for Vygotsky's approach. Indeed, the following statement by Vygotsky (1978) could easily have served as part of the assumptions that guided Lucy's argument: "as soon as speech and the use of signs are incorporated into any action, the action becomes transformed and organized along entirely new lines" (p. 24). However,

Vygotsky did not see distinctions such as the one between count and mass nouns because they are grounded in the "combinatorial properties" of lexical items.

Vygotsky's approach to word meaning generally begins with sign–object referential relationships in the indicatory function and ends with sign–sign meaning relationships in scientific and genuine concepts. If one considers grammatically based distinctions in word meaning, such as the difference between count and mass nouns, one sees an additional link in this process—namely, by learning a lexical unit's combinatorial properties as defined by a grammar, a child masters an aspect of its meaning. For example, in grasping the fact that we say "two pieces of wood" but "two chairs" in English, the child has understood that "wood" is a mass noun and "chair" is a count noun. This is not a distinction that can be learned through ostensive definition, and it does not reflect the necessary and "real" state of affairs in material reality ("chair" is not a count noun in all languages). Rather, it is learned by mastering the privileges of occurrences of numerals and lexical specification, such as "pieces of" in English.

My review of the distinction between count and mass nouns touches on only one of the many grammatically based distinctions overlooked by Vygotsky. Several additional issues and hypotheses would emerge with a more comprehensive examination of complex grammatical relationships. However, it does provide one more example of my general claim that the inclusion of grammatical analysis in Vygotsky's semiotic approach raises several questions that he never addressed. Indeed, because he did not utilize grammatical analysis, he could not "see" these questions. The complex relationship between grammatical specification and higher mental functions still awaits thorough investigation.

Discourse Referentiality

While recognizing the implications of grammatical theory for Vygotsky's approach, it would be a mistake to assume that a theory of grammar can simply replace his semiotic analysis. Vygotsky's approach deals with issues that go beyond propositional referentiality—specifically, it deals with how signs mediate social and psychological processes in real spatiotemporal settings. Thus his account of semiotic mediation must consider relationships between sign tokens and their unique contexts, that is, it must deal with discourse referentiality.

Discourse referentiality entails the general issue of reference, or what

Quine (1973) terms the "apparatus for speaking of objects" (p. 81). Furthermore, the objects involved still can range from being concrete to being quite abstract. However, instead of the decontextualized referential potential of expressions, the focus now shifts to the issue of "computing the referential value of the sign with relation to the situation of speaking . . . in which the instance of the sign occurs" (Silverstein, 1980b, p. 1). When explaining the nature of pragmatic referentiality, Silverstein states:

> Here we are no longer dealing with the fixed, constant contribution to referentiality of the propositional level, which linguists attempt to specify in terms of class characteristics common to all entities referred to, but rather with the specific entities referred to and the way language keeps track of them. The most interesting such devices from our point of view in this discussion are the reference-maintaining devices. A simple example from English is the chunk of discourse "Some man was walking down the street the other day. He . . . ," where the unit "he" indicates that the referent of this noun phrase is *the same as* the referent of the noun phrase instance "some man" that occurred earlier.   (1977, p. 6)

Thus the interpretation of "he" is dependent on factors in addition to its case role in the proposition and its lexical content (that is, + singular, + animate, + human, + masculine, and so on).

The notion of discourse referentiality provides the foundation for reexamining and extending Vygotsky's account of the regulative function of speech. I shall begin with what he termed the "psychological segmentation"—that is, segmentation into psychological subject and predicate—of egocentric and inner speech. Vygotsky was quite concerned with the "predicative syntax" of these speech forms. He argued that predicativity consists of the tendency to preserve "the predicate and associated parts of the sentence at the expense of deleting the subject and other words associated with it" (1934a, p. 293).

In order to make this argument, Vygotsky had to distinguish the psychological subject and predicate from the grammatical subject and predicate. On the basis of ideas from the psychologically oriented linguistics of his day, he concluded that "the lack of correspondence between grammatical and psychological subject and predicate has been established" (ibid., p. 271). He agreed with Vossler that "there hardly exists a more incorrect path for the interpretation of the mental sense of a linguistic phenomenon than the path of grammatical interpretation. By following this path one is inevitably led to misunderstandings resulting from the discrepancy of the psychological and grammatical segmentation of speech" (ibid., p. 271).

Vygotsky continued his account of the psychological and grammatical segmentation of speech with the following example:

> Consider the sentence "The clock fell."[2] In it "the clock" is the subject, and "fell" is the predicate. Imagine that this sentence is uttered twice in different situations and consequently expresses two different thoughts using one and the same form. I direct your attention to where the clock lies and ask how that happened. I receive the answer, "The clock fell." In this case the notion of the clock was already in my consciousness, the clock is the psychological subject, which the speech is about. The notion that the clock fell emerges second. In this case "fell" is the psychological predicate, that which is said about the subject. In this case the grammatical and psychological segmentation of the sentence coincide, but they also may not coincide.
>
> Working at a table I hear the noise caused by a falling object and ask what fell. In response I am answered with the same sentence, "The clock fell." In this case the notion that something fell is my consciousness first; "fell" is what is spoken about, that is, the psychological subject. What is to be said of this subject, what emerges second in consciousness, is the notion of clock, which in this case is the psychological predicate. In essence this idea can be expressed as follows: what has fallen is the clock. In this case the psychological and grammatical predicate would coincide, but in our example they do not. Our analysis shows that in a complex sentence any member can be the psychological predicate. When something is the psychological predicate, it carries the logical stress, the semantic function of which is the setting off of the psychological predicate. (Ibid., p. 272)

On the basis of these and other examples, Vygotsky defined the psychological subject as "what is being talked about in a given phrase" or what is "in the consciousness of the listener first" (ibid.), and he defined the psychological predicate as "what is new, what is said about the subject" (ibid.).

This account of psychological subject and predicate has much in common with the notions of "theme" and "rheme" (for example, Firbas, 1966) and "given" and "new" information (for example, Halliday, 1967) that have come to play an important role in functional linguistics. The distinction outlined by W. Chafe (1974, 1976) between given and new information is especially similar to Vygotsky's distinction between psychological subject and predicate. Chafe defines these notions as follows: "Given (or old) information is that knowledge which the speaker assumes to be in the consciousness of the addressee at the time of the utterance. So-called new information is what the speaker assumes he is introducing into the addressee's consciousness by what he says" (1976, p. 30). Like Vygotsky, Chafe uses the notion of consciousness in his analysis. In fact he goes so far as to say that "the key to this distinction is the notion of consciousness" (ibid.).

The striking similarities between the two theorists' accounts indicate that Vygotsky's notion of psychological segmentation involves essentially the same distinction as Chafe's account of given and new information. As I have noted (Wertsch, 1979b), there are differences between them because Vygotsky was concerned with speech to oneself, whereas Chafe focused on speech for others. However, the two accounts of form–function relationships have much in common. This fact is useful because Chafe has provided a more detailed analysis of relevant linguistic devices and hence has provided a means for extending and testing Vygotsky's claims (compare Wertsch, 1979b).

The central methodological concern that arises when considering given information is how to examine it on the basis of objective criteria. To say that given information is what is being talked about or what is in consciousness first (Vygotsky) or to say that it is knowledge that is assumed to be in consciousness (Chafe) begs the question of how this is known to be the case. Fortunately there are objective criteria for clarifying and testing one's intuitions: one can examine the speech form itself and the context in which it occurs. Both Chafe and Vygotsky utilized the speech form evidence to some degree, but they failed to provide a systematic account of contextual factors and their relationship to such forms. This led them to outline approaches that cannot account for important aspects of discourse referentiality.

My reformulation of the relationship between speech and context begins by focusing on the speech form. In Vygotsky's analysis of "The clock fell," nothing in the surface form changed when the sentence was used in different contexts.[3] In most cases, however, objective changes in the form of the utterance itself occur. There is a tendency toward what Chafe (1976) has called the "attenuation" of the surface structure forms associated with given information, that is, the psychological subject. He pointed out that the portion of an utterance conveying given information is characterized by lower pitch, weaker stress, and a tendency for nouns to be pronominalized. Vygotsky was dealing with the most extreme form of attenuation—deletion—when he argued that the psychological subject is deleted.

In an analysis of attenuation in egocentric speech, I have examined the contextual factors involved in determining what portions of an utterance are reduced or deleted entirely (Wertsch, 1979b). The action pattern of a child using egocentric speech as well as the objects in the speech context need to be taken into consideration. For example, consider the following segment of egocentric speech of a two-year-old putting together a puzzle containing animal figures:

1. Hmm? Oh wh-oh, me got duck. Snake. Snake. Break.

2. Puppy.

3. Ta goo do. This snake, snake. Hey brak. Oh. Snake.

4. Ooh. Waa. Owass. Eee-Eee. Ja open. Simmin. He go out. Hey monkey.

Since this egocentric speech (Wertsch, 1979b, p. 93) comes from a two-year-old, it is not surprising that it is quite primitive—it includes several instances of what Kohlberg and his colleagues (1968) term "word play" (as in utterance 3, "Ta goo do").

More important for my present purposes, however, is the nature of the attenuation. The action pattern being executed by the child at the time of speech is the crucial factor here. The lack of mention of the puzzle frame reflects the fact that it provides the presupposed background framework in which repeated actions with pieces are carried out. What changes (that is, what is new) in each of these actions is the identity of the piece (such as a duck, or a snake); what stays constant (what is given) is the identity of the object in which these pieces are located or are to be inserted.

Thus a crucial contextual determinant of attenuation in this case is the action pattern being executed. This can be shown by altering the action pattern. For example, if one were to change the action from one in which several pieces are inserted in one puzzle frame to one in which a single piece is to be inserted into several different puzzle frames, one would expect utterances to refer to a new puzzle frame rather than to a new piece. Such a change shows that the action pattern being executed in the context of speech plays a role in determining what is and is not mentioned.

This does not mean, however, that the pattern of attenuation in egocentric speech can be determined solely on the basis of the pattern of action in the speech context. In addition, other factors such as the physical presence of objects influence what is and what is not said. Children's egocentric speech typically does not mention absent objects no matter what action pattern is involved. This fact about the dual determination of what is and what is not said in egocentric speech raises some problems for an account based on any simple notion of consciousness. Instead of dichotomizing information neatly into what is and what is not in a speaker's consciousness, one must deal with multiple determinants and forms of presupposition.

The problem with a dichotomous account of information is exacerbated by the fact that the information is not always mentioned in equally nonattenuated ways, as reflected in cases of egocentric speech reported in one of my studies (Wertsch, 1979a). Utterances such as "a little one," "this one," and "a white" were reported when a child mentioned pieces of a puzzle. These utterances all involve attenuation (pronominalization or partial deletion) despite the fact that they are "new" in terms of the action pattern involved. In utterance 4 above, "he" seems to be an additional instance of this. All of these utterances, then, present a seeming contradiction—they are used to mention new information, but their form meets the criteria for given information or the psychological subject.

The problems I have noted are connected with the notion of consciousness as formulated by Vygotsky and Chafe. This notion has been formulated such that attenuation is linked with the simple presence or absence of information in a speaker's consciousness. In place of such a notion of consciousness, I would argue that the general concept of pragmatic presupposition is an appropriate analytic tool for examining attenuation in self-regulative speech.

Pragmatic presupposition is an issue of discourse referentiality and hence is concerned with indexical relationships between utterance (or more generally, sign token) and context. An utterance is presupposing to the extent that information from the context is "required" (that is, is presupposed) to compute its referential value. As Silverstein points out in his analysis of referential indexes or shifters:

> For . . . shifters . . . we could furthermore say that the aspect of the speech situation [is] presupposed by the sign token. That is, a given shifter token is uninterpretable referentially without the knowledge of some aspect of the situation.
>
> A particularly clear case of such presupposition is the operation of deictics, in English, for example, this and that in the singu-

lar . . . The referent of the token . . . must be identifiable, must "exist" cognitively, for the deictic itself to be interpretable. (1976, p. 33)

In the examples from Wertsch (1979b) used above, information from the context was obviously necessary to identify the referent. In these cases the property of the speech situation that made it possible for the referent to "exist cognitively" was the physical presence of the object in the extralinguistic context. This second extralinguistic contextual correlate of attenuation contrasts with the first factor identified earlier: the action pattern being executed in the context. The two contextual factors (and others as well) frequently operate in tandem, but they need not do so. They are analytically distinct and can in fact vary independently. By dealing with both, however, it becomes clear that several factors in a speech event context may serve simultaneously as grounds for attenuation.

Extralinguistic and Intralinguistic Indexical Relationships

In his definition of discourse referentiality, Silverstein pointed out that in addition to the extralinguistic context, the context of a speech event includes "the prior language context in discourse" (1980b, p. 1). Thus the extralinguistic context is only one aspect of the speech situation that can determine what exists cognitively and hence what can be presupposed. Objects may also exist in a speech situation because they are introduced through speech. In Silverstein's example of "Some man . . . He," the object (the man) exists cognitively not because it is physically present in the extralinguistic context, but because its existence and identity have been created through speech. It is possible to compute the reference value of the attenuated form "he" because a linguistically created object is now presupposed. In such cases pragmatic presupposition is grounded in intralinguistic rather than extralinguistic indexical relationships.

Recent research in developmental psycholinguistics sheds light on the relationship between the emergence of extralinguistic and intralinguistic indexical relationships. The research indicates that children first master extralinguistic indexical relationships and then, using many of the same formal devices, differentiate the intralinguistic indexical function. Findings by investigators such as Greenfield and P. Zukow (1978) show that the extralinguistic context begins to play a role in speech at a very early age. Greenfield and Zukow examined the verbal output of children who had demonstrated the ability to use vocabulary items to express several aspects of particular extralinguistic contexts but were at the stage of holophrastic, or single-word, speech and therefore could utter only a single word at a time.

When examining the children's speech, Greenfield and Zukow posed the following research question: "Given a child at the one-word stage who is encoding a complex event but is limited to uttering but a single word, can we characterize which element of the referential event will be selected for verbal expression?" (1978, p. 287). To answer this question they used several procedures to examine young children's one-word utterances. For example, the method of selective imitation determined which aspect of an adult's utterance would be repeated by the child. In all cases the objects mentioned by the child were physically present in the setting. One class of utterances to be imitated in this context involved a constant object and a variable location. In each of the mother's utterances (M) listed below, the same toy bird was to be placed by the child (C) in a different location and the child was to repeat her mother's utterances:

M: (M places stroller, chair, highchair, and box near C; M hands the bird to C.) Sit the bird in the stroller.
C: Sit.
M: (M hands the bird to C again.) Sit the bird in the chair.
C: Chair.
M: (M hands the bird to the C again.) Sit the bird in the highchair.
C: Highchair.
M: (M hands the bird to C again.) Put the bird in the box.
C: Box (Based on Greenfield and Zukow, 1978, p. 312)

In this sequence of utterances once a repeated action pattern is established (after the first turn by the mother and child), the child's selective imitation of her mother's utterances was limited to what changed, that is, to the location of the object. The recurring aspect in this action pattern and the object used in it (the toy bird) were not mentioned. Thus even at this early stage of development, there is evidence that pragmatic presupposition, based on extralinguistic indexical relationships, influences speech patterns. Here the context is defined by objects and action patterns that are physically present in the event of speaking.

The mastery of linguistic forms that utilize intralinguistic indexical relationships has been found to occur much later in ontogenesis. In this connection, A. Karmiloff-Smith's (1979) examination of how children (from three to eleven years of age) master the use of determiners in French is relevant. Among her findings is that children have a strong tendency to use determiners in French to establish extralinguistic reference well before they can use them to create and maintain reference solely through linguistic means.

This pattern is reflected in several of Karmiloff-Smith's studies. In one study of the production of anaphoric devices, an experimenter manipulated a little boy-doll and a little girl-doll such that first one and then the other carried out an operation on an object (pushing it, jumping into it, touching it, knocking it over). In the condition I shall examine, three identical objects were available, but both dolls operated on only one of them. The procedure called on the experimenter to make one doll carry out an action on the object and ask the child to report what had occurred and then make the second doll carry out the same action on the same object and again ask the child to report what had occurred. This procedure is represented as follows (after Karmiloff-Smith, 1979, p. 124).

E's action	Child's expected response
Boy-doll acts on X	Le garçon a fait tomber une des X/une X [The boy knocked over one of the Xs / an X]
Girl-doll acts on same X	La fille *l'a* fait tomber/ a fait tomber *la* X/ *la même* X [The girl knocked *it/ the same* X over]

The result of interest for my purposes is the subjects' use of determiners in the second utterance. In particular, I am concerned with the children's ability to use a referring expression that reflects the intralinguistic indexical relationship between first and second mention of the object being manipulated (knocked over in the case above).

Karmiloff-Smith (1979, p. 134) reports results that show a clear developmental trend in the use of referring expressions, a trend that continues well into later stages of childhood (eleven years of age). To obtain a clearer picture of what occurred in this study, consider the actual types of items used by the subjects. Items that were scored as adequate referring expressions were definite article plus localizer, anaphoric definite article, definite article plus re-verb, definite article plus "same," and anaphoric pronoun. The most frequently used inadequate referring expressions were deictic definite articles, which generally decreased with age. Karmiloff-Smith makes the following comment on this category:

> It was of course necessary to make a distinction between those children who first used, say, an indefinite referring expression and then used the definite article in reference to the second action on the same object, and those who used the definite article for both the first action and the second action on the same object. It is these latter responses that were classified as "deictic definite article," since the definite article for the first action is clear from the context but has no previous linguistic mention.   (Ibid., p. 126)

In cases coded as deictic definite article, the evidence indicated that the use of the definite article was motivated by extralinguistic indexical relationships (specifically, deixis) rather than by intralinguistic indexical relationships (anaphora). The second most frequently used inadequate referring expressions for second mention were indefinite articles. Here again, the use of these referring expressions indicated failure to recognize intralinguistic indexical relationships. For example, a child who uses an expression such as "a pencil" to identify the same object a second time has failed to recognize the potential intralinguistic connection created by the previous utterance. Karmiloff-Smith summarizes her results from such production experiments in the following terms:

> Linking intralinguistically is a difficult problem for the small child, which he is only able to attempt by multiple marking . . . The results of this experiment lend support to the explanatory hypothesis that the definite article functions first as a deictic . . . Thus the definite article clearly points to the referent under focus of attention, irrespective of the fact that it is different from the one just mentioned. In other words, the definite article is not used to link referents intralinguistically . . . The evidence adduced from this experiment is perhaps the clearest support of the hypothesis concerning the deictic nature of the definite article, and it is also backed from the results of other experiments.   (Ibid., pp. 140–141)

In addition to studies of speech production, Karmiloff-Smith conducted experiments on comprehension. In order to examine children's comprehension of anaphoric devices, she carried out a study that generally reversed the procedure of the production study just outlined. In this comprehension study, she asked children between the ages of three years, nine months and ten years, ten months to use two dolls and several other objects to perform an action described by the experimenter. Karmiloff-Smith (1979, p. 204) reports the same basic developmental pattern as found in her studies of children's speech production. Extralinguistic indexical relationships (in this case reflected in the use of the indefinite articles) are utilized quite early in children's development, but intralinguistic indexical relationships (reflected in the use of the anaphoric definite article) are mastered much later. Karmiloff-Smith points out that the differences here cannot be explained simply on the basis of a contrast between definite and indefinite reference since "the definite article in its deictic function is understood very early" (ibid.).

Karmiloff-Smith draws the following general conclusions from her series of production and comprehension studies.

> Small children . . . rely more heavily on extralinguistic features to clarify reference. It is not until the second phase [roughly from five to eight years] that, in cases of ambiguity, children endeavor to make use of intralinguistic means, first by overmarking and finally, in the third phase [roughly from eight to twelve years], by using the adult system . . . It may therefore be reasonable to hypothesize that from eight or nine years an essential linguistic development takes place, that is, the child can make more abstract analysis of an utterance and no longer requires stress on intralinguistic clues nor salience of extraliniuistic clues. (1979, pp. 226–227)

Using a somewhat different set of experimental procedures and materials, Hickmann (1980a, 1980b, 1982, 1985) has extended this line of reasoning. In her study four-, seven-, and ten-year-olds and adults were asked to watch a short film of puppets carrying out discourse and action and then narrate the content of the film to someone who supposedly knew nothing about it. This narrative context was structured such that the subjects could not rely on any extralinguistic indexical relationships to establish and maintain reference. It therefore contrasts with Karmiloff-Smith's experimental settings where objects were always present in the extralinguistic context. One of the measures used by Hickmann to evaluate subjects' performance was the first mention of referents in their narratives. She categorized all instances of first mention of a referent as effective, ineffective, or mixed. A first mention was coded as effective if it fell into a category such as indefinite article (for example, "a dog"), indefinite existential clause ("There was a dog"), or indefinite "topic clause" ("This story was about a frog"). A first mention was coded as ineffective if it fell into a category such as definite article (for example, "the frog"), third person pronoun ("He said 'Hi'"), or inappropriate possessive construction ("Her(?) friend had a box"). Finally, a first mention was classified as mixed if it fell into a category such as definite "topic clause" (for example, "This story was about the elephant and a lion").

As in Karmiloff-Smith's studies, Hickmann's findings support the claim that mastery of pragmatic presupposition based on intralinguistic indexical relationships is a late development in childhood. In Karmiloff-Smith's studies it was only around the age of eight that children systematically begin to utilize intralinguistic relationships when producing or comprehending an expression that is the second mention of an object. In Hickmann's study, only between the ages of seven and ten did children seem able to introduce referents such that their existence and identity were appropriately created and therefore could serve as the foundation for pragmatic presupposition.

Implications of the Distinction Between Extralinguistic and Intralinguistic Indexical Relationships

The distinction between extralinguistic and intralinguistic indexical relationships and the successive mastery of these relationships in ontogenesis have major implications for the semiotic mediation of higher mental functions. With the mastery of intralinguistic indexical relationships, a child can begin to operate on a new category of objects: objects whose existence and identity are created through speech. Now speech is beginning to serve as its own context.

Two sets of implications for Vygotsky's approach derive from children's mastery of linguistic devices for representing intralinguistic indexical relationships: one relates to self-regulative speech and the other to concept development.

Research from developmental psycholinguistics indicates that whereas children's speech reflects extralinguistic indexical relationships from an early age, intralinguistic indexical relationships come to be utilized effectively in speech only much later (between the ages of eight and twelve years). This fact is of crucial importance for an account of self-regulative speech. It means that until a relatively late point in childhood, attenuation in self-regulative speech is based primarily on extralinguistic indexical relationships. Evidence from psycholinguistic research indicates that children do not develop efficient means for representing intralinguistic indexical relationships until after this point.

The type of object represented and manipulated in self-regulative speech changes with the emergence of the ability to represent intralinguistic indexical relationships. Instead of being limited to representing objects that are physically present in the extralinguistic context, the child can now also represent objects whose existence and identity can be created through speech alone. This constitutes an extension and revision of Vygotsky's account of the development of self-regulative speech. His comments imply that once egocentric speech has gone underground to form inner speech, there are no further changes in the nature of self-regulative speech. He saw the emergence of inner speech as occurring roughly by the age of seven.

Based on the evidence I have reviewed, the representation of intralinguistic indexical relationships is apparently not mastered until after this age. Therefore, a major change in the semiotic mediation of higher mental processes seems to occur *after* the emergence of inner speech. A new type of object becomes a part of mental representation and higher mental processes in general. The existence and identity of this new type of object are still tied to the context of speech, but now the context is intralinguistic as well as extralinguistic. Thus one can now deal with objects that are not physically present as well as with those that are.

One of my assumptions has been that evidence drawn from studies of the production and comprehension of external speech utterances is relevant to claims about the internal representational means. Some readers may object to this hypothesis, arguing instead that internal cognitive and representational abilities may exist independently of, and earlier than, their external manifestation in speech. That is, it might be argued that the production and comprehension studies I have reviewed do not necessarily provide insight into the origins of children's internal representational abilities.

Such counterargument, however, fails to understand the relationship between internal representation and external semiotic processes. In the cases I have examined, evidence about external speech performance is relevant because the representational skills at issue are tied directly to the requirements imposed by linguistic activity. The very issues of intralinguistic indexical relationships, linguistically created objects, and the like confront the child with specific semiotic challenges, which give rise to internal representational mechanisms. This is not to say that abstract objects can be represented only through speech; but the task of creating and maintaining reference is something that constantly confronts the child in discourse and hence is a prime motivating force for developing certain representational skills. Requirements for how objects must be referred to in discourse (for example, their existence and identity must be clearly indicated) impose a unique set of requirements on the form of mental representation involved. It is hard to imagine how these representational requirements could arise solely through participating in noncommunicative, nonsemiotic activities. Such requirements are built into the nature of the linguistically mediated interaction in which the child is called upon to participate. Simply by speaking with others, children are confronted with the need to deal with objects that exist cognitively because they have been introduced through speech.

Thus I would argue that instead of viewing the mastery of external speech as deriving from the mastery of internal representational means, one should be aware that the causal connection may run in the opposite direction for certain semiotic processes: internal representational means emerge in response to the requirements of producing and comprehending external speech. It is on the basis of this assumption that I see the implications of recent research in developmental psycholinguistics for an account of egocentric and inner speech.

Research on discourse referentiality also has implications for Vygotsky's approach with respect to his account of concept development. His notion of genuine concepts is concerned with relationships among abstract sign types. Because these relationships are defined by the semiotic system in which such sign types exist, the issue for Vygotsky was one of propositional or semantic referentiality. Thus his account of genuine concepts is based on theoretical principles that are analytically distinct from those that govern discourse referentiality.

While recognizing the analytic distinction separating propositional from discourse referentiality, I would argue that an account of the ontogenetic transitions that lead up to the mastery of genuine concepts must consider issues of discourse referentiality. By recognizing this fact one can fill in a major gap in Vygotsky's account of concept development. Although he identified the stages of complexes, pseudoconcepts, and concepts, Vygotsky did not provide an adequate explanation of how and why the child progresses from one stage to another. He attributed this development to the demands placed on the child by communication with adults. At this general level I am in complete agreement with him. However, he viewed these communicative demands primarily in the form of sign–object relationships (in the case of complexes and pseudoconcepts), at least until the child enters school. With the onset of schooling, Vygotsky argued, the child is introduced to sign–sign relationships by producing and understanding abstract, or decontextualized, definitions and scientific concepts. Vygotsky's description of scientific concepts indicates that he viewed them as providing the child's first real experience with relationships among signs.

Such an account, however, overlooks some crucial areas of semiotic functioning that involve other modes of sign–sign relationships. By mastering the linguistic devices involved in the kinds of intralinguistic indexical relationships I outlined earlier, the child makes an important first step in the development of sign–sign relationships that culminates in genuine concepts.

Such a claim does not, of course, assume that the sign–sign relationships found in scientific concepts can be reduced to those in intralinguistic indexical relationships. The former involve sign types and exist independently of context of use, whereas the latter involve contextualized sign tokens and are inherently context bound. Rather, the connection between the two is at a level concerned with intralinguistic relationships in general. Any comprehensive examination of intralinguistic relationships and their role in cognitive development would include a long list of such relationships. In my brief account here of how children develop the ability to use language to operate on itself, I shall consider only three types of intralinguistic relationship.

First, I would argue that intralinguistic indexical relationships play a role in this development. The mastery of the linguistic means required to create and maintain reference is important in this connection. Recall that since I am concerned here with the ability to create and maintain reference through linguistic means alone, this aspect of discourse referentiality contrasts with that based on extralinguistic indexical relationships. In M. A. K. Halliday and R. Hasan's (1976) terminology, the contrast is one between endophoric and exophoric reference. With the emergence of the ability to represent and operate on intralinguistic indexical relationships, one sees the development of one way that language can serve as its own context. The referents are still nonlinguistic objects, but the existence and identity of the referents are created and maintained through speech. Table 2 represents the objects and relationships involved in this first type of intralinguistic relationship.

The second type of relationship is another form of intralinguistic

Table 2 Intralinguistic indexical relationships: type I (endophoric reference)

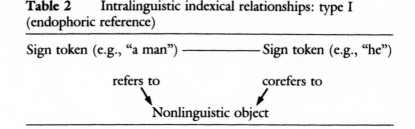

Sign token (e.g., "a man") ——————— Sign token (e.g., "he")

refers to   corefers to

Nonlinguistic object

indexical relationship (that is, a relationship between sign tokens). Unlike the first type of relationship, where the referent was nonlinguistic, now the referent itself is linguistic. Thus both the referent and the referring expression concern actual discourse (sign tokens). Following Hickmann (1980a, 1985) and Silverstein (1976, 1985), I shall term this use of speech "metapragmatic." Hickmann (1985) has noted that one of the metapragmatic uses of speech occurs "when speech refers to speech—for example, when a speaker uses speech in one situation in order to represent speech that was uttered in another situation" (p. 241). For example, in reported speech utterances such as "He answered, 'I don't know,' " the speaker refers to and predicates something about an actual segment of discourse. The sign token "he answered" refers to a linguistically constituted speech event. Furthermore, the reference value of the sign token "I" must be computed in light of the linguistically constituted referent. It refers to the speaker of the reported utterance, not to the speaker of the entire utterance.

A complete account of metapragmatic uses of speech and metapragmatic devices would involve a host of complex issues that I shall not examine here (see Hickmann, 1985, and Silverstein, 1976, 1985, for a review of these issues). My main point in raising the issue is to identify a second way that language can begin to serve as its own context. In the first type of intralinguistic relationship, the use of pragmatic devices already involved a context created by speech. In that case, the issue was how it is possible to use language to establish the existence and identity of a nonlinguistic referent. In the second type of intralinguistic relationship, an utterance, its participants, and other components of the speech situation can become referents. Thus, to say that language serves as its own context in metapragmatic uses of speech means something quite different. The objects and relationships in-

Table 3 Intralinguistic indexical relationships: type II (metapragmatic uses of speech)

Sign token a ——————————— Sign token b (refers
(e.g., "I don't know," to a) (e.g., "He said, 'I
uttered by speaker A) don't know,' " uttered
by speaker B to report
speaker A's utterance)

volved in metapragmatic uses of speech are schematically presented in Table 3.

Hickmann (1985) has carried out several investigations of the use of metapragmatic devices such as reported speech. She has found that, as is true of devices for representing the endophoric reference, metapragmatic devices are mastered quite late in childhood. For example, in a study of how four-, seven-, and ten-year-olds used reported speech when narrating the contents of a film, Hickmann observed that "overall, both the 7- and 10-year-old children used framing devices consistently when reporting the participants' speech . . . when the 4-year-old children did focus on the participants' speech, they often used frames inconsistently or did not use them at all" (1985, pp. 250–252). Hickmann provides the following example of a four-year-old's narrative where the lack of metapragmatic framing devices is particularly striking. (Quotation marks have been inserted by Hickmann at those points where she assumes there is a change of speakers; A2 refers to the second adult experimenter in the setting.)

> The donkey is angry . . . because "I put my toys in the box . . . Now I bring that to school. (A2:uh-huh) I think you're trying to *trick* me . . ." "I'm not . . ." "*You* are—*you* h— *you* . . . took it. I'm very angry at you."
>
> "No . . . you don't understand me! (A2: uh-huh) W— well I . . . I'm your friend. Let's go and play." "OK." (Laughs) (1985, p. 252)

On the basis of such patterns of narrating speech events, Hickmann (1985) concludes that four-year-olds have not yet mastered the metapragmatic devices needed to use language to represent linguistic referents: "Generally, when objectifying speech events that occurred in another speech situation, these children [the four-year-olds] tended

Table 4   Intralinguistic relationships in genuine concepts
(metasemantic uses of speech)

Sign type ─────── Sign type(s)	
(e.g., the scientific concept socialism)	(e.g., a system of society in which the means of production are owned by the state)

not to indicate a clear separation between the reported message and the narrative message in the immediate speech situation." (p. 252).

I have outlined two forms of intralinguistic indexical relationships because they seem to be important keys in understanding the emergence of the third type of intralinguistic relationship, which comprises what Vygotsky termed "genuine concepts." The intralinguistic relationships involved in genuine concepts are schematically presented in Table 4.

Tokens of sign types such as socialism can refer to specific instances of a type of social formation. In such cases, indexical relationships are involved. However, when considering terms from the standpoint of whether or not they are used as genuine concepts, the focus is on intralinguistic relationships among types. Thus it is possible to define, discuss, and argue about scientific concepts without regard to any particular context of use. Following Silverstein (1985), I shall term this the "metasemantic" function of language.

In all three types of intralinguistic relationship (endophoric reference, metapragmatic function of language, and metasemantic function of language), language is used in one way or another to operate on itself. Of course there are crucial differences in the ways this occurs, a point that I have emphasized throughout my discussion. However, I would argue that processing speech which involves intralinguistic indexical relationships is an aspect of experience that may play an important role in the emergence of the ability to understand the intralinguistic relationships among types that Vygotsky saw as the essence of genuine concepts. It is an aspect of linguistic experience that he overlooked in his account of concept development. The importance of such early precursors to abstract (that is, decontextualized) linguistic and higher mental processes is only beginning to be recognized.

I have used the notions of propositional and discourse referentiality to extend Vygotsky's account of decontextualized and contextualized sign functioning. In so doing I have identified several points where Vygotsky's semiotic analysis can be extended and revised. In particular, I have emphasized (a) the revisions necessary in Vygotsky's semiotic analysis if one were to take the sentence rather than the word as the unit of analysis, and (b) the importance of distinguishing between extralinguistic and intralinguistic context.

Although I have dealt almost exclusively with intrapsychological functioning, the revisions I have proposed have in all cases been grounded in others' analyses of social speech. By now, however, this should not appear an anomaly. Rather, it simply manifests Vygotsky's general assumption about the social origins of individual forms of semiotic mediation and mental processes. In the case of the phenomena I have mentioned, as well as in many others I have not, the close relation between social and individual functioning is a strength rather than a weakness in a Vygotskian analysis of semiotic mediation.

CHAPTER 6

Semiotic Mechanisms in Vygotsky's Genetic Law of Cultural Development

According to Vygotsky's general genetic law of cultural development, all higher mental functions appear first on the interpsychological plane and then on the intrapsychological plane. This claim is central to Vygotsky's approach, but the processes it entails have not yet been examined in any great detail. Vygotsky was most specific about it in connection with his account of egocentric and inner speech, where he analyzed the forms of semiotic mediation that make possible the transition from interpsychological to intrapsychological functioning. In that analysis, however, he focused almost exclusively on the latter. My concern here is with properties of interpsychological processes that make possible the transition to the intrapsychological plane.

An assumption that underlies everything I shall have to say on this topic is that interpsychological functioning is inextricably linked with intrapsychological functioning. This claim has emerged repeatedly in connection with the general point about the social origins of higher mental functioning in the individual. The specific point I have in mind here, however, is that in the transition from interpsychological to intrapsychological functioning, any change in the former involves a corresponding change in the latter. It is sometimes assumed that there is a sudden, clean shift from social to individual functioning—a child works with someone on a task and then begins to carry it out independently. But to characterize the transition in this way is to miss the main point about its dynamic, namely, that a series of changes typically occurs on the interpsychological plane and that each is reflected in a change in intrapsychological functioning. Of course, these changes are not always in the form of quantitative increments; many are qualitative.

The notion of situation definition—the way in which objects and events[1] in a situation are represented or defined (Wertsch, 1984)—is needed in the analysis of interpsychological functioning. It allows one to characterize the fact that interlocutors may differ and may change in their representations of the same set of objects and events. This difference may be particularly great in the kind of interpsychological functioning of primary interest to Vygotsky: adult–child interaction in the zone of proximal development. A child often does not understand the definition of the objects or the functional significance of behaviors that are assumed by an adult. In one sense the adult and child are in the same situation because the same concrete objects and events are perceptually available to both. In another sense, however, they are not in the same situation because they do not define these objects and events in the same way.

When interlocutors such as an adult and a child in the zone of proximal development approach a setting with dissimilar situation definitions, it may at first be difficult to see how they could carry on effective communication. After all, they represent many aspects of the setting in quite different ways. To understand this apparent problem, one needs to invoke the notion of *intersubjectivity*. Intersubjectivity exists when interlocutors share some aspect of their situation definitions. Typically this overlap may occur at several levels, and hence several levels of intersubjectivity may exist.

In discussing intersubjectivity I shall focus primarily on the work of R. Rommetviet and his colleagues (for example, Rommetveit, 1974, 1979a–1979g, 1985; Blakar and Rommetveit, 1979: Hundeide, 1985), since their position is compatible with a Vygotskian approach to interpsychological functioning.

The issue of how greater or lesser degrees of intersubjectivity between speaker and hearer are created, maintained, and reestablished lies at the foundation of Rommetveit's approach to the study of human communication. According to him, "Communication aims at transcendence of the 'private' worlds of the participants. It sets up what we might call "states of intersubjectivity" (1979c, p. 94).

Rommetveit's approach contrasts with many contemporary analyses that begin with the implicit or explicit claim that when interlocutors come together in a speech situation, they share a fund of "background knowledge" that provides an agreed-upon foundation for communication. He argues that this assumption has led investigators to overlook the issue of how communicative behavior creates and transforms a situation and to focus instead on how an utterance simply adds to preexisting information.

Rommetveit has emphasized that any situation, event, or object has many possible interpretations and that speech serves to impose a particular interpretation and create a temporarily shared social reality. He sees the issue as one of how the "meaning potential" of linguistic units and structures provides a "rough draft of a contract" that can be defined or specified only by considering its role in the communicative context:

> The basic problem of human intersubjectivity becomes . . . a question concerning in what sense and under what conditions two persons who engage in a dialogue can transcend their different private worlds. And the linguistic basis for this enterprise, I shall argue, is not a fixed repertory of shared "literal" meanings, but very general and partially negotiated drafts of contracts concerning categorization and attribution inherent in ordinary language. (1979f, p. 7)

In Rommetveit's account, what any particular observer "sees" going on in a situation is an entirely private affair. However,

> it can be talked about and hence—at least under certain conditions and in some sense—become a temporarily shared social reality. The solitary observer may thus try to transform his "private" outlook on the situation into a social reality simply by telling some other person about it. Once the other person accepts the invitation to listen and engage in a dialogue, he leaves behind whatever his preoccupations might have been the moment "silence was transformed into speech" (Merleau-Ponty, 1962, p. 182). From that moment on the two of them are jointly committed to a temporarily shared social world, established and continually modified by acts of communication. (1979g, p. 10)

Among the illustrations Rommetveit uses to elaborate this point is the following:

> What is being said may . . . impose a definite structure upon what is seen or upon the situation in which it is being said . . . I may

be told, for instance, as I am watching a large and derelict building: "There was not enough profit from production." What I am not told at all—but yet am forced to assume in order to make sense of what I hear—is that the building in front of me is a factory or a business building of some sort.   (1979b, p. 70)

Thus when interlocutors enter into a communicative context, they may have different perspectives or only a vague interpretation of what is taken for granted and what the utterances are intended to convey. Through semiotically mediated "negotiation," however, they create a temporarily shared social world, a state of intersubjectivity. The writings of Rommetveit and his colleagues show that there are many complex aspects to interlocutors' understanding of the speech situation. The issues involved can extend from basic trust in the other's communicative abilities and good intentions to the way a particular referent is categorized or understood.

Because an adult and a child operating in the zone of proximal development often bring divergent situation definitions to a task setting, they may be confronted with severe problems of establishing and maintaining intersubjectivity. The challenge to the adult is to find a way to communicate with the child such that the latter can participate at least in a minimal way in interpsychological functioning and can eventually come to define the task setting in a new, culturally appropriate way. During early phases of development, intersubjectivity usually cannot be created at the level of verbal formulations and abstract definitions of the task. Instead, communication typically must be grounded in context-bound signs. This communication, which operates on the basis of a minimal level of shared situation definition (that is, intersubjectivity), lays the groundwork for the transition to intrapsychological functioning.

The Transition from Interpsychological to Intrapsychological Functioning

The usefulness of the notions of situation definition and intersubjectivity for a Vygotskian approach can be demonstrated by some concrete examples. The setting that provides the basis for situation definitions in these examples is relatively simple. It involves using small objects (the "pieces") to construct one object (the "copy") in accordance with another (the "model"). My account of interaction in this setting will focus on these objects and the goal-directed action in which they are embedded. It does not explicitly examine other aspects of the interaction, such as its affective dimensions.

The goal-directed action that is at the core of an adult's situation definition of this setting can be analyzed in terms of strategic steps. The number of steps is positively correlated with the level of detail used to analyze the action. My analysis, which will not go into great detail here, identifies the following three strategic steps:

1. Consult the model to determine the identity and location of the piece needed next.

2. Select the piece identified in step 1 from the pieces pile.

3. Add the piece selected in step 2 to the copy.

The strategic steps in this description of the goal-directed action are interdefined. An account of each presupposes the others in some way. In addition, the action (made up of the strategic steps) and the objects are interdefined. The objects are appropriately understood only if their roles in the action are specified, and the action can be fully described only by invoking information about the objects. Hence the situation definition in this setting involves the interrelated components of goal-directed action (with its strategic steps) and the objects (pieces, copy, model).

What I have said so far characterizes an adult's typical definition of the situation. Young children, however, often do not see the setting this way. They may agree with the adult only in certain minimal respects about how objects and actions should be understood. By identifying the points on which there is adult–child accord, one can recognize points of intersubjectivity in the zone of proximal development. Many such points can be found in the transition from interpsychological to intrapsychological functioning. For example, four points were identified in my study of American mothers interacting with their preschool children (Wertsch, 1979a). These points reflect four levels in the transition from interpsychological to intrapsychological functioning. The first level is characterized by the fact that the child's situation definition is so different from the adult's that communication is very difficult. The adult may attempt to direct the child through the strategic steps, but the child's understanding of the objects and goal-directed action is so limited that the child may not interpret the adult's utterances appropriately. In one case the child's response to his mother's utterance about a puzzle piece depicting a truck window was to shift his attention to the real windows in the room where they were working. Even minimal agreement about the definition of objects in this setting seems to have been missing, thus leading to this misunderstanding. The issue of intersubjectivity about the goal-directed action never arose here since the adult and child differed in a fundamental way about the definition of the objects involved; communicating on the basis of the adult's situation definition was impossible.

At the second level of intersubjectivity, the adult–child interaction is not so restricted by the child's limited situation definition. The child at least seems to share the adult's basic understanding of objects in the setting, namely, that they depict pieces of a truck. However, the child does not yet understand the nature of the goal-directed action in which these objects are embedded and consequently often fails to make the inferences necessary to interpret the adult's other-regulative utterances. For example, the child may know that the truck pieces are to go in the copy puzzle but does not understand that the model must be matched. This level is generally characterized by the fact that the child is beginning to participate successfully in the task setting, but the child's understanding of the task situation is still far from being in complete agreement with the adult's. Thus communication problems arise because the child does not see all the implications of an utterance in other-regulation.

At the third level of intersubjectivity, the child can respond appropriately to other-regulation by making the inferences needed to interpret the adult's directives even when they are nonexplicit and rely on an adult-like situation definition. While the process is still carried out on the interpsychological plane, the fact that the child can make the appropriate inferences indicates that intrapsychological functioning is beginning to account for much of the child's performance. The adult no longer has to specify all the steps that must be followed in order to interpret a directive since the child can carry these out on the basis of a fairly complete situation definition. Indeed, in some cases it seems that the child is functioning independently and that the adult is simply providing reassurances that what the child is doing is correct.

At the fourth and final level identified by Wertsch (1979a) in the transition from interpsychological to intrapsychological functioning, the child takes over complete responsibility for carrying out the goal-directed task. Egocentric speech may appear during and shortly after the shift to intrapsychological functioning. This self-regulative form of semiotic mediation typically shares many structural and functional properties with the communicative speech previously used by the dyad. This is a semiotic manifestation of the fact that the child has mastered the situation definition with which the adult originally approached the task. At this point there is almost complete intersubjectivity between adult and child on the situation definition, a fact that makes further other-regulation unnecessary.

While my focus here has been on interpsychological functioning, it is important to realize that each time I noted an increase in the level of shared situation definition, I was implicitly dealing with a transfer of responsibility for the task to intrapsychological functioning by the child. More and more of what had been accomplished on the inter-psychological plane was therefore being carried out on the intra-psychological plane.

This reciprocal relationship has been examined in detail in several other studies (for example, Wertsch, McNamee, McLane, and Budwig, 1980; McLane, 1981; Rogoff, 1984; Sammarco, 1984; Wertsch, Minick, and Arns, 1984; Brown and Ferrara, 1985). All have been concerned with the ways in which responsibility for executing a task shifts from the adult–child dyad to the child. In several studies the situation definition was grounded in the goal-directed action (involving the three strategic steps) and the objects (pieces, copy, model) outlined earlier. The focus of these studies was on variation in the form and style of interpsychological functioning, but in all cases the correlated intra-psychological functioning was also reflected in the analysis.

J. McLane (1981) examined the difference between mother–child and child–child interaction; J. Sammarco (1984) examined mother–child interaction involving children both with and without language comprehension deficits; and Wertsch, N. Minick, and F. Arns (1984) examined mother–child and teacher–child interaction in rural Brazil. Many complex modes of social interaction were observed, with varying implications for the transition to intrapsychological functioning.

In these studies a multilevel analysis was used to examine the execution of each of the three strategic steps. This analysis concerned the distribution of task responsibility between the tutor and the tutee. The first level specified who physically carried out the step of looking at the model, picking up a piece from the pieces pile, or inserting the piece in the copy. If (and only if) the tutee physically carried out a step, a second level of analysis assessed whether the behavior was self-regulated or other-regulated. Major differences appeared in the analyses of these two levels. For example, whereas middle-class American mothers and Brazilian teachers almost never physically carried out the steps of picking up or placing a piece, such behavior was not unusual for rural Brazilian mothers, American children acting as tutors, and American mothers working with children with language disorders. By picking up or placing the pieces, these latter sets of tutors gave almost no strategic responsibility to their tutees, thus minimizing the required intrapsychological participation on their part. Furthermore, when a tutee did execute a step, the use of other-regulation varied widely among the groups of dyads.

Even from the first two levels of analysis, it is possible to identify major differences among dyads' forms of interpsychological functioning. These differences exist between American mothers and five-and-one-half-year-old children when acting as tutors for three-and-one-half-year-olds (McLane, 1981) between mothers and teachers working with six-year-olds in rural Brazil (Wertsch, Minick, and Arns, 1984), and between mother–child interaction involving preschool children with and without language comprehension deficits (Sammarco, 1984; Wertsch and Sammarco, 1985). In none of these cases is there a claim that the unique pattern of social interaction is attributable to the tutor or tutee alone, but in some cases the findings suggest one or the other more strongly. For example, findings from a study by Arns (1980) indicate that the tutees could have functioned at a higher level than was allowed by the rural Brazilian mothers. The required level of the children's intrapsychological functioning seems to have been significantly determined by the tutors' behavior. Conversely, in the Sammarco (1984) study language comprehension disabilities on the part of the tutees seem to have had a major impact on the level of interpsychological and intrapsychological functioning. The overall point from the studies is that children may participate in quite different forms of interpsychological functioning, and these differences affect how a child participates on the intrapsychological level in a task setting.

While forms of interpsychological and intrapsychological functioning differ significantly, there seems to be at least one common tendency in how children in these studies come to master the situation definition of the task: they first participate in the execution of the goal-directed task on the interpsychological plane, and only subsequently do they recognize and master the strategic significance of their behaviors. Rather than understanding the task and then doing it, the children seem to have done the task (as a participant in interpsychological functioning) and then understood it.

Perhaps the most revealing cases of how this developmental sequence works can be found in within-session, microgenetic transitions. Wertsch and Hickmann (in press) have analyzed several cases of mother–child interaction in a task setting of constructing a copy puzzle in accordance with a model and have documented some striking within-session transitions from interpsychological to intrapsychological functioning. Among the factors cited as encouraging this transition were (1) a cognitive readiness on the part of the child, (2) a willingness on the part of the adult to transfer strategic responsibility to the child, (3) adults' use of "reflective assessments" to inform the child of the significance of his or her behaviors (4) the explicitness of the adults' directives, and (5) the possibility for the dialogic structure of interpsychological functioning to be mastered on the intrapsychological plane through the differentiation of language functions. All five factors are presumably involved in ontogenetic as well as microgenetic transitions, but their relative contribution (especially that of the child's cognitive readiness) is more difficult to specify in ontogenesis.

These studies have viewed the transition from interpsychological to intrapsychological functioning in terms of how the child can master the situation definition that had guided interpsychological functioning. The process involves entering into interaction on the basis of primitive intersubjectivity with the tutor (usually an adult) and then going through one or more situation "redefinitions" (Wertsch, 1984) until a mature, culturally appropriate situation definition provides the ground for self-regulation.

My review of the research has stressed that a change on the interpsychological plane is necessarily coupled with a change on the intrapsychological plane. This finding belies any account that regards the transition as an undifferentiated period of interpsychological functioning followed neatly by an undifferentiated period of intrapsychological functioning. Furthermore, it highlights the fact that by characterizing interpsychological functioning in a task setting, one necessarily characterizes intrapsychological functioning. Indeed this procedure provides information about individual processes that often can be obtained in no other way.

Semiotic Mechanisms in the Transition

If a task is executed correctly and smoothly on the interpsychological plane, why should a transition to individual functioning occur? The problem of why transitions should occur is notoriously difficult for most theories of cognitive development, but in this case the solution may be relatively straightforward. It would seem to be grounded in the tendency of adults to encourage increasing participation or independence in task performance by children as an inherent aspect of socialization. As Arns (1980) has shown, the timing and procedures for encouraging independent functioning may vary widely depending on cultural and socioeconomic factors, but the transition is a necessary part of socialization anywhere.

Hence, one must deal with the specific mechanisms whereby individual competency is encouraged. An adult often cannot simply provide an explanation or one set of directives and then insist that the child begin to function independently. The nature of the transition is typically more subtle, gradual, and complex. Given Vygotsky's central theme about sign mediation, I shall focus especially on the semiotic mechanisms involved in the transition. Such a focus not only provides essential information about the eventual "quasi-social" processes in the individual; it also holds the key to understanding how and why the child is pushed along the path toward redefining situations in accordance with adult views and thereby comes to function as a mature member of the culture.

The two semiotic mechanisms I shall examine here are referential perspective and abbreviation. The former concerns ways of entering into interpsychological functioning; the latter seems to play a role primarily in making the transition to intrapsychological functioning. In both cases the mechanisms create and transform various aspects of intersubjectivity in a communicative setting where the interlocutors do not share the same situation definition.

Referential Perspective

To function effectively on the interpsychological plane, interlocutors must be able to direct one another's attention to specific objects and events. This behavior involves reference. For my purposes, I shall examine the case in which a speaker uses a sign (verbal or nonverbal) to identify a nonlinguistic referent in the speech situation. This mechanism involves extralinguistic indexical relationships (that is, relationships between sign tokens or unique utterance events and nonlinguistic objects or events).

A fundamental fact about referring is that the same referent can be identified in a variety of ways (that is, by using different referring expressions). For example, assume the following object is the referent that a speaker wishes to identify: ○. The speaker can choose from a variety of referring expressions, such as:

1–a. . . . the round thing . . .

1–b. . . . the white thing . . .

1–c. . . . the round white thing . . .

Although any one of these expressions may be used to identify the referent, they obviously differ in some important respects. The notion of referential perspective that I shall develop here is intended to account for this difference. The referential perspective, or "mode of presentation" (Frege, 1960), involved in an act of referring is the perspective or viewpoint utilized by the speaker in order to identify a referent. Referential perspective is necessarily involved in any act of referring. Furthermore, the perspective from which a referent is identified may vary. Thus in 1–a the object is identified in terms of a shape category; in 1–b it is referred to in terms of a color category; and in 1–c it is identified from a perspective that combines the two categories.

There may appear to be cases in which a speaker does not introduce a perspective when referring. For example, one might argue that it is possible to identify the referent in the example above by using nonverbal pointing and/or expressions such as the following:

2–a. . . . that . . .

2–b. . . . that one . . .

This line of reasoning assumes that such verbal and nonverbal means can be used to identify a referent but do not categorize it and therefore do not involve the introduction of a perspective. While I would agree with the claim that different levels and types of perspective exist, I would not agree that no perspective is involved in cases of nonverbal pointing and/or deictic expressions. The speaker's communicative act necessarily defines a referent in a minimal way—namely, in terms of relative spatiotemporal contiguity between the referent and the speaker, as in "that" versus "this."

The fact that a speaker introduces some perspective in any referring act is only the starting point in my argument. The main questions I wish to address are concerned with how and why a speaker introduces a particular perspective. These questions lead to a consideration of the range of semiotic options available to a speaker when introducing a perspective into a speech situation and the reasons for selecting one of these options over another. My analysis is based on the fact that when identifying a referent, a speaker may introduce different amounts of information about referential perspective into the speech situation by choosing different types of referring expressions. In examining this issue I shall proceed from expressions that minimize the amount of information about a speaker's perspective introduced into the speech to expressions that maximize such information (Wertsch, 1980a).

One of the most important semiotic devices that allow speakers to identify an intended referent while minimizing information about their perspective is deixis. Deixis falls under the category of what Peirce (1931–1935) termed "indexical signs." The general analysis of indexical signs has been extended by Silverstein (1976). I shall be concerned here with what he terms "presupposing referential indexes." Deictics such as nonverbal pointing or "this" or "that" in English are perhaps the best examples of this kind of index. An appropriate use of deictics assumes that the referent already exists cognitively (that is, the referent is presupposed) for the interlocutors. Given that the existence and identity of the referent are presupposed and that a deictic referring expression serves simply to point out this referent, the use of such a referring expression introduces only a minimal amount of information about referential perspective into the speech setting. This is what Morris (1971) had in mind when he stated that "an indexical sign does not characterize what it denotes (except to indicate roughly the space–time coordinates)" (p. 102).

Thus a speaker who uses expressions such as "that" to identify the intended referent introduces very little information about a particular way of perceiving or thinking of the object. This fact does not mean that the speaker and listener cannot or do not think of the referent in some more complex way. It simply means that the speaker has not explicitly introduced such information into the speech situation.

A further point about referring expressions is that levels of indexicality rather than its simple presence or absence are involved in an overall account. Thus the use of nonverbal pointing alone, without an accompanying verbal utterance, to identify a referent may introduce even less information about referential perspective than does an utterance such as "that" or "that one" because it may not signal relative proximity of the object to the speaker. Conversely, expressions such as "the round thing" and "the white thing," which rely more heavily on symbolic signs than "that" and "that one," still involve an element of indexicality due to the presence of "the."

A second way that a speaker minimizes the information about referential perspective that is introduced into a speech situation is to use a "common referring expression" (Wertsch, 1980a). This concept is borrowed from R. Brown's (1970) analysis of how a child is introduced to the way that everyday objects are identified in speech. Brown argued that while we can use a variety of expressions to refer to an object, there is typically a "most common name" (a categorization) in a speech community that is based on the function the object normally or most commonly has:

> The name of a thing, the one that tells what it "really" is, is the name that constitutes the referent as it needs to be constituted for most purposes. The other names represent categorizations useful for one or another purpose. We are even likely to feel that these recategorizations are acts of imagination, whereas the major categorization is a kind of passive recognition of the true character of the referent. (p. 10)

In the case of the referent introduced earlier, "the round thing" or "the white thing" could be used as a common referring expression. In the case of any actual utterance event, one of these categorizations may indeed be most appropriate and informative for identifying the referent. The very definition of a common referring expression guarantees that the chances of this being true are fairly high. However, the use of a common referring expression typically is not maximally informative because the information it uses is redundant. The redundancy does not arise because the information is available in the spatiotemporal organization of the speech event. Rather, it is redundant because the common referring expression is the one that the listener would have been likely to choose if forced to make a choice with no additional contextual information. Thus to identify the referent above by using common referring expressions such as "the round thing" or "the white thing" is to add little new information since it categorizes the object in the same way that the listener would be most likely to categorize it.

There is also a third semiotic mechanism that allows a speaker to maximize the amount of information about referential perspective that is introduced into the speech context. This kind of referring expression can introduce a perspective that is informative about the specific way that the speaker views the referent in the speech event. This "context-informative" referring expression (Wertsch, 1980a) introduces more information into the speech situation than either a common or a deictic referring expression does in the sense that it categorizes the referent in a way that would not already be obvious to someone who does not understand the situation definition. The mother's use of the expression "window" at the first level in the transition from inter- to intrapsychological functioning is an example of a context-informative referring expression (Wertsch, 1979a).

Deictic and common referring expressions, with their associated perspectives, may serve as a "default" option vis-à-vis context-informative expressions. A default option can be used when a speaker wishes to identify a referent without introducing a context-informative referential perspective.

The ranking of these three types of referring expressions in terms of informativeness—from deictic to common to context informative—has several implications for their use in communication. In general, higher levels of intersubjectivity are associated with, but do not require the use of, more informative referring expressions. By incorporating an account of the three types of referring expressions into an analysis of adult–child interaction, it is possible to gain certain insights into a dyad's success at attaining intersubjectivity on a situation definition. In my 1980a study, mother–child interaction was examined in a setting where the interlocutors were to use puzzle pieces in order to construct one puzzle (the "copy") in accordance with another (the "model"). When properly completed, the copy puzzle depicted a truck that was identical to the one in the model.

In this study I compared the performance of a dyad involving a two-and-one-half-year-old with that of a dyad involving a three-and-one-half-year-old on one segment of the task, the segment having to do with the pieces depicting the wheels on the truck. In the case of the two-and-one-half-year-old, interpsychological functioning with his mother was at the first level (Wertsch, 1979a) and never really dealt with the goal-directed action of constructing the copy puzzle in accordance with the model. Rather, the interaction was constantly disrupted by the fact that the child seemed to categorize objects in the task setting in a way quite different from his mother's. An excerpt from the discourse making up the interpsychological functioning reflects this lack of intersubjectivity:

3. C: Look it, crackers. Look. (C looks at the pieces pile; C picks up an inner wheel piece from the pieces pile; C picks up an outer wheel piece from the pieces pile.)

4. M: Crackers. They sort of look like crackers. (C puts the outer wheel pieces in his hand onto the pieces pile; C picks up an outer wheel piece from the pieces pile.)

5. C: Crackers. (C puts the inner wheel piece in his hand back onto the pieces pile.)

6. M: Mm–hm. (C picks up another outer wheel piece from the pieces pile.)

7. C: Look, look . . . Look at the crackers. (C picks up several additional nonwheel pieces from the pieces pile.)

8. M: They look like crackers. But they aren't crackers. But they aren't crackers. I think what we're supposed to do here is make this truck. (M pats the model puzzle.)

9. M: Can we do that? (M points to the empty frame where the copy puzzle is to be made.)

10. M: Make this truck (M pats the copy puzzle frame) to look like this truck. (M pats the model puzzle; C puts all the pieces in his hand back onto the pieces pile.)

11. M: Where are the wheels? (M points to the wheel pieces in the model puzzle; no response from C.)

12. M: I think we're supposed to leave this truck (M points to the model puzzle) all together and make a truck right here (M points to the empty frame for the copy puzzle) that looks like this one. (M points to the model puzzle.)

13. M: Let's find the wheels for this truck.

14. C: What's this? (C picks up the truck body piece from the pieces pile.)

A cursory examination of this excerpt reveals that the child was not very successful at "transcending his private world." He apparently never understood that the pieces represented wheels on a truck. It seems that throughout the interaction he viewed the pieces as circles or crackers rather than as wheels. Because of the child's constant inability to negotiate or "buy into" a situation definition that would be more appropriate for carrying out this culturally defined task, the adult was forced to adjust her communicative moves such that they could be interpreted within his alternative framework. One of the semiotic mechanisms that made it possible for the mother to interact with her child within the confines of his situation definition was referential perspective.

In the course of this dyad's entire problem-solving session, the mother used twenty-eight referring expressions in her attempts to refer to wheels (Wertsch, 1980a). The interaction was marked by the use of several different referential perspectives. She used four context-informative referring expressions (as in utterances 11 and 13), four common referring expressions, and twenty deictic referring expressions. Of the twenty deictic referring expressions four were instances of nonverbal pointing alone, and the remaining sixteen involved verbal expressions such as "they," "this," and "it."

In this interaction the pattern of the mother's choice of referring expressions provides particular insight into the problems the dyad was having in establishing a temporarily shared social reality, or intersubjectivity. At the beginning of the interaction the child understood or defined the wheel pieces in terms of "crackerness" rather than "wheelness" (as in utterances 3, 5, and 7). The mother attempted to impose a different situation definition on the task setting both by saying that the wheel pieces were not really crackers (utterance 8) and by introducing context-informative referential perspectives based on wheels (utterances 11 and 13) and trucks (utterances 8, 10, 12, and 13). Even as she was introducing these referential perspectives into the speech situation, however, she "hedged her bets" by relying extensively on nonverbal pointing. Thus in all cases except in utterance 13, the mother accompanied her context-informative referring expressions having to do with a truck or a wheel with a nonverbal pointing behavior. In the only instance where she did not supplement her context-informative referring expression with deixis (utterance 13), the child's response (utterance 14) was inappropriate.

Thus when the child shifted his attention to the appropriate aspects of the task setting, he could have been doing so either because he was categorizing the objects as the adult was or because he was simply following the minimally informative deictic referring expression. If he were acting on the basis of the former, he would be accepting the adult's situation definition and "transcending his private world." If he were acting on the basis of the latter, he would be entering into only a minimal level of intersubjectivity. That is, he would be attending to the same referent but categorizing it in a different way from the adult's.

The subsequent excerpts indicate that this child was attending to the referents for the latter reason. Later in the session the mother again introduced a context-informative referential perspective concerned with wheels, but she again accompanied her expressions with a deictic referring expression, such as "this." Even later, she switched entirely to using verbal and nonverbal deixis when identifying referents. She then introduced another referential perspective by asking the child whether the object he was holding was "a circle." He responded by defining the wheel piece as a circle; that is, he "bought" this referential perspective or categorization. "A circle" is a common referring expression and represents a default option because it is not closely tied to the specific situation definition (building a truck puzzle that has wheels). Thus the mother and child were able to agree that the referents were circles, and so it then was possible to continue their joint cognitive activity by using diectic and common referring expressions.

Near the end of the segment of interaction, the mother reintroduced the context-informative referential perspective based on wheels. This pattern of reintroducing context-informative referring expressions after an initial lack of success (and the associated switch to default options) characterizes the interaction of several of the mothers in my study (1979a). It often appeared to be a semiotic challenge to the children to determine whether they were capable of redefining the objects in the communicative setting in a task-appropriate way. In the case just mentioned, it seems that this challenge did not meet with success. The child continued to display behaviors that indicated he was not categorizing the objects as wheels. For example, at a later point in the interaction, after continuing to refer to other pieces as crackers he put them in his mouth as if to eat them.

The excerpts of interaction between this two-and-one-half-year-old and his mother can be summarized as follows. The mother and the child did not define the goal-directed task and the objects in the setting in the same way. After initial attempts to introduce a context-informative referential perspective based on the functional significance of pieces in a perceptual array depicting a truck, the mother switched to communicative moves that did not require this situation definition. One of the ways that she did this was to switch from context-informative referring expressions to common and deictic referring expressions (default options). While she obviously continued to understand that the puzzle depicted a truck, she ceased (at least temporarily) introducing referential perspectives that posed semiotic challenges to the child to enter into intersubjectivity on her terms, that is, to use the same situation definition. One could argue that she never really required the child to interpret her utterances strictly on the basis of a situation definition involving a truck since she supplemented virtually all of her context-informative reference with deictic reference.

In contrast to the problems that this two-and-one-half-year-old had in transcending his private world, or understanding the adult's situation definition, children in the same task setting often are capable of entering into a level of intersubjectivity that permits productive joint cognitive activity. For example, in another excerpt of an interaction between a three-and-one-half-year-old boy and his mother in the same task setting (Wertsch, 1980a), the child seemed to realize immediately which pieces were wheels. He responded appropriately to the mother's initial introduction of a context-informative referential perspective based on "wheelness." Although she subsequently used a deictic referring expression, the initial success at agreeing on referential perspective indicates that the switch was not motivated by a need to operate on the basis of a more primitive situation definition. In this case the deictic referring expression was not functioning as a default option. Unlike the two-and-one-half-year-old, this three-and-one-half-year-old child quickly and smoothly entered into a state of intersubjectivity with his mother in connection with defining the puzzle as a truck, and the mother did not find it necessary to switch referential perspective in an attempt to arrive at some shared situation definition.

To summarize, I examined two cases of adult–child interpsychological functioning in a task setting. These cases differed greatly with respect to the level of intersubjectivity attained. The examination demonstrated that when confronted with a lack of intersubjectivity in such interactional settings, an adult can utilize options in referential perspective to establish and maintain communication.

Two major points can be made about the use of referential perspective in these interactions. First, it again reflects the inherent link between interpsychological and intrapsychological functioning. The switches from one referential perspective to another obviously reflected attempts to establish a level of interpsychological functioning. In many instances, however, establishing such a level necessarily involves a specification of the interlocutors' intrapsychological representation of the situation. Any switch in one is inherently linked with a switch in the other.

My second point concerns the nature of the relationship between referential perspective and intersubjectivity, that is, between referential perspective in interpsychological and hence intrapsychological functioning. In the case of the two-and-one-half-year-old above, it appears that the mother often was forced to change referential perspective in order to bring the common situation definition "down" to the child's level. However, she continued to try to introduce context-informative referential perspectives that would lure the child "up" to her situation definition. The latter represents what I term a "semiotic" challenge. It is an attempt to communicate by using a semiotic mechanism whose understanding would require the child to redefine the situation in a manner more like that of a mature member of the culture. There is nothing inherently better or worse about representing the round pieces in the puzzle task as wheels. In fact, the model-copying procedure could be executed perfectly without doing so. Such a representation was, however, the one chosen spontaneously by all the adults in my studies (1979a, 1980a) and hence something on which they all tried to establish intersubjectivity with children.

The notion of a semiotic challenge points out what might be termed a "creative" use of language (compare Silverstein, 1976). Instead of using signs, in this case linguistic signs, such that they presuppose another person's existing intrapsychological situation definition, they are used to encourage the creation of a new one, on both the interpsychological and the intrapsychological planes. In the particular cases examined earlier, their use indicated an adult's attempt to lure a child into a new situation, that is, to create a new situation definition in social and individual functioning.

Because referential perspective is one device that seems particularly well suited for this subtle but powerful process of setting up semiotic challenges, it is often used and, I believe, is quite effective. In a nutshell, referential perspective is a semiotic mechanism whose use can lead a child to think differently by talking differently. The changes it induces represent a form of development that meets the criteria I mentioned earlier.

Abbreviation

A second semiotic mechanism involved in the transition from inter-psychological to intrapsychological functioning is abbreviation, the reduction of fully expanded, explicit linguistic representation. Vygotsky examined this phenomenon in his account of inner speech. He claimed that the "first and most important" property of inner speech is its "unique abbreviated syntax." Furthermore, he analyzed egocentric speech to obtain concrete evidence about the "fragmentary, abbreviated nature of inner speech as compared with external speech" (1934a, p. 292).

In these and other comments about abbreviation Vygotsky dealt only with the intrapsychological plane of functioning. I shall argue that abbreviation plays an important role in interpsychological func-tioning as well. Specifically, it is instrumental in the changes in adult–child interpsychological functioning that are tied to changes in the child's intrapsychological functioning.

The starting point for such an argument is to recognize the rela-tionship between linguistic representation and a situation definition. All aspects of a situation definition may be explicitly and exhaustively reflected in speech, or only some of them may appear. This is a matter of degree. As fewer and fewer aspects are explicitly represented, the level of abbreviation rises.

Just as there are many referential perspectives a speaker may take toward an object, there are many ways in which a speaker may represent a situation definition when providing other-regulation. A speaker may use quite explicit (nonabbreviated) utterances when a listener shares relatively little of the situation definition, but with greater intersub-jectivity the speaker's utterances need not be so detailed, or explicit, because the listener can be relied upon to understand more abbreviated directives.

These issues were examined in an analysis of adult–child interaction where mother–child dyads were assigned the task of constructing a copy puzzle in accordance with a model (Wertsch and Schneider, 1979). That is, the study involved the general structure of the objects and goal-directed action used in earlier illustrations. Again, the strategic steps that comprise the action in the adult's situation definition are (1) consult the model to determine the identity and location of the piece needed next, (2) select the piece identified in step 1 from the pieces pile, and (3) add the piece selected in step 2 to the copy. The major difficulty for young children in carrying out this goal-directed action consistently seems to be in coordinating information from the model and the copy. The coordination required is reflected in step 1. There it is specified that one must look at the model, but in order to obtain relevant information from it one must also know what comes next in the copy.

The nature of abbreviation in this context becomes obvious when one considers the fact that the listener must utilize information both from the model and from the copy in order to respond appropriately to a directive that deals with only one of them. It is especially important to recognize that in order to comply with a directive that seems to be concerned only with the copy, the listener may be called upon to identify and carry out substeps in connection with the model. For example, utterances 15 and 16 would be used to direct the listener to carry out some action concerning the copy, but to comply, the listener must consult the model:

15. Put the next piece in the copy puzzle.

16. What do you need in the copy puzzle now?

In this task setting the listener can identify what piece is needed or what piece is next only by checking the model. That is, utterances 15 and 16 are abbreviated with respect to the implicit substep of checking with the model.

Although it is possible to distribute directives along a multivalued continuum of abbreviation, a simple, dichotomous distinction was used between "abbreviated" and "nonabbreviated" directives (Wertsch and Schneider, 1979). Abbreviated directives were defined as those that do not specifically instruct the listener to consult both the model and the copy in their puzzle-making task but in fact implicitly require the listener to make a comparison between the two. Utterances 15 and 16 do not specifically direct the listener to be concerned with both the copy and the model, but they in fact require the listener to do so in order to respond appropriately. Nonabbreviated directives were defined as directives with which the listener can comply without having to carry out any implicit substeps involving both of the puzzles (ibid.). Examples of nonabbreviated directives are utterances 17 and 18:

17. Find the blue piece in this puzzle.

18. Put the red piece next to the orange in that puzzle.

The listener can respond appropriately to both utterances by dealing with only one of the two puzzles. There is no need to be aware that two puzzles are involved in the task and that a specific functional relationship exists between them.

The distinction between abbreviated and nonabbreviated directives is not based on how the listener actually responds to the directive (ibid.). It is based solely on an analysis of the directive utterance, without regard to the response it elicits. This point is important since in the task setting virtually every utterance by the adult is a directive, and if the listener understands the task very well, even a nonabbreviated directive such as 17 or 18 may be followed by several steps beyond those required to respond to that directive alone. It is possible for the listener to "see where the speaker is going" with a nonabbreviated directive and to respond as if he or she were complying with an ab-breviated utterance.

We examined the verbal directives used by eighteen middle-class American mothers when directing their two-and-one-half-, three-and-one-half-, or four-and-one-half-year-old children through the task of making the copy puzzle in accordance with the model (Wertsch and Schneider, 1979). In those cases where information from the model was required for correct placement of pieces in the copy, we categorized the directive as either abbreviated or nonabbreviated.

Several differences were found among the three groups of dyads. For my purposes here, the findings about the "mix" of abbreviated and nonabbreviated directives used by the mothers is of greatest in-terest. The mothers switched from a predominant use of nonabbre-viated verbal directives to a predominant use of abbreviated verbal directives as the age of the children increased. That is, directives ad-dressed to older children were likely to require them to carry out implicit substeps or subdirectives in order to respond appropriately, whereas those addressed to younger children were less likely to require the recognition and execution of implicit substeps.

The following excerpts of mother–child interaction illustrate the nature of these differences (ibid.). The first excerpt involves a two-and-one-half-year-old child and her mother.

19. C: (C looks at the pieces pile.) Now what do you think?

20. M: Well, what colors do you still need?

21. C: (C looks at the copy puzzle; then C looks at the pieces

pile.) Uh (C looks at the copy puzzle), there's no purple on there. (C looks at the pieces pile.)

22. M: That's right.

23. C: I need (C looks at the copy puzzle) two colors for those two empty spaces. (C looks at the pieces pile.)

24. M: So where does the purple go?

25. C: Where's this (C picks up purple cargo square from the pieces pile) purple go, you think?

26. M: Where (C looks at the copy puzzle), is it over here?

27. C: (C looks at the model puzzle.) It's, oh, I mean only (C points to the purple cargo square in the model puzzle) in the, it's on, it's right (C points to purple cargo square in the model puzzle) above the yellow.

28. M: Okay.

29. C: (C inserts the purple cargo square correctly in the copy puzzle.)

In this segment of discourse the mother's utterances 20 and 24 are abbreviated directives, since an appropriate response by the child would require her to deal both with the model puzzle and with the copy puzzle. In contrast, utterance 26 is a nonabbreviated directive, since in order to respond appropriately, the child must be concerned with one or the other puzzle (in this case, the model) but need not carry out any implicit subdirectives that involve consulting both puzzles.

Utterance 30 represents the discourse that occurred in an episode for a four-and-one-half-year-old girl and her mother:

30. M: Now (C looks at the copy puzzle) what else do you need? (C looks at the model puzzle; then C picks up the black cargo square; then C looks at the copy puzzle; then C looks at the model puzzle; then C looks at the copy puzzle; then C inserts the black cargo square correctly in the copy puzzle.)

In this case the only directive in the episode was an abbreviated directive. The child did not in fact provide a verbal response here, but the directive is still abbreviated in our coding system because any appropriate response (verbal or nonverbal) would have required information both from the model puzzle and from the copy puzzle.

In addition to illustrating age differences, these two excerpts exhibit a general fact about the way that abbreviated verbal directives function in adult–child interaction. When an abbreviated directive such as utterance 20 or 24 was addressed to a younger child, the child often did not provide the appropriate response. For example, after hearing utterance 20, the two-and-one-half-year-old did not shift her eye gaze to the model. We interpreted this to be a reflection of the child's failure to recognize and carry out the implicit subdirectives involved in utterance 20. Conversely, in the case of the older child, the abbreviated directive was followed by an appropriate sequence of behaviors. This was interpreted as reflecting the four-and-one-half-year-old's ability to identify and carry the subdirectives implicit in utterance 30.

In order to analyze differences in the children's ability to recognize and carry the implicit subdirectives in abbreviated verbal directives, we examined their responses to this type of utterance. Specifically, we identified the subset of all abbreviated verbal directives that resulted in the correct insertion of the piece in the copy puzzle without any further assistance from the adult. While it is true that adults used abbreviated directives with the younger children, such utterances seldom led directly (that is, without further adult intervention) to the correct placement of the pieces in the copy puzzle. Conversely, older children identified and carried out all the implicit subdirectives necessary to select and insert the piece correctly significantly more often than younger children did.

The two segments of mother–child interaction presented above reveal why these particular empirical results were obtained in the study (Wertsch and Schneider, 1979). The example of the interaction between the two-and-one-half-year-old and her mother represents a common pattern of interaction in dyads involving younger children. If the mother used an abbreviated directive at all, she often had to "break it down" by using subsequent nonabbreviated directives. Thus it should not be surprising that in the case of younger children (a) the directive mix included relatively more nonabbreviated directives, and (b) the correct insertion of a piece in the copy puzzle seldom followed directly from the use of an abbreviated directive. These tendencies were reversed in the case of older children.

The results reported in these studies on abbreviation (Wertsch and Schneider, 1979) are similar to those reported by Arns (1980); Wertsch, Minick, Arns (1984); McLane (1981); and Sammarco (1984) with regard to "direct" and "indirect" other-regulation. The analysis of direct and indirect other-regulation was a part of the multilevel analytic technique mentioned earlier. After determining that a child's execution of a strategic step was other-regulated, these investigators identified the type of other-regulation used. Direct other-regulation corresponds roughly with what we termed nonabbreviated directives (Wertsch and Schneider, 1979), whereas indirect other-regulation corresponds with abbreviated directives. In all the studies, significant differences in indirect other-regulation were found between groups. For example, Wertsch, Minick, and Arns (1984) reported that in rural Brazil teachers were much more likely than mothers to use indirect other-regulation when directing six-year-olds through a model-copying task. Such results indicate that the teachers were providing more complex semiotic challenges to the children than were the mothers. Because they were faced with more frequent indirect other-regulation when dealing with teachers, the children were required to operate on the intrapsychological plane with a more sophisticated situation definition. This in turn offered more opportunities for taking over full responsibility for the task than were to be found with rural Brazilian children dealing with their mothers. Such differences are the essence of how interpsychological functioning can vary in its tendency to induce the transition to intrapsychological function.

As in my account of referential perspective, I wish to make two points about the role of semiotic abbreviation in the transition from interpsychological to intrapsychological functioning. First, analyses such as Wertsch and Schneider's (1979) reveal once again the inherent link between interpsychological and intrapsychological functioning. Changes on the interpsychological plane typically reflect changes in the child's intrapsychological functioning. Thus any analysis of interpsychological functioning is seen to be ipso facto an analysis of intrapsychological functioning.

Second, abbreviation is another mechanism that allows a tutor to pose semiotic challenges to a tutee. By using an abbreviated directive, a tutor is inviting a tutee to identify and carry out the implicit substeps involved in a task setting. If this challenge is not met, the tutor always has the option of switching back to nonabbreviated directives, thereby taking over responsibility once again for certain aspects of the situation definition. The fact, however, that a tutor can switch between abbreviated and nonabbreviated directives means that the tutor has another mechanism for posing semiotic challenges and luring the tutee into a culturally appropriate situation definition.

The process at issue here is what Rommetveit has examined in so much of his writing. What an adult says to a child in interpsychological functioning in the zone of proximal development may "impose a definite structure . . . upon the situation in which it is said" (1979b, p. 70). The transitions in intrapsychological functioning are often products of what the child is not told at all—but yet is forced to assume in order to make sense of what is heard.

I have extended Vygotsky's comments on the general genetic law of cultural development by examining the communicative mechanisms that make possible the transition from interpsychological to intrapsychological functioning. In order to understand this transition, one must specify in more detail than has been done the semiotic means used in social interaction. They provide the key to the origins and transition of intrapsychological functioning. One must first specify the situation definition at issue and then identify ways in which various levels of intersubjectivity can be created through devices such as referential perspective and abbreviation. In all the cases examined here, I emphasized the inextricable link between the levels of interpsychological and intrapsychological functioning, and I noted the potential for using these devices to pose semiotic challenges that would encourage the child to view situations in a culturally more appropriate way.

CHAPTER 7

Units of Psychological Functioning: Consciousness, Word Meaning, and Action

Vygotsky's constant reference to mental functions calls for a closer examination of the role they play in his approach—in particular, whether they should be viewed as a fundamental unit of psychological analysis. For example, when arguing that semiotic mechanisms mediate human activity, was he claiming that they mediate individual mental functions? Or when outlining the transition from interpsychological to intrapsychological functioning, was he claiming that this transition takes place within the framework of specific mental functions?

Evidently this is not what Vygotsky had in mind. For him, the complexities of actual psychological activity could not be accounted for in terms of isolated mental functions. He saw that humans do not operate within the boundaries of, say, an isolated "memory mode" or "perceptual mode." Rather, he viewed mental functioning as a larger, complex whole in which individual functions participate:

> Memory certainly presupposes the activity of attention, perception, and comprehension. Perception necessarily takes in that same function of attention, recognition, or memory, and comprehension. However, in previous as well as contemporary psychology this obviously correct idea of the functional unity of consciousness and the indissoluble connection of the various forms of its activity has remained on the periphery. (1934a, p. 190)

Vygotsky's claims about interrelationships among mental functions may appear obvious. However, in psychological research we often seem not to recognize the interrelationships. We devote studies and even journals and subdisciplines to a single mental function, such as memory, as if we could consider it in isolation from other aspects of psychological activity.

Vygotsky struggled with this issue throughout his career. Rejecting artificial divisions and abstractions, he assumed that one must study psychological activity in all its complexity, not in isolation. He also assumed that one must conduct objective empirical studies of this complex psychological activity, which led him to search for a manageable unit of analysis. The unit had to be subject to objective observation and manipulation, but it could not be derived through artificial divisions or abstractions of real psychological activity. It had to be a microcosm of the complex interfunctional processes that characterize actual psychological activity. Vygotsky's insistence on studying complex psychological activity gave rise to his interpretation of *consciousness,* and his attempt to identify a unit of analysis led him to his investigations of *word meaning.*

Vygotsky's Notion of Consciousness

Marxist philosophy and contemporary psychological theories jointly influenced Vygotsky to make consciousness the most fundamental construct in his approach. As V. P. Zinchenko (1985) has noted, "Consciousness was always the major object in Vygotsky's research. He evaluated the productivity of a particular psychological theory in terms of its actual or potential contribution to the study of consciousness" (p. 99).

Given the centrality of consciousness in Vygotsky's approach, it is important to consider how he defined it. His first major paper in psychology was devoted to this topic, which he chose because he saw that psychology was threatened by a form of behavioristic reductionism—namely, Bekhterev's reflexology. He strongly objected to the notion that consciousness could be abolished as a scientific construct and that the study of human psychology could be based solely on the analysis of reflexes or sums of reflexes. He viewed reflexology, along with other forms of behavioristic reductionism, as representing one of the two horns of the dilemma that constantly haunted psychology. The other was represented by idealist approaches in which psychology was considered the study of the self-contained world of purely subjective phenomena. This approach readily recognized the existence of consciousness but defined it such that it could be studied only through nonobjective methods like introspection. Investigators were forced to choose between those two incompatible approaches, generating what Vygotsky (1982a) called the "crisis in psychology."

The crisis consisted of the fact that no overarching theoretical framework was available for an integrated, internally consistent explanation of human psychology. Research theories, findings, and hypotheses were not interrelated and in many cases even seemed contradictory. Borrowing from F. Bretano, Vygotsky wrote that "there exist many psychologies, but there does not exist a unified psychology" (1934a, p. 18). He pointed out the serious ramifications of this state of affairs:

> The absence of a unified scientific system that would embrace and combine all of our contemporary knowledge in psychology results in a situation in which every new factual discovery . . . which is more than a simple accumulation of details *is forced* to create its own special theory and explanatory system. In order to understand new *facts and relationships* investigators are forced to create their own psychology—one of many psychologies. (Ibid.)

Vygotsky's decision to focus on consciousness as a fundamental object of investigation was motivated by his desire to avoid these forces of fragmentation. As Leont'ev and Luria (1956) noted in their introduction to a volume of Vygotsky's collected writings, he played a pivotal role in the discussions on "the struggle for consciousness" in Soviet psychology that went on between 1921 and 1927. He was striving to avoid the fatal weaknesses of "vulgar behaviorism" on the one hand and a "subjectivistic understanding of mental phenomena as internal . . . states that are accessible only through introspection" (1956, p. 6) on the other.

Since the prevailing emphasis in 1924 was based on a form of behavioristic reductionism, Vygotsky's main concern in his early work was to introduce the notion of consciousness into an objective psychology rather than to criticize it in subjective approaches. In his 1924 presentation Vygotsky argued that one of the ironic consequences of reflexology's refusal to deal with consciousness in scientific research was that it was forced to reinstate a form of idealist–materialist dualism:

The exclusion of consciousness from the domain of scientific psychology to a considerable extent preserves all the dualism and spiritualism of earlier subjective psychology. Bekhterev asserted that his system of reflexology did not contradict the hypothesis of the soul. He depicts subjective or conscious phenomena as second-order phenomena, as specific internal phenomena accompanying combinatory reflexes. Here, dualism is reinforced by the fact that a special science, subjective reflexology, is admitted as a future possibility, even as an inevitability.   (1979, p. 8)

Vygotsky argued that it was possible to avoid this dilemma by viewing consciousness as the objectively observable *organization* of behavior that is imposed on humans through participation in sociocultural practices. This "organizational criterion" served as the foundation of his understanding of consciousness.

Unlike other Soviet psychologists such as Leont'ev (1959, 1975, 1981) and Rubinshtein (1957), Vygotsky never produced extended treatises on his concept of consciousness. In fact, other than in his 1924 paper, the only places where he addressed this issue were the introductory and concluding sections of several articles and volumes. A review of his comments, however, reveals that by the end of his life he understood consciousness broadly as the subjective reflection of material reality by animate matter. This understanding, which is similar to the Marxist-Leninist accounts devised later in Soviet psychology, is evident in the following statements from the beginning and ending pages of *Thinking and Speech* (1934a):

> When it is said that there is a dialectical leap not only from non-comprehending matter [inanimate matter] to sensation but also from sensation to thinking, it is meant that thinking reflects reality in consciousness in a qualitatively different way than direct, non-mediated sensation . . .
> We have attempted to study experimentally the dialectical transition from sensation to thinking and to show that reality is reflected differently in thinking than in sensation . . . If consciousness in the form of sensation and consciousness in the form of thinking are governed by different modes of reflecting reality, they represent different types of consciousness.   (pp. 10, 318)

Although Vygotsky may have had these broad epistemological criteria in mind when speaking of consciousness, in his writings his primary concern was with uniquely human forms of reflecting reality that emerge in a sociocultural milieu. Thus most of his writings dealt with only a subset of the issues in his methodological treatment of consciousness.

Vygotsky's use of the term "reflection" in his comments on consciousness deserves special comment. The term derives from the "theory of reflection" developed by V. I. Lenin (1929). Because it often is not recognized as a technical term, it can easily be misinterpreted, particularly in two ways. First, reflection should not be understood as the passive reception of sense data. A crucial aspect of Vygotsky's understanding of human consciousness is that humans are viewed as constantly constructing their environment and their representations of this environment by engaging in various forms of activity. The process of reflection is just as much concerned with the organism's active transformation of reality and representation of reality as with the reception of information. This is a cornerstone of all versions of the theory of activity that now dominate Soviet psychology.

Second, the use of the term "reflection" in the definition of consciousness should not be taken to mean that self-reflection, self-consciousness, or conscious awareness is necessarily involved. Although such processes play an important role in Vygotsky's account of advanced stages of human consciousness, as in his analysis of scientific concepts, they represent only some of its possible modes.

This issue has often been a source of confusion in understanding and translating Vygotsky's work. For instance, in a passage of the English version of *Thinking and Speech* "consciousness" is defined as "awareness of the activity of the mind—the consciousness of being conscious" (1962, p. 91). The apparent contradiction between this definition and my interpretation results from incorrect translation rather than from a lack of consistency on Vygotsky's part. In this passage he was dealing with conscious realization or conscious awareness (*osoznanie*) rather than the broader notion of consciousness (*soznanie*). However, both terms, *osoznanie* and *soznanie,* were translated into English as "consciousness." An examination of the original Russian passage reveals that Vygotsky was arguing that conscious awareness (*osoznanie*) is a special form of consciousness (*soznanie*). It is a form that exists when consciousness itself becomes the object of consciousness.

As already noted, a major criterion for Vygotsky's definition of consciousness is its organizational properties. Vygotsky's concern with the organizational criterion was evident even in his 1924 paper, where he argued for the need to study the organization or structure of reflexes as well as the nature of the isolated reflex itself. Vygotsky's later accounts of consciousness were much less tied to issues in reflexology, but the issue of organization remained central.

In these later accounts Vygotsky apparently had a hierarchy in mind in which the components at one level of description become subcomponents of more inclusive components at the next higher level. In general, his preference was to focus on higher-level components. His assumption was that whenever investigators isolate a subcomponent for analysis, they run the risk of ignoring its properties that can be understood only by virtue of its being part of a higher-level component.

At the highest level of Vygotsky's hierarchy, the component is consciousness itself. This component is comprised of two basic subcomponents—intellect and affect. Until one addresses the issue of how these two subcomponents are related, one's account of consciousness will remain essentially incomplete:

> The separation of the intellectual side of our consciousness from its affective, volitional side is one of the fundamental flaws of all of traditional psychology. Because of it thinking is inevitably transformed into an autonomous flow of thoughts thinking themselves. It is separated from all the fullness of real life, from the living motives, interests, and attractions of the thinking human. (1934a, p. 14)

Although Vygotsky made several statements about the need to integrate affective and intellectual phenomena in the study of human functioning, he devoted very little effort in his empirical research to exploring the affective side of consciousness. As one of his students, Bozhovich (1977), has pointed out, he was beginning to examine this issue near the end of his life. However, his death cut this research short. Bozhovich (1979, 1980, 1980–81) and her colleagues (Bozhovich, Slavina, and Dovitskaya, 1976) subsequently took on this task as one of their major research concerns. Vygotsky's students (for example, Leont'ev, 1959, 1975, 1981) have also touched on this issue in their work. On the basis of Vygotsky's few comments on this topic and the development of his ideas by his followers, his approach to affect clearly was concerned with how it provides the integrating and motivational forces for consciousness.

If the highest level in Vygotsky's hierarchy took consciousness as the component and affect and intellect as the subcomponents, the next level focused on the intellect as the component and "higher mental functions" such as memory, attention, thinking, and perception as the subcomponents. It was at this level that Vygotsky carried out most of his research. Again here he viewed the tendency to isolate individual subcomponents and to ignore their role in the component (in this case, intellectual consciousness) as a fundamental weakness in the psychology of his day:

> The atomistic and functional analysis that has dominated scientific psychology in the recent decade has resulted in the examination of individual psychological functions in isolation . . . The problem of the connection among these functions, the problem of their organization in the overall structure of consciousness has all this time remained outside the investigators' attention. (1934a, p. 4)

Any discussion of Vygotsky's ideas on the organization properties of this "functional unity" of consciousness would be incomplete, if not misleading, if it did not make the point that his concern was with dynamic or dialectical, rather than static, organization. Just as important as the existence of interfunctional connections is the fact that these connections continually change. He argued that a fundamental weakness of previous psychological accounts was that they were based on "the false postulate . . . of unchanging permanent interfunctional connections in consciousness' (1934a, p. 4). In opposition to this, he argued that interfunctional relationships are characterized by constant transformation and mutual influence. Thus I shall henceforth speak of the *dynamic organization* of consciousness. This aspect of Vygotsky's understanding of consciousness is reflected in his treatment of components at all levels. While recognizing K. Lewin's contribution to the understanding of the relationship of affective and intellectual functioning, Vygotsky criticized him for failing to emphasize the continual changes, dialectical negations, and mutual influences involved. Vygotsky argued that he failed to recognize "the dialectical law that in the course of development causes and effects change places. Once higher mental formations have emerged on the basis of certain dynamic preconditions, these formations themselves influence the processes that spawned them . . . *Above all the interfunctional connections and relationships among various processes, in particular intellect and affect, change*" (1956, p. 467).

In connection with the intellectual side of consciousness, where he had most to say, Vygotsky was concerned with the dynamic organization of higher mental functions. He was concerned that now the "same" activity may be carried out by relying on different combinations or "mixes" of higher mental functions at different ages or in different task settings:

> The memory of older children is not only different from the memory of younger children; it also plays a different role in the older child's cognitive activity. Memory in early childhood is one of the central psychological functions upon which all the other functions are built. Our analyses suggest that thinking in the very young child is in many respects determined by his memory, and is certainly not the same thing as the thinking of the more mature child . . . *For the young child, to think means to recall; but for the adolescent, to recall means to think.* (1978, pp. 50–51)

This passage reveals that the notion of dynamic organization was central to his account of the ontogenesis of the intellectual side of consciousness. He argued that change in the interrelationships among higher mental functions rather than the development of the individual functions themselves was the primary cause of the development of consciousness: "the psychological development of the child is not so much the development and perfection of separate functions as the change in interfunctional relationships . . . The fate of each functional part in the development of consciousness depends on the change of the whole, and not vice versa" (1934a, pp. 189–190).

In Vygotsky's view, the problem with investigating a particular ability or function in isolation from others is that such an approach presupposes that one and the same entity, such as memory, can be identified and observed at different stages of development. As opposed to this, he argued that the very nature of the role of memory in intellectual consciousness changes with age. For him, memory itself therefore changes—it is not a single, identifiable process across development. This aspect of his approach obviously conflicts with approaches that view memory development in terms of quantitative increments, regardless of whether these increments are in terms of reflexes, associations, units of information-processing capacity, or whatever. Thus instead of focusing on static structure, Vygotsky emphasized change, transformation, and dialectical negation as inherent aspects of the organizational principles of human consciousness. Although this aspect of his thinking is particularly evident in his account of consciousness, it characterized his approach to other issues as well. In fact one could say that a general mode of argumentation for him was to select two or more phenomena that are typically examined as separate entities or as parts of a static organizational framework and observe how they interact and play off one another during the course of development.

Word Meaning as a Unit of Analysis

Vygotsky proposed word meaning as a unit for analyzing consciousness. The need to specify a unit of analysis arose from the fact that there is no manageable way to investigate consciousness in general as Vygotsky defined it. His notion of consciousness is useful in constructing an overall theoretical framework, but it presents severe problems to investigators wishing to conduct concrete psychological research. The problems arise over the possibility of examining any higher mental function or delimited segment of complex psychological activity while recognizing the functional unity of consciousness. If, as Vygotsky argued, no aspect of consciousness can be adequately characterized without taking into consideration its relationships with all other aspects, where is one to begin? The investigator is confronted with the necessity of studying all aspects of mental life in order to answer questions about any single one. Vygotsky's response to this seemingly intractable dilemma was to search for a new unit of analysis. The criteria he established had a powerful impact on the rest of his theoretical approach. As Zinchenko (1985) has noted, any choice (either explicit or implicit) about a unit of psychological analysis influences all other aspects of a theoretical approach:

> As is known, the problem of units for psychological research has confronted every school of scientific psychology. In the past, a variety of phenomena have been singled out in this capacity. For example, sensations (in associationism), figure–ground (in Gestalt psychology), the reaction or reflex (in reactology and reflexology, respectively), set (in set psychology), and the behavioral act (in behaviorism) have served as units. In neobehaviorism in particular Tolman treated the problem of analytic units as central . . . In Western European psychology, Piaget discussed the problem in particular detail. He singled out reversible operations in this connection . . . In contrast to reversible operative structures, other investigators have viewed mnemonic and motor schemes as the units of analysis. This is characteristic of Bartlett (1932) and sev-

eral of his followers in contemporary Anglo-American psychology. (1985, p. 95)

Vygotsky attempted to deal with the problem by proposing a unit of analysis that provides a cross section of the interfunctional complexity of consciousness. He argued for identifying a "microcosm" of consciousness that reflects all its aspects. His ideas on this issue can be traced to many sources, but one of the most important was the work of Marx. In certain respects Vygotsky viewed himself as trying to create an "enabling theory-method" for psychology that parallels Marx's for the investigation of socioeconomic phenomena. In an unpublished notebook Vygotsky (1978) observed that:

> the whole of *Capital* is written according to the following method: Marx analyzes a single living "cell" of capitalist society—for example, the nature of value. Within this cell he discovers the structure of the entire system and all of its economic institutions. He says that to a layman this analysis may seem a murky tangle of tiny details. Indeed, there may be tiny details, but they are exactly those which are essential to "microanatomy." Anyone who could discover what a "psychological" cell is—the mechanism producing even a single response—would thereby find the key to psychology as a whole. (Cole and Scribner, 1978, p. 8)

Thus in order to pursue his study of human consciousness, Vygotsky viewed his task as one of identifying an investigable microcosm. He began with a distinction between two methods for analyzing psychological structures: analysis into elements (*elementy*) and analysis into units (*edinitsy*). The latter he saw as the correct mode of analysis for psychology, a fact reflected in his comment that the analysis into elements is "responsible for all the failures that have beset investigators" interested in complex problems in psychology (1934a, p. 7), whereas analysis into units is the "only correct way" to approach these problems.[1] Using an illustration from chemistry, Vygotsky compared the analysis of psychological structures into elements with the analysis of chemical substances into elements. He warned that in chemistry as well as in psychology such an approach is fundamentally incapable of answering certain questions and therefore can be misleading if used in isolation. For example, if someone who is interested in why water extinguishes fire were to use analysis into elements, "he would be surprised to find out that hydrogen burns and oxygen sustains fire.

From these properties of the elements, he would never be able to explain the properties of the whole" (1934a, p. 7).

Vygotsky argued that similar anomalies can arise in psychological research. His criticism of analysis into elements is based on the fact that "the essential feature of such analysis is that it results in products that are alien to the whole being analyzed; it results in elements that do not contain the properties of the whole as such" (ibid.). When considering analysis into units, Vygotsky wrote:

> By unit we mean a product of analysis that, as distinct from elements, retains *all the basic properties of the whole*. These properties of the whole are not distributed among its living parts. It is not the chemical formula of water, but the study of the molecule and molecular movement that is the key to explaining the properties of water. Similarly, the living cell that preserves all the basic qualities of life of the living organism is the real unit of biological analysis.   (1934a, p. 9)

According to Vygotsky, it is units, rather than elements, that are required in the study of the dynamic interfunctional organization of consciousness. The particular unit that Vygotsky chose for this task was word meaning. In his opinion it fulfilled the requirements he had laid down for a "psychological cell" or unit: "At every step actual research shows that the word plays a central role in consciousness as a whole, not in its individual functions" (ibid., p. 318).

Thus he viewed the word as capable of reflecting the interfunctional organization of consciousness instead of individual mental functions. This fact led him to view the word as a genuine microcosm of consciousness: "Consciousness is reflected in the word, as the sun is reflected in a droplet of water. The word is related to consciousness as a miniature world is related to a large one, as a living cell is related to an organism, as an atom to the cosmos. It is a miniature world of consciousness. The meaningful word is a microcosm of human consciousness" (ibid.).

All of these comments came from Vygotsky's *Thinking and Speech* (1934a). His detailed examination of these forms of activity was motivated by the assumption that "thinking and speech turn out to be the key to understanding the nature of human consciousness" (1934a, p. 318). He viewed the emerging relationship between thinking and speech as a privileged case of the general problem set of relationships involved in the dynamic organization of consciousness: "The problem of thinking and speech belongs to the set of psychological problems in which the main issue is the relationship among various psychological functions, among various forms of the activity of consciousness. The central moment of this entire problem is, of course, the question of the relationship of thought and the word" (ibid., p. 4).

Vygotsky pointed out that too often the word had been approached from the perspective of analysis into elements. In particular, researchers had often been led to examine sound in isolation from meaning. This point played a role in his critique of formalism, but Vygotsky also saw it as arising in psychology. In this discipline he viewed the isolation of sound from meaning as leading to oversimplified associationist accounts of meaning:

> As matters stood in associationist psychology, so they stand in principle in modern structural psychology. In the word we always knew only one side, its external side that confronts us. Its other, internal side—its meaning—like the other side of the moon always was and remains unstudied and unknown. Incidentally, it is in this other side that the possibility of solving an extremely interesting problem remains concealed. This is the problem of the relationship between thinking and speech. It is precisely in the meaning of the word that the center of that unity is found. This is the unity we term verbal thinking.   (Ibid., p. 9)

Thus Vygotsky urged that analysis into units be applied to the study of word meaning as well as to the study of the relationship between thinking and speech. It is only by understanding the relationship between sound and meaning in the word that we can understand the relationship between thinking and speech. In this program word meaning serves as an ideal unit because "meaning can be viewed equally as a phenomenon that is speechlike in nature and as a phenomemon related to the area of thinking. It is impossible to deal with word meaning as we earlier spoke so freely about the elements of the word, considered separately. What does word meaning represent? Speech or thinking? It is speech and thinking at one and the same time because it is a unity of verbal thought" (ibid., p. 10).

These and other excerpts from Vygotsky's writings reveal his reasons for examining word meaning in such depth. For him it was the ideal microcosmic unit for analyzing human consciousness.

Weaknesses in Vygotsky's Account

I have already argued that Vygotsky's account of the word and word meaning needs revision in light of theoretical advances in the study of propositional and discourse referentiality. Clearly there are strictly semiotic reasons for revising his account. I would also argue that his notion of word meaning as a unit for analyzing human consciousness does not meet some of the requirements he himself established for such a unit. Going back to the distinction Davydov and Radzikhovskii (1985) make between "Vygotsky the methodologist" (or metatheoretician) and "Vygotsky the psychologist," I am concerned with a conflict between the theoretical requirements Vygotsky established for a unit of analysis and the unit he actually proposed. Recall that Vygotsky's fundamental claim was that "the meaningful word is a microcosm of human consciousness." He assumed that word meaning could act as a "psychological cell" or unit of analysis in which all the processes and interrelationships of human consciousness are reflected. If one remembers what Vygotsky meant by consciousness, however, one will see that this is not really so. While word meaning may be a unit for analyzing the *semiotic mediation of human consciousness,* it is not a unit for analyzing human consciousness itself.

Vygotsky's notion of human consciousness is grounded in the notion of dynamic organization, which involves the changing interrelationships among mental functions such as memory, attention, and thinking. Given the central role that dynamic interfunctional relationships play in the macrocosm of consciousness, one must know how they are reflected in the microcosm of word meaning. In fact, they are not reflected there. In no sense are mental functions such as memory or attention, let alone their interrelationships, reflected in word meaning. If one considers word meaning as defined by the sign-type–sign-type relationships of genuine concepts, one sees that Vygotsky's concern was categorization and systems of categorization inherent in the linguistic code. Such categorization serves an essential role as a means for *mediating* consciousness, but it is not consciousness itself.

A somewhat different point applies to Vygotsky's notion of the sense (*smysl*) of a word: "The sense of a word . . . is the aggregate of all the psychological facts emerging in our consciousness because of this word" (1934a, p. 305). At first glance this would seem to be much more compatible with Vygotsky's notion of consciousness than is meaning. However, even in this case several problems remain. The most severe grows out of Vygotsky's claim that a word changes its sense in various contexts. His account provides no principled way of defining contexts or understanding their role in determining sense. Furthermore, as with meaning (*znachenie*), it is unclear how various mental functions such as memory and attention could be represented in a microcosm of word sense. What he was examining here still seems to be a unit for analyzing semiotic mediation rather than a unit for analyzing human consciousness.

Another criticism of Vygotsky's notion of word meaning as a microcosm of human consciousness emerges when one considers the relationship between the natural and cultural lines of development. In essence, Vygotsky failed to provide an adequate account of the natural line of development, and he failed to specify what it is that is transformed by social forces. His account of word meaning is directly tied to this weakness. Specifically, Vygotsky said almost nothing about the relationship between the natural line of development and word meaning. His account of the early indicatory function of speech provides some clues as to how social semiotic processes can "come into contact" and transform the products of the natural line, and an account of propositional referentiality could take this analysis somewhat further. But this does little to resolve the fundamental weakness of his account— the absence of an adequate account of the natural line. He does not specify very much about what it is that interpsychological semiotic processes transform.

One is here again confronted with a problem that can be understood only if one distinguishes between "Vygotsky the methodologist" and "Vygotsky the psychologist." Vygotsky the methodologist proposed a general account of the ontogenesis of human consciousness in which natural and social forces come into contact and become mutually determining. Vygotsky the psychologist said almost nothing about the natural line of development. As a result, his writings on the mechanisms of psychological development suggest an interpretation that conflicts with his general metatheoretical or methodological approach. Namely, it suggests that with the onset of language learning, the child's development can be explained solely in terms of learning word meanings. In this view the development of human consciousness could be reduced to the learning of semiotic codes. This and other related criticisms have been leveled at Vygotsky. For example, A. V. Brushlinskii (1979) has argued that inherent in Vygotsky's approach is a biological-social dualism. Brushlinskii cites the following excerpt from B. E. Varshava and

Vygotsky (1931) to support his claim: "As soon as a child acquires a command of language, the entire internal development of the *child* from his *animal* stage (biological) becomes truly human (social) development" (Brushlinskii, 1979, p. 39).

Brushlinskii's criticism is based on the assumption that in Vygotsky's account the natural line of development ceases at a certain point and the social line begins; furthermore, the two are viewed as quite separate, and the emergence of the social line represents an entirely new form of development that has no connection with the natural line. It is certainly possible to interpret certain portions of Vygotsky's writings in this way. However, I would again argue that Vygotsky's general methodological approach calls for something else; it calls for an account of how the natural and social forces of development enter into emergent interactionism. Again, a major reason for his failure to act in accordance with this general methodological prerequisite is that at the time he was writing, very little was known about early development in the natural line. The discoveries by Piaget about sensorimotor intelligence were yet to be made.

When one considers all these problems, it becomes clear that Vygotsky's account of word meaning is not a good unit for analyzing the development of human consciousness. It does not provide the theoretical mechanisms needed to understand how the natural and social lines of development enter into emergent interactionism. Rather, Vygotsky used it primarily to explain the onset and development of the social line.

Thus I have touched on three weaknesses in Vygotsky's account of word meaning: (1) his failure to situate word meaning in a broader account of propositional and discourse referentiality; (2) his failure to fulfill his own requirements for a unit of analysis, namely, that it serve as a microcosm of the dynamic interfunctional relationships that define consciousness; and (3) his failure to explain adequately the relationship between natural and social forces of development. Of course, some sort of semiotic unit clearly does play a central role in Vygotsky's approach; however, such a unit serves a different role in Vygotsky's approach from the one he assigned it. Instead of being a microcosm or cell of human consciousness, it is a unit of the *semiotic mediation* of consciousness.

The interpretation I have been using so far is most consistent with Vygotsky's general methodological framework. If one accepts this claim, one is left with the question, What is the appropriate unit for analyzing consciousness as Vygotsky defined it? For an answer, I shall turn to one of the major contributions of Vygotsky's students and followers: the *theory of activity*.

The Theory of Activity and Units of Analysis

The major goal of any school of Soviet psychology is to create a Marxist psychology. As the history of that discipline in the USSR has shown (compare Kozulin, 1984), the interpretation of this charge may vary widely. During some periods it has produced reductionistic, "vulgar materialistic" approaches; in others it has led to the creation of theories of consciousness. Vygotsky drew on certain aspects of Marx's theory to formulate his approach to psychology. In particular, he attempted to build on Marx's method (for example, genetic analysis, holistic units of analysis), Marx's claims about the social origins of human consciousness (from the Sixth Thesis on Feuerbach), and Engels's claims about mediation by tools and signs. Vygotsky's approach, however, does not draw on many other aspects of Marxist theory.

In the years since Vygotsky's death, several Soviet psychologists have attempted to utilize other aspects of Marx's ideas to develop psychological theory. They have argued, for instance, that psychology must be founded on Marx's First Thesis on Feuerbach. This point in Marx's writings has given rise to various attempts to create a theory of activity in Soviet psychology. At the beginning of his paper "The Problem of Activity in Psychology" Leont'ev wrote:

> The importance of this category [that is, activity] hardly needs to be emphasized. We need only recall Marx's famous theses on Feuerbach, in which he said that the chief defect of earlier metaphysical materialism was that it viewed sensuousness only as a form of contemplation, not as human activity or practice. Therefore, the active aspect of sensuousness was developed by idealism, the opposite of materialism. Idealism, however, understood it abstractly, not as the real, sense activity of man. (1981, p. 41)

For my purposes, one of the most important tenets of the theory of activity is its recognition that a new unit of analysis is needed to carry out the Vygotskian enterprise. Instead of focusing on the study of psychological entities such as skills, concepts, information-processing units, reflexes, or mental functions, it assumes that we must begin with a unit of *activity*. Vygotsky himself came quite close to introducing the notion of activity into his approach. Many of Vygotsky's Soviet colleagues and students have argued that his ideas can be most profitably and consistently interpreted if the concept of activity (*deyatel'nost'*) is accepted as the fundamental category in his approach. In fact Vygotsky's ideas have been developed and extended in the USSR largely in the formulation of the "theory of activity." Investigators such as Davydov (1972), Gal'perin (1969), A. A. Leont'ev (1981), P. I. Zinchenko (1939, 1981), and V. P. Zinchenko (1985) have been instrumental in explicating this theory. The major figure responsible for its general formulation, however, has been A. N. Leont'ev (1959, 1975, 1981).

All these colleagues and students of Vygotsky have emphasized that most of the essential roots of the theory of activity may be traced to Vygotsky's own writings. Various hypotheses have been advanced for why Vygotsky himself did not reformulate his ideas into a theory of activity. Some scholars have argued that he would have moved in that direction had he lived longer. Others, such as Davydov and Radzikhovskii (1985), have claimed that Vygotsky was in fact very close to proposing such a theory.

Davydov and Radzikhovskii (1985) note that Vygotsky had two concerns in mind when outlining his account of consciousness. He was concerned with rejecting reductionistic interpretations of mental phenomena in which consciousness would be abandoned as a scientific concept and all psychological phenomena would be reduced to neurophysiological or behavioristic phenomena. But he also wanted to avoid any form of "substantialism," in which consciousness would be set forth as a second substance that coexists with the material substance of the brain. Davydov and Radzikhovskii point out that much of Vygotsky's admiration of William James stemmed from the fact that the latter had rejected substantialism. Although Vygotsky was not greatly influenced by many other aspects of James's writings on consciousness, this rejection of substantialism is something he found quite compatible with his own ideas. In his article "Does Consciousness Exist?" James (1904) argued that consciousness is a *function,* not an essence or a substance.

This accords very well with an important dictum of Vygotsky's favorite philosopher, Spinoza. Following Spinoza, Vygotsky argued that investigators are often misled in their attempts to understand the relationship between mental and neurophysiological phenomena because their analyses are based on the false assumption that they are dealing with two substances rather than with two attributes of one substance:

> Thinking . . . itself is nothing other than a function of the brain. The mental does not have an independent existence. According to Spinoza's definition, thinking is not a substance, but an attribute. A mental phenomenon never exists by itself, it is always only the internally necessary moment of a more complex psychophysiological process. Consequently, the very problem of the independent functioning of the mind rests upon a false assumption, namely, that mental processes flow in parallel or in interaction with physiological processes. That is, this problem in the final analysis is founded on the psychophysiological hypothesis of a parallelism or interaction. (Vygotsky, 1960, p. 408)

In more recent years Soviet philosophers and psychologists concerned with the role of ideal phenomena in dialectical materialism have examined this issue in greater detail. E. V. Il'enkov has pointed out that Spinoza's claim represented an important advance in the history of philosophy because it provided an alternative to Descartes' dualism:

> There are not two different and originally contrary objects of investigation—body and thought—but only *one single* object, which is the *thinking body* of living, real man . . . only considered from two different and even opposing aspects or points of view. Living, real thinking man, the sole thinking body with which we are acquainted, does not consist of two Cartesian halves—"thought lacking a body" and a "body lacking thought". In relation to real man both the one and the other are equally fallacious abstractions and one cannot in the end model a real thinking man from two equally fallacious abstractions. (1977, p. 31)

Il'enkov used the following analogy of Spinoza to illustrate this point: "Thinking is not the *product* of an action but the *action itself,* considered at the moment of its performance, just as walking, for example, is the mode of action of the legs, the 'product' of which, it transpires, is the space walked" (ibid., p. 35).

The antireductionism and antisubstantialism that characterize Vygotsky's basic position provide the first point in Davydov and Radzikhovskii's argument that he was close to founding a theory of activity. The next point in their argument is concerned with how the two attributes of thought and material extension could be united within a monistic system. As proponents of the theory of activity in Soviet psychology have long argued, the key to this monistic system is the notion of human activity. The germ of this idea was available to Vygotsky in Spinoza's insistence that one not abstract the corporeal or mental attributes of "living, real thinking man." As Il'enkov noted, the concept that activity must serve as the starting point in one's analysis follows directly from Spinoza's rejection of Cartesian dualism:

> But you can find the functional determination of thought only if you do not probe into the *thinking body* (the brain), but carefully examine the real composition of its objective activities among the other bodies of the infinitely varied universum. Within the skull you will not find anything to which a functional definition of thought could be applied, because thinking is a function of external, objective activity. And you must therefore investigate not the anatomy and physiology of the brain but the "anatomy and physiology" of that "body" whose active function *in fact* is thought, that is, the "inorganic body of man", the "anatomy and physiology" of the world of his culture, the world of "things" that he produces and reproduces by his activity. (1977, pp. 73–74)

There is an ongoing debate in the USSR over how much an activity-based approach extends or even distorts Vygotsky's basic ideas. I shall not go into all the complexities of this problem here nor provide a complete outline of the theory of activity as it exists in contemporary Soviet psychology. Such accounts are available elsewhere (compare Leont'ev, 1959, 1975; Smirnov, 1975; Wertsch, 1981a, 1981b; Kozulin, 1984). Instead, I shall outline a proposal for what the notion of activity in a Vygotskian approach would entail. My account will draw on recent advances in Soviet psychology and philosophy, but in several respects it will be more closely tied to Vygotsky's ideas than many contemporary Soviet proposals have been.

In accordance with recent proposals by Leont'ev (1975, 1981), several distinct but interrelated levels of analysis or abstraction can be identified in a theory of activity. Associated with each level is a specific type of unit. At the first, most global level of analysis is the unit of an activity. As Leont'ev (1975) points out, the use of the term "activity" (*deyatel'nost'*) here must be distinguished from the use of this term in connection with the general "theory of activity" (*teoriya deyatel'nosti*). When speaking of the *unit* of activity, one is dealing with specific real activities as opposed to human activity in general, and one is speaking of a particular level of analysis as opposed to the more general theory that encompasses all levels of analysis. In my discussion this difference in the use of the term "activity" will be clear from the context. Leont'ev has defined an activity as:

> the nonadditive, molar unit of life for the material, corporeal subject. In a narrower sense (that is, on the psychological level) it is the unit of life that is mediated by mental reflection. The real function of this unit is to orient the subject in the world of objects. In other words, activity is not a reaction or aggregate of reactions, but a system with its own structure, its own internal transformations, and its own development. (1981, p. 46)

The level of analysis concerned with activities is seldom included in Western approaches to cognitive psychology. Perhaps the construct in contemporary Western social science that is most similar to this level of analysis in the theory of activity is the notion of "frame" as outlined by E. Goffman (1974). As in Goffman's analysis, the notion of an activity focuses on socioculturally defined contexts in which human functioning occurs. Among the activities mentioned by Vygotsky's students (for example, El'konin, 1972) are play, instructional (formal educational) activity, and labor or work. One of the most important characteristics of an activity is that it is not determined or even strongly circumscribed by the physical or perceptual context in which humans function. Rather, it is a sociocultural interpretation or creation that is imposed on the context by the participant(s).

The next level of analysis in Leont'ev's system focuses on a unit that is more compatible with Vygotsky's original formulation and with Western psychology: the unit of a goal-direction *action* (*deistvie*). According to Leont'ev (1975, 1981), to say that an individual is engaged in a particular activity says nothing about the specific means–end relationships that are involved. It simply tells us that the individual is functioning in some socioculturally defined context. The best indication that the two levels of analysis must be distinguished is that an action can vary independently of an activity:

> One and the same action can be instrumental in realizing different activities. It can be transferred from one activity to another, thus revealing its relative independence. Let us turn . . . to a crude illustration. Assume that I have the goal of getting to point N, and I carry it out. It is clear that this action . . . can realize com-

pletely different activities. The converse is also obvious: one and the same motive can give rise to different goals and, accordingly, can produce different actions.   (Leont'ev, 1981, p. 61)

To relate this back to my earlier list of activities, the goal-directed action of moving from one point to another could be executed while participating in different activities, such as play, work, or instruction.

Leont'ev (1975, 1981) has proposed that the third level of analysis in the theory of activity is concerned with an *operation* (*operatsiya*). Whereas an action is associated with a goal, an operation is associated with the concrete conditions under which the action is carried out. It is through operations that a generalizable goal-directed action is instantiated in a real spatiotemporal setting:

> [An] important aspect of the process of goal formation is making the goal concrete or selecting the conditions of its attainment . . . Any goal—even one such as "reaching point N"—exists objectively in some objective situation. Of course, the goal can appear in the subject's consciousness in abstraction from this situation, but the same cannot be said for the *action*. Thus, apart from its intentional aspect (*what* must be done), the action has its operational aspect (*how* it can be done), which is defined not by the goal itself, but by the objective circumstances under which it is carried out. In other words, the *performed* action is in response to a task. The task is the goal given under certain conditions . . . I shall label the means by which an action is carried out its operations . . . If we imagine a case in which the goal remains the same and the conditions under which it is given change, then only the operational composition of the action changes.   (Leont'ev, 1981, pp. 62–63)

Thus the operational aspect of a goal-directed action such as "reaching point N" may vary depending on the distance involved, obstacles on the route to point N, and so on. The following schematic representation can be used to summarize the levels of analysis in Leont'ev's theory of activity:

Activity—Motive
Action—Goal
Operation—Conditions.

Although Leont'ev's account was not founded on semiotic theory, the distinction he made between an action and its operational instantiation is similar to the type–token relationship outlined in the analysis of signs in chapter 4. Operations are the token instantiation of actions;

under different conditions the same action will be instantiated in different ways. Because of this relationship between actions and operations, it is natural to consider them together. Whenever one makes a claim about an action, one could also consider it from the perspective of its "operational composition."

Zinchenko (1985) has recently utilized Leont'ev's ideas in order to identify an appropriate unit of analysis in Vygotsky's approach. He has argued that in place of word meaning, the appropriate unit of analysis for Vygotsky's account of consciousness is a *tool-mediated action* (*orudinnoe deistvie*). Zinchenko's proposed revision meets the general theoretical provisions established by Vygotsky for such a unit while avoiding the problems inherent in Vygotsky's attempt to use word meaning in this capacity.

This advance is based on a recognition of the appropriate role of word meanings and other semiotic phenomena. Instead of arguing that they *are* units of analysis, Zinchenko has proposed that they *mediate* such units. In his account of tool-mediated action Zinchenko does not go into detail on the distinction between tools and signs. He subsumes both tool mediation and semiotic mediation under the more general heading of "tool-mediated." Since his focus is on identifying a general unit for analyzing consciousness in Vygotsky's system, this may be appropriate. However, I would argue that any complete account of this unit would have to take into consideration the unique properties of semiotic phenomena.

The power of Zinchenko's argument can be appreciated when one considers it from the perspective of my earlier criticisms of Vygotsky's claim that word meaning can serve as a unit for analyzing consciousness. This claim provides no clear insight into how the natural and social lines of development became intertwined and mutually determining. His notion of the indicative function of speech does suggest a means whereby an adult can come into contact with and begin to regulate a child's early activity, but it says nothing about what this early activity is and how it is transformed by semiotic mediation. In examining this problem Zinchenko asserts:

> It is interesting to trace what might be termed the reverse genesis of meaning, both in reference to its role as a primary unit for the analysis of mind and in reference to the units that constitute its immediate preconditions. We note immediately that the genetically primary units for analysis must meet one additional requirement that was not foreseen in Vygotsky's system of requirements.

In proposing the genetically primary "cell" or "the undeveloped beginnings of the fully developed whole" as a unit of analysis, Davydov (1972) noted that such a "cell" must have an actual sense-contemplative form.   (1984, p. 101)

When Zinchenko and Davydov speak of the "sense-contemplative" (*chuvstvenno-sozertsaemaya*) form of this cell, they are speaking of its properties as practical sensorimotor action (sensorimotor in the broadest sense). In the terminology used by Vygotsky, their claim is that we must provide an account of the processes of the natural line of development. Drawing on the ideas of K. Holzkamp (1973) about "object activity," Zinchenko has pointed out that "in principle, this experience is richer than the system of verbal categories that one masters. In Vygotsky's account of the development of concepts, the stage of generalization that he called 'pseudoconcepts' corresponds most closely to the concept of 'object meaning' " (1984, p. 102). Holzkamp had in mind the subject's experience arising from individual practical activity. The claims in this statement are quite consistent with Vygotsky's about the role of categorization and generalization. As soon as one employs categorization to engage in "genuine social interaction," one necessarily captures certain aspects of one's rich experience and ignores others.

Thus Zinchenko's claim about the role of tool-mediated action is twofold. On the one hand, he is concerned with identifying genetically primary units. Hence his comments about the sense-contemplative form of early action. On the other hand, he recognizes that once semiotic mediation is incorporated into practical action, the action undergoes a qualitative transformation. It is not simply the same action with an improved means of mediation and representation. The point is that while one cannot understand tool-mediated action without understanding its origins, one cannot reduce a tool-mediated action to its origins. An adequate analysis of action must take into account its genetic origins as well as the transformations it undergoes as a result of becoming intertwined with a sign system.

Another of my criticisms was that word meaning is not really a unit that reflects the interfunctional relationships that define consciousness. Of course this is the most serious criticism one can raise, since it means that the analytic unit chosen by Vygotsky cannot fulfill the very requirements he assigned to it. Again, Zinchenko's notion of a tool-mediated action suggests a way out of this quandary. By beginning with the notion of a tool-mediated action rather than a mental function or word meaning, it is possible to fulfill the general theoretical requirements Vygotsky proposed for an analytic unit of consciousness. Specifically, it provides a unit that necessarily incorporates the defining criterion of Vygotsky's notion of consciousness and its development: the dynamic organization of interfunctional relationships.

When one considers a goal-directed, tool-mediated action such as that involved in constructing an object in accordance with a model (compare chapter 6), one sees that perception, memory, thinking (or problem solving), and attention are all necessarily involved and co-ordinated in a unit of actual psychological life. The analytic unit involved is fundamentally different from the units typically employed in psychological research. It encompasses several moments that psychologists often try to abstract and isolate (for example, mental functions), and it focuses on a kind of unit that they often fail to recognize. It is a unit that "cuts across" the units typically employed. Most important for my present purposes, it makes possible the study of consciousness as defined by Vygotsky. Given the fact that for him the fundamental defining criterion of consciousness is its dynamic interfunctional organization, the notion of a tool-mediated action provides a "manageable microcosm" within which consciousness may be studied.

Up to now I have emphasized the properties of action that exempt it from the criticisms I have made of Vygotsky's unit of analysis, word meaning. In addition, action as an analytic unit retains most of the bona fide strengths that Vygotsky saw in word meaning. It retains in particular the strength of being a unit that is not tied solely to inter-psychological or intrapsychological functioning. Just as word meaning transcends the boundary between individual and social, so does action.

As noted by Wertsch, Minick, and Arns (1984), the distinction between interpsychological and intrapsychological functioning is to be found at the level of operations in Leont'ev's theory of activity. This fact can be illustrated by considering once again the goal-directed action outlined in chapter 6. Recall that the action of making a copy object in accordance with a model can be broken down into three strategic steps.[2] Studies such as those by Arns (1980), McLane (1981), Sammarco (1984), and Wertsch, Minick, and Arns (1984) have examined these steps with regard to whether they are executed on the inter-psychological or intrapsychological plane.

In terms of levels of analysis in Leont'ev's theory of activity, these studies assume that the same goal-directed action is involved regardless of the plane of its execution. The plane of its execution is an issue of the operational composition of the action. Thus the analytic level in

Leont'ev's theory concerned with action fulfills Vygotsky's requirement that a unit be applicable to interpsychological as well as intrapsychological functioning. It is also compatible with Vygotsky's account of mediation.

So far when dealing with mediation, I have used noncommittal terms such as "functioning" when referring to what is mediated. By now it should be clear that the notion of action is an appropriate and much more specific candidate for this role. It provides the framework within which mediation operates, a claim reflected in Zinchenko's (1985) term "tool-mediated action." Just as it is crucial to understand, say, that "assimilation" and "accommodation" are terms that apply to a schema in Piaget's approach, I would argue that it is essential to understand that terms such as "mediation," "interpsychological," and "intrapsychological" apply to action in a Vygotskian analysis.

Vygotsky's proposal for using word meaning as a unit of analysis in his theoretical framework is flawed in several respects. While continuing to accept his claims about the importance of semiotic phenomena in human mental functioning, I have argued that word meaning (or any other semiotic unit for that matter) is a unit of *semiotic mediation* of mental functioning, not a unit of mental functioning itself. I have also considered, and rejected as incorrect, the possibility that individual mental functions (memory, thinking) could serve as units of analysis in Vygotsky's approach.

Because these functions are defined in terms of their changing interrelationships—their dynamic organization—in consciousness, they cannot properly be considered in isolation. Instead, an appropriate unit of analysis in Vygotsky's theoretical framework must be a "microcosm of consciousness" itself; it must be capable of reflecting all the complex interfunctional relationships that characterize human consciousness. In addition to meeting this formidable requirement, such a unit must be amenable to objective investigation.

For these reasons, following Zinchenko (1985) I have argued that tool-mediated, goal-directed action is the appropriate unit of analysis in Vygotsky's approach. The analytic unit of action avoids the shortcomings of word meaning while preserving its strengths. With regard to the latter, it is a unit that applies to the interpsychological as well as the intrapsychological plane, and it provides an appropriate framework for mediation.

CHAPTER 8

Mind and Society

I n attempting to explicate Vygotsky's claims about the social origins
and social, or "quasi-social," nature of human consciousness, I have
examined several issues concerned with interpsychological functioning,
such as intersubjectivity, abbreviated directives, and the dialogic form
of semiotic mediation. In all these cases the term "social" has referred
to dyadic or small-group communicative processes.

Such interpsychological functioning is not the only kind of social
phenomenon envisioned by Vygotsky. He also recognized "social institutional" processes, which are the primary focus of Marxist social
theory. Although Vygotsky's project of reformulating psychology along
Marxist lines calls for an account of the relationship between social
institutional forces and human consciousness, his concrete research on
social phenomena never went beyond the level of interpsychological
processes. Thus he did not deal with a variety of classic issues in Marxist
social theory, such as commodity fetishism, the commodification of
labor and of the individual, and alienation.

Although these would seem to be the primary issues one would
address in reformulating psychology along Marxist lines, recall that
Vygotsky was also struggling with psychological and semiotic issues
as defined by the theories of his time. This fact, plus his premature
death, prevented him from reaching the point where he could explore
in detail how human consciousness is related to social institutional
forces.

Before considering some ways in which Vygotsky's approach can be extended to deal with this problem, it is worth noting that its solution remains elusive. Indeed increasing disciplinary specialization and isolation make it even less likely that the problem will be recognized, let alone resolved, today than half a century ago. The relationships among levels of analysis and among disciplines in the social sciences are all too seldom examined in contemporary writings in the West.

In certain respects the problems under consideration here are similar to those encountered earlier regarding the relationship between the natural and social lines of development. In that case the concern was with ways in which various forces enter into emergent interactionism. I shall again be concerned with multiple forces of development and corresponding sets of explanatory principles, but the goal will now be to arrive at an expanded account of social forces and their relationships to human mental processes in the individual.

I shall do this by extending Vygotsky's account of social processes beyond the interpsychological level to the social institutional level. While my proposals are compatible with Vygotsky's ideas, my comments will go into areas that he never examined in detail. Furthermore, my comments are not intended as an exhaustive treatment of the issues involved. Rather, they are a preliminary, partial inventory of problems that could be addressed from a Vygotskian perspective when trying to understand the relationship between social institutional forces and individual consciousness. The three topics in my inventory are (a) Leont'ev's notion of activity, (b) Vygotsky's account of the decontextualization of mediation means, and (c) Vygotsky's account of inner speech.

Leont'ev's Notion of Activity

In my brief overview of the theory of activity outlined by Vygotsky's student and colleague A. N. Leont'ev (1972, 1975, 1981), I argued that the notion of tool-mediated, goal-directed action is the appropriate unit of analysis in Vygotsky's approach. In making this argument in chapter 7, I mentioned two levels of analysis identified by Leont'ev: actions and operations (that is, the operational composition of actions).

The third level of analysis is activity. As I have noted elsewhere (Wertsch, 1981a, 1981b), the Russian term *deyatel'nost'* has no adequate English equivalent. "Activity" is usually the closest approximation. To understand what Leont'ev had in mind when using this term,

I must return briefly to his general theoretical framework. Leont'ev viewed activity as a "nonadditive, molar unit of life for the material, corporeal subject" (1981, p. 46); that is, he believed that an activity cannot be reduced to other units of analysis, such as stimulus–response ties, information-processing units, actions, or operations. Of course this theory does not mean that other units and levels of analysis cannot be used in conjunction with the level concerned with activities—this is precisely Leont'ev's point in his trilevel analysis. However, these other levels of analysis complement rather than replace analysis at the level of activity.

The three levels of analysis must be kept separate from one another because Leont'ev was trying to provide three distinct types of answers to what L. Eckensberger and J. Meacham (1984) cite as a fundamental question for any theory of action or activity: the question of what an individual or group is doing in a particular setting. A response can be formulated at the levels of activity, of action, and of operations.

Leont'ev's attempt to specify what someone is doing at the level of activity concerns the social institutional milieu in which psychological processes occur. Given his concern with formulating a Marxist psychology, it is not surprising that Leont'ev viewed labor as the prototypic form of human activity. Indeed, the theory of activity may be viewed as an attempt to elaborate Marx's account of labor by identifying its implications for psychological processes and by providing an analogous examination of other social institutions and their psychological implications. The fundamental role of social institutional factors in defining activity is evident from Leont'ev's claim that

> human psychology is concerned with the activity of concrete individuals, which takes place either in a collective—that is, jointly with other people—or in a situation in which the subject deals directly with the surrounding world of objects—for example, at the potter's wheel or the writer's desk. However, if we removed human activity from the system of social relationships and social life, it would not exist and would have no structure. With all its varied forms, the human individual's activity is a system in the system of social relations. It does not exist without these relations. The specific form in which it exists is determined by the forms and means of material and mental social interaction (*Verkehr*) that are created by the development of production and that cannot be realized in any way other than in the activity of concrete people. It turns out that the activity of separate individuals depends on

their place in society, on the conditions that fall to their lot, and on idiosyncratic, individual factors.   (1981, p. 47)

A fundamental tenet of Marxist accounts of social institutions is that they are in a constant process of historical change. They are part of sociohistorical processes such as the rise of the commodity form and the commodification of labor and the individual. As a result, the psychological correlates of social institutions are also viewed as historically specific in Leont'ev's approach. Of course, this accords well with Vygotsky's desire to incorporate social history as a genetic domain into his approach. With these general points in mind, let me turn once again to the specific properties of activity and how they can help one understand behavioral patterns such as those manifested by the dyads in the model–copy task.

For my purposes an activity can be thought of as a social institutionally defined setting. An activity or activity setting is grounded in a set of assumptions about appropriate roles, goals, and means used by the participants in that setting. In terms of the levels of analysis in the theory of activity, one could say that an activity setting guides the selection of actions and the operational composition of actions, and it determines the functional significance of these actions. For example, the functional significance or "sense"[1] of getting to point N in Leont'ev's example (see chapter 7) will vary depending on whether this action is executed in the activity setting of, say, labor or schooling.

The more important question here is how the implicit assumptions of an activity setting determine the selection of actions and their operational composition. The guiding and integrating force of these assumptions is what Leont'ev called the motive of an activity. For Leont'ev a motive is not a construct that can be understood in biological or even psychological terms. Rather, it is an aspect of a sociohistorically specific, institutionally defined setting. Among other things, the motive that is involved in a particular activity setting specifies what is to be maximized in that setting. By maximizing one goal, one set of behaviors, and the like over others, the motive also determines what will be given up if need be in order to accomplish something else.

Given this description of a motive, I turn to the two specific activities of interest here—labor and schooling.[2] The motive of labor generally is productivity. When someone is engaged in the activity setting of labor, productivity will be maximized, and other possible motives will be given secondary status. In contrast, the motive of a formal schooling activity[3] may be defined as "learning for learning's sake." In this activity setting other motives play a secondary role, and actions and operations executed in their service will be altered or foregone if they interfere seriously with the maximization of learning.

In labor activity, errors are viewed as expensive interferences with productivity. Consequently, they will be avoided if at all possible. In model–copy tasks such as the ones used in the studies noted earlier, how can someone who understands the task organize his or her collaboration with someone who does not understand it in order to maximize productivity? The obvious solution is for the experienced member of the dyad to take responsibility for all aspects of the task that are potentially difficult and to allow the novice to carry out only those aspects that can be executed without complete understanding. Such a division of responsibility will maximize the efficient, correct execution of the task and will minimize expensive mistakes.

In schooling activity quite different assumptions define the setting. Instead of maximizing productivity, students' learning is accorded highest priority. When carrying out a goal-directed action on the interpsychological plane, joint cognitive functioning will be organized such that students can make maximal gains in learning. The implication is that if mistakes are instructive, they will not be avoided as they are in labor activity; indeed, tutors may even be willing to encourage errors by students because of the assumption that one can learn from mistakes.

Thus instructional activity and labor activity differ sharply in their motives and in their hierarchies of what is to be maximized. Of course, instruction or learning can also occur in labor activity settings, and production of some sort can occur in instructional activity settings. But when these two motives come into conflict, the definition of the activity setting will determine which is given priority and which is sacrificed.

My colleagues and I conducted a study in rural Brazil in which we examined adult–child dyads carrying out a task of making a copy farmyard in accordance with a model (Wertsch, Minick, and Arns, 1984). The child in each of the dyads was a six-year-old. In half the dyads the adult was the child's mother, and in the other half, a teacher. The mothers had spent very little time in formal schooling settings (none had more than four years of education), whereas the teachers had all completed at least eleven years of education and had continued to work in a formal schooling setting.

On the basis of a fine-grained analysis of the dyads' interaction in this task setting, two distinct patterns in the operational composition of the action emerged. On the one hand the Brazilian mothers organized interpsychological functioning such that they took on a great deal of the responsibility for executing (that is, operationalizing) the strategic steps in the goal-directed action. On the other hand the Brazilian teachers organized interpsychological functioning such that the children in the dyads were given the bulk of the responsibility for executing the goal-directed task. We argued that the reason for this diference in the operational composition of the goal-directed action lies in how the adults in these two groups construed or created the setting. Specifically, the mothers interpreted this joint cognitive functioning in terms of a labor activity setting, whereas the teachers interpreted it in terms of an instructional activity setting.

The Brazilian mothers organized interpsychological functioning on the assumption that efficient error-free execution of the goal-directed action had highest priority. They retained responsibility for most aspects of the task and allowed their children to execute only those relatively easy steps that they could be expected to carry out flawlessly. In an instructional activity setting, where learning for learning's sake is the motive and efficient, error-free task execution is accorded secondary status, quite different assumptions prevail. The Brazilian teachers structured interaction such that students were encouraged to participate in all aspects of the task, even if they made mistakes. That is, learning was given a high enough priority that errors were not viewed as being so expensive as to be avoided; indeed they seemed to be encouraged if they could foster increased mastery of the task.

We went on to examine the possibilities for why these two sets of adults differed in their definition of the activity setting. The answer lies in the level of experience the adults in the groups had had with various social institutional contexts. As noted earlier, all the mothers in this study had attended school for no more than four years, whereas all the teachers had attended school for a minimum of eleven years and had continued to function in schoollike settings after completing their education.

These facts make it understandable why the teachers were willing and able to organize interpsychological functioning in accordance with the assumptions of instructional activity, whereas the mothers were not. To say that the Brazilian mothers did not organize joint cognitive functioning in this way does not, however, mean that their performance was random or simply deficient. The organization of their performance makes perfect sense given another activity setting, namely, labor. This was the activity setting in which these adults carried out tasks with children on a day-to-day basis. As investigators such as J. Lave (1977a, 1977b) have pointed out, much learning does occur in such settings, but the process whereby it is accomplished is more properly viewed as apprenticeship rather than schoollike instruction.

To summarize, in outlining the analytic level concerned with activity in Leont'ev's theoretical framework, I have identified one of the ways in which Vygotsky's approach can be extended to deal with the psychological consequences of social institutional phenomena. The notion of an activity setting with its motive provides a means for relating social institutional and individual psychological phenomena. In the study I reviewed, differential experience with various activity settings resulted in dissimilar interpretations of an experimental situation. Because these dissimilar interpretations were associated with different forms of interpsychological functioning, a Vygotskian approach predicts different intrapsychological outcomes as well.

In my discussion of activity settings I used the terms "assumptions" or "implicit assumptions." These terms reflect the fact that institutionally defined settings are often not readily recognized or accessible to conscious reflection by the individuals participating in them. In studies such as ours (Wertsch, Minick, and Arns, 1984), for example, it is unlikely that any of the adults made a conscious decision to operate in accordance with labor as opposed to instructional activity or vice versa. Rather, when participating in activity settings, subjects usually do not identify the setting consciously. If asked, they may not even be able to identify what it is that organizes their performance.

A further point is that activity settings are not determined by the physical context. Rather, they are created by the participants in the setting. This is evident from the empirical results I have reviewed, which show that two sets of dyads, operating in the same physical context and even executing the same goal-directed action, create quite distinct activity settings. Naturally, some physical contexts are more conducive to creating certain activity settings than others, but this relationship cannot be reduced to mechanistic determination.

These points about activity settings pose the following problem: If an experienced member of a culture is not conscious of the assumptions involved, and if there are few straightforward clues from the concrete environment, how are children to understand and master activity settings? Such settings would appear to be quite elusive, especially since adults (such as those in our study) seldom describe or explain them. It is possible to do little more than to raise this question here. It does seem to me, however, that the answer lies in what Rommetveit (1974) has termed "prolepsis," a communicative process whereby individuals must identify others' implicit assumptions in order to interpret their utterances. Rather than viewing communication as a process that presupposes fixed and shared background knowledge and involves the transmission of information, Rommetveit suggests that a listener often must create background knowledge as part of "what is made known" in communication. That is, an understanding of the activity setting emerges for the junior participant as a "by-product" of communicating in it.

The general issue of the relationship between activity settings and mental processes has only recently begun to receive serious attention in Western psychology.[4] In several cases this interest has been motivated, at least in part, by Leont'ev's writings (compare Bronfenbrenner, 1979a, 1979b; Laboratory of Comparative Human Cognition, 1983; Scribner, 1984). Bronfenbrenner has called for an "ecological psychology," a major thesis of which is that "human abilities and their realization depend in significant degree on the larger social and institutional context of individual activity" (1979a, p. xv). With regard to the ecological settings of interpsychological functioning, Bronfenbrenner has criticized existing studies by noting that "the pervasive use of a dyadic parent–child model leaves out of consideration the possibility that forces external to the two-person system could influence the effectiveness of outcomes" (1979b, p. 896). It is precisely this kind of criticism to which studies grounded in Leont'ev's theory of activity can reply. By examining the social institutional settings in which interpsychological functioning occurs, one can understand much more about this functioning than when it is considered in isolation. This, in turn, should provide much needed information about the emergence of intrapsychological functioning. It is only by constructing a theoretical framework within which social institutional, interpsychological, and intrapsychological levels of analysis can be linked, but not reduced to one another, that one will be able to answer questions about the relationship between activity settings and the individual. This is a goal that remains to be fulfilled in the Vygotskian approach.

Vygotsky's Account of the Decontextualization of Mediational Means

Vygotsky viewed mechanisms of semiotic mediation as providing a basic metric by which change in various genetic domains can be measured. In particular, the decontextualization of mediational means played an essential role in his account of social history and ontogenesis. This form of decontextualization is possible because of one of the latent potentials of language: the potential of sign types and their systemic interrelationships to serve as objects of reflection. To identify this latent potential, however, does nothing to specify the forces that lead to its being used. That is, an account of decontextualization provides an analysis of the "grooves" along which certain changes will occur if they do occur, but it does not specify why and when such change should take place.

To address this question one must turn once again to social institutional phenomena. An obvious place to begin is with formal schooling, as did Luria (1975b) and Vygotsky and Luria (1930) in the sociohistorical domain, and Vygotsky (1934a) in his account of the ontogenesis of scientific concepts. Formal schooling has also been the focus of investigators such as Cole and Bruner (1971), Scribner and Cole (1973, 1981), J. Goody (1977), and Olson (1980), who have sought to clarify and extend Vygotsky's ideas. These and others have argued that the special speech styles and cognitive processes involved in the decontextualization of mediational means are closely tied to subjects' participation in schooling. Furthermore, Scribner and Cole (1981) have identified "literacy practice" (see chapter 2) as the essential phenomenon that results in the cognitive consequences typically associated with schooling.

This line of research has provided convincing answers to certain questions, but it has not addressed the issue of why literary practice and the decontextualization of mediational means occur in social history. This is more than a question about the time of onset of such phenomena; it also concerns their very nature, since the character of literary practice is probably influenced by other aspects of the sociocultural milieu in which it appears.

One way to pose this question is to ask whether literary practice is not a manifestation of some larger social institutional phenomenon. If so, one would have a framework for understanding why such practice emerges when it does in social history and how its psychological consequences are related to those of other institutions. A line of inquiry that may help answer these questions is the social theory of figures such as Marx (1977), M. Weber (1968, 1979), and G. Lukács (1971). Of particular interest is the notion of "reification," which plays an extremely important role in the dialectical theory of society. My comments here will be based primarily on the account of reification proposed by Lukács in 1923 (Lukács, 1971). Although he drew heavily on Marx, his ideas have not been incorporated into Soviet philosophy or psychology. Indeed, his analysis of reification was attacked almost immediately upon its publication by Soviet commentators (see Breines, 1972). Hence my comments constitute a proposal for approaching a problem raised by Vygotsky's theory rather than a report on existing Soviet research.[5]

In developing his account of reification, Lukács was greatly influenced by the ideas of his teachers Weber and G. Simmel. Weber's notion of rationality seems to have been of particular importance. For my purposes the essential point about Weber's notion of rationalization is that it is a process wherein objects and events come to be viewed in terms of abstract categories rather than their qualitatively unique particularity. Weber's notion of rationality can be found in many spheres of social institutional action (what corresponds to activity in Leont'ev's approach). For example, in outlining categories of economic action, he defined "formal" rationality as follows: "A system of economic activity will be called 'formally' rational according to the degree in which the provision for needs, which is essential to every rational economy, is capable of being expressed in numerical, calculable terms, and is so expressed" (1978, p. 85). Hence this form of rationality involves categories that go beyond the point of simply being abstract; the fact that they are numerical and calculable means that they are interrelated in an abstract system.

For Weber, rationality is not only characteristic of economic action but is manifested in other spheres of action and social institutions as well. In this connection bureaucracy, regardless of the socioeconomic formation (for example, capitalism or socialism) in which it appears, is especially important. Weber viewed bureaucracy and bureaucratic domination as phenomena that are inherently linked to the tendency to consider individuals and actions in terms of abstract, formal categories rather than their unique particularity. Among the consequences of bureaucratic domination, he cited the following:

The tendency to "levelling" in the interest of the broadest possible basis of recruitment in terms of technical competence . . . The dominance of a spirit of formalistic impersonality: *"Sine ira et studio,"* without hatred or passion, and hence without affection or enthusiasm. The dominant norms are concepts of straightforward duty without regard to personal considerations. Everyone is subject to formal equality of treatment; that is, everyone in the same empirical situation. This is the spirit in which the ideal official conducts his office. (1978, p. 225)

Thus for Weber, rationalization, and hence abstract categorization, is an aspect of many forms of modern social organization.

Although Lukács (1971) reported that his first reading of Marx was "through spectacles tinged by Simmel and Max Weber" (p. ix), the writings of Marx himself become the central theoretical impetus for his notion of reification. Specifically, Marx's account of the commodity, commodity fetishism, and the commodification of labor[6] in capitalism was central to the development of this notion. Whereas Marx's theory is often interpreted as asserting that ideological and epistemological aspects of human consciousness are reflections of underlying economic causes, Lukács (1971) argued that a dialectical method reveals that " 'ideological' and 'economic' problems lose their mutual exclusiveness and merge into one another" (p. 34). More recently, M. Postone (1983) has similarly argued about the epistemological constraints suggested by Marx's account of labor. The general point is that certain aspects of human consciousness in capitalist society (the only social formation studied extensively by Marx) are integral to any account of the society.

According to S. Buck-Morss (1977), "Lukács's most original contribution" (p. 26) was that "he maintained that the commodity structure, whose mysteries Marx had dispelled in the first chapter of *Capital,* permeated every aspect of bourgeois society, including the very patterns of bourgeois thought. The problem of commodities, he asserted, was 'the central structural problem of capitalist society in all its aspects'; it was the 'model of all the objective forms of bourgeois society, together with all the subjective forms corresponding to them' " (p. 26). In order to understand the nature of Lukács's contribution, one must turn to Marx's analysis of the commodity. In the first chapter of *Capital,* Marx (1977) specified the properties of the commodity in capitalist society. The most important is that by coming into contact in the marketplace, products, including labor, acquire a dual nature. They come to have exchange value as well as use value. The use value of an object is dependent on its physical properties; it is the value of its use in non-economic human activity. Thus the use value of an article of clothing may be to keep its wearer warm. When products are exchanged, however, a second form of value is typically involved in capitalism. This is exchange value, a quantitative abstraction derived from specifying how many units of one product can be exchanged for another.

As noted by Marx, the quantitative aspect specified by the exchange value of objects is defined quite independently of their qualitative aspect, that is, their use value. Thus the fact that either one coat or ten pounds of tea can be exchanged for twenty yards of linen is a fact about quantitative equivalence that operates independently of the qualities of the specific objects at issue. The "common element" of objects that makes exchange possible

> cannot be a geometrical, physical, chemical, or other natural property of commodities. Such properties come into consideration only to the extent that they make the commodities useful, that is, turn them into use-values. But clearly, the exchange relation of commodities is characterized precisely by its abstraction from their use values. Within the exchange relation, one use-value is worth just as much as another, provided only that it is present in the appropriate quantity.   (Marx, 1977, p. 127)

The distinction between use value and exchange value is not original with Marx. His original contribution derives from his claims about labor as the source of value and about the commodification of labor. He argued that when products of labor enter into exchange relations, labor itself is given exchange value and hence becomes a commodity, that is, it acquires a twofold character. The exchange value of labor is abstracted from its use value, thereby giving rise to a qualitatively homogeneous, quantifiable, "abstract labor" that allows the equation of all qualitatively distinct forms of human labor. Furthermore, Marx argued that the phenomenon of abstract labor is not recognized by its producers:

> Men do not . . . bring the products of their labor into relation with each other as values because they see these objects merely as the material integuments of homogeneous human labour. The reverse is true: by equating their different products to each other in exchange as values, they equate their different kinds of labour

as human labour. They do this without being aware of it. (1977, pp. 166–167)

Humans fail to recognize the implication of the commodification of their labor because they do not see beyond the material form of the objects they produce; they fail to understand the abstract labor that is associated with their products' exchange value. This misperception is what Marx (1977) termed "commodity fetishism." It arises through the failure to see that abstract, commodified labor, rather than some mysterious property of the commodities themselves, determines the exchange value of commodities.

With the rise of commodity fetishism, Marx argued that human relations come to take on the appearance of thinglike relations:

> Since the producers do not come into social contact until they exchange the products of their labour, the specific social characteristics of their private labours appears only within this exchange. In other words, the labour of the private individual manifests itself as an element of the total labour of society only through the relations which the act of exchange establishes between the products, and, through their mediation, between the producers. To the producers, therefore, the social relations between their private labours appears as what they are, that is, they do not appear as direct social relations between persons in their work, but rather as material [*dinglich*] relations between persons and social relations between things. (Ibid., pp. 165–166)

Lukács drew heavily on Marx's account of the commodity and the objectification of social relations in outlining his concept of reification. Lukács wrote that the basic essence of commodity structure is that "a relation between people takes on the character of a thing and thus acquires a 'phantom objectivity', an autonomy that seems so strictly rational and all-embracing as to conceal every trace of its fundamental nature: the relation between people" (1971, p. 83). The main point of Lukács's account of reification is that the commodity structure appears in all aspects of capitalist society; it permeates all aspects of consciousness:

> The transformation of the commodity relation into a thing of "ghostly objectivity" cannot therefore content itself with the reduction of all objects for the gratification of human needs to commodities. It stamps its imprint upon the whole consciousness of man; his qualities and abilities are no longer an organic part

of his personality, they are things which he can "own" or "dispose of" like the various objects of the external world.   (Ibid., p. 100)

Under this general claim about the commodification of consciousness, Lukács made specific points about philosophy. He argued that modern philosophy, which is often assumed to be independent of the social conditions of the society in which it is developed, "springs from the reified structure of consciousness" (ibid., pp. 110–111). In particular, he focused his critical comments on Kant. He argued that Kant represents the culmination of a line of philosophers extending at least from Descartes who focus on abstract, rational, calculable categories at the expense of the active subject and concrete particularity. In Kantian philosophy:

> The ideal of knowledge represented by the purely distilled formal conception of the object of knowledge, the mathematical organisation and the ideal of necessary natural laws all transform knowledge more and more into the systematic and conscious contemplation of those purely formal connections, those 'laws' which function in—objective—reality without the intervention of the subject. But the attempt to eliminate every element of content and of the irrational affects not only the object but also, and to an increasing extent, the subject.   (1971, p. 128)

Of course Kant and Descartes predate modern capitalism. In Lukács's view, however, their ideas represent a philosophical precursor to the reified consciousness that would come to pervade society with the spread of the commodity form. The focus of consciousness is most readily recognized in modern technology, but it governs the understanding of social relations as well. According to Lukács, "all human relations (viewed as the object of social activity) assume increasingly the objective forms of natural science and of the abstract substrata of the laws of nature" (ibid., p. 131).

My comments on Weber, Marx, and Lukács are not intended as a review or defense of their approaches. Instead, my intention is to identify some fundamental issues in social theory that have major implications for a Vygotskian approach to human consciousness. The principal issue concerns the social institutional forces that lead to abstract categorization in human activity, ideology, and mental processes. Rather than viewing such categorization solely in terms of mental processes, the social theory of Marx and Lukács suggests that psychological phenomena comprise only one of several moments in a larger sociohistorical process. Furthermore, to say that formal schooling is the institution associated with certain psychological phenomena is to identify only the tip of the iceberg in this instance. Such a claim begs the question of why schooling emerges when it does and as it does in social history.

Although Vygotsky viewed abstract reasoning as a product of history, he never carried out a detailed examination of the sociohistorical forces that gave rise to it. What the ideas of figures such as Weber, Marx, and Lukács add to the picture is a proposal for how to do this. Their ideas suggest that social institutional processes, with their unique, nonreducible set of explanatory principles, are primary (analytically if not genetically). Thus while Vygotsky's ideas about the decontextualization of mediational means provide an account of the grooves along which change can occur, one must invoke constructs in social theory (for example, bureaucratization, commodification, reification) in order to account for how and why various semiotic potentials will be utilized.

Finally, in addition to examining the processes of reification in the subject, psychological theories must be capable of recognizing reification in their own constructs. Scholars such as Buck-Morss (1975), J. Broughton (1981), and J. Youniss (1983) have raised this issue in connection with Piagetian theory. Their questions are perhaps not surprising given Lukács's comments on Kant and Piaget's avowed neo-Kantianism. I would argue that similar questions need to be raised about Vygotsky's account of human consciousness. Do his assumptions about the decontextualization of mediational means reflect a reificatory tendency in his theory? If so, could a theory that is more self-critical avoid this? These are questions that have been notoriously difficult to answer regarding other theories (compare Broughton, 1981), but I would argue that they must be addressed in a Vygotskian approach if it is to be a truly sociohistorical theory.

Vygotsky's Account of Inner Speech

Earlier I identified a research question concerning the relationship between social institutional and psychological phenomena by focusing on one of the latent potentials of language, the potential inherent in the relationships among sign types. It is the only semiotic potential that Vygotsky examined concretely in his account of social history. Specifically, it underlies his account of the decontextualization of mediational means as outlined in chapter 2.

As noted in chapters 4 and 5, however, Vygotsky's semiotic analysis also involves a second latent potential in human language, a potential based on contextualized sign tokens. Several aspects of his analysis of social, egocentric, and inner speech rely on the indexical connections between sign tokens and their extra- and intralinguistic contexts. Given the fact that such contextual relationships play a central role in Vygotsky's account of semiotic mediation in ontogenesis, one might expect them to assume the role of a metric for social history as well.

Although Vygotsky did not go into detail on the issue of how contextualized sign functioning might be related to social history, several of his comments suggest that he saw some sort of relationship between these two phenomena. His comments on this issue usually concern egocentric and inner speech, the speech forms in which contextualized sign functioning predominates. For example, in the final paragraphs of a chapter on the genetic roots of thinking and speech, Vygotsky made the following comment on the verbal thinking associated with egocentric and inner speech:

> By acknowledging the historical character of verbal thinking, we must apply all the methodological tenets established by historical materialism for human social history to this form of behavior. Finally, one must expect beforehand that the very type of historical development of behavior will turn out to be directly dependent on the general laws of the historical development of human society. (1934a, pp. 101–102)

"The methodological tenets established by historical materialism" concern social history at the macrosociological, institutional level. Therefore this statement by Vygotsky amounts to a claim about the relationship between a psychological phenomenon and social institutional processes.

This general claim could be translated into concrete terms in several ways. My approach is to examine changes in intralinguistic indexical relationships. These relationships play a role in speech on the interpsychological plane (see chapters 4 and 5), but they are especially important in egocentric and inner speech. Vygotsky's notion of sense, as opposed to meaning, is particularly relevant for the present discussion.

In order to explicate Vygotsky's account of sense such that it could help relate psychological and social institutional phenomena, additional ideas must be incorporated. The ideas I have in mind come from the writings of M. M. Bakhtin (1968, 1981, 1984; Voloshinov, 1929[7]).

Like Vygotsky, Bakhtin (1984)[8] was concerned with the issue of contextualized significance. Indeed, he used the term "metalinguistics" to distinguish his methods and object of study from those of linguistics. According to Bakhtin, metalinguistics studies "language in its concrete living totality, and not language as the specific object of linguistics, something arrived at through . . . [an] abstraction from various aspects of the concrete life of the word" (1984, p. 181). Bakhtin (1984) argued that "of course, metalinguistic research cannot ignore linguistics and must make use of its results" (p. 181), but it goes beyond the boundaries of linguistics in that it examines the organization of signs and their significance in social context (that is, "concrete living reality").

Unlike Vygotsky, who provided only the general outline of an account of contextualized significance, or sense, Bakhtin endeavored to understand "language in its concrete living totality." The basic theoretical construct he used in this effort was dialogicality. For him "dialogic relationships (including the dialogic relationships of a speaker to his own discourse) are the subject of metalinguistics" (1984, p. 182).

Bakhtin's notion of dialogue encompasses much more than the process of interlocutors' taking sequential turns in conversation. It applies to any phenomenon in which two or more "voices" come into contact. The voices may be those of two individuals engaged in overt dialogue (Voloshinov, 1973), those of an author and a character in "novelistic discourse" (Bakhtin, 1981), or those of two conflicting positions in intrapsychological, internal functioning (Voloshinov, 1973, 1976).

Bakhtin's notion of dialogue underlies his approach to a wide range of issues in aesthetics, philosophy, and psychology. For instance, it provides the foundations for his account of human consciousness, an account that bears many similarities to Vygotsky's. Like Vygotsky, Bakhtin relied on the notion of inner speech in order to account for the social, semiotically mediated nature of psychological processes in the individual (for example, Voloshinov, 1973, 1976). However, Bakhtin emphasized the dialogic nature of inner speech more than Vygotsky did. Vygotsky occasionally mentioned "inner dialogue" (1934a, p. 301) and seemed to assume that inner speech has certain dialogic properties (see chapter 4), but Bakhtin saw dialogic relationships as the very essence of inner speech."

> The units of which inner speech is constituted are certain whole entities somewhat resembling a passage of monologic speech or whole utterances. But most of all, they resemble the alternating

lines of a dialogue. There was good reason why thinkers in ancient times should have conceived of inner speech as inner dialogue . . . Only by ascertaining the forms of whole utterances and, especially, the forms of dialogic speech, can light be shed on the forms of inner speech as well as on the peculiar logic of their concatenation in the stream of inner speech. (Voloshinov, 1973, p. 38)

At least two key points in Bakhtin's approach to dialogicality are of particular interest when trying to extend Vygotsky's account of inner speech or, more broadly, when trying to propose a Vygotskian account of mind and society. First, Bakhtin formulated his account of dialogue in terms of voices. As M. Holquist and Emerson (1981) note, for Bakhtin a voice is "the speaking personality, the speaking consciousness" (p. 434). Essential to Bakhtin's approach to the speaking consciousness is the assumption that it is sociohistorically specific. That is, the voices that come into contact in dialogue are not those of isolated, ahistorical individuals; they are ideological perspectives or "axiological belief systems" (Bakhtin, 1981, p. 304) that can adequately be understood only in terms of a specific sociohistorical setting. Hence Bakhtin was concerned with the voice of a merchant as opposed to that of a laborer in nineteenth-century England, the voice of a peasant as opposed to that of an aristocrat in eighteenth-century Russia, and the like. This does not mean that speakers are mere puppets on a sociohistorical stage; it does mean, however, that voices are always sociohistorically situated, regardless of whether or not the speakers are aware of this.

In addition to viewing voices themselves as sociohistorically situated, Bakhtin (1981; Voloshinov, 1973) argued that forms of their contact and interanimation are socially and historically specific. This is most apparent in his accounts of carnivalization (Bakhtin, 1968) and novelistic discourse (Bakhtin, 1981). For example, he viewed the history of novelistic discourse in terms of the increasing contact and interpenetration of the author's and character's voices, a process that he viewed as culminating in Dostoevsky's creation of the truly "polyphonic" novel (Bakhtin, 1984).

A second key point in Bakhtin's analysis concerns the uniquely semiotic properties that determine the nature of voices and their contact in dialogue. While he insisted that these phenomena must always be viewed in terms of their sociohistorical setting, he by no means believed that they would be accounted for solely in terms of sociological principles. Rather, semiotic principles account for voices and dialogue. Like Vygotsky, Bakhtin assumed that language provides grooves along which certain forms of functioning and genetic transition occur.

To illustrate these points, consider the devices Bakhtin outlined in his account of the dialogic contact of voices, the "hybrid construction" used in certain forms of discourse in the novel. In his terminology a hybrid construction is "an utterance that belongs, by its grammatical (syntactic) and compositional markers, to a single speaker, but that actually contains mixed within it two utterances, two speech manners, two styles, two 'languages,' two semantic and axiological belief systems" (Bakhtin, 1981, p. 304).

The fact that no formal markers separate the two voices involved in hybrid construction makes the interanimation of the voices and the possibilities for authorial commentary more subtle, but for that very reason more powerful in a sense, than in other forms of the dialogic interanimation of voices. Bakhtin used the following example from Dickens's *Little Dorrit* (bk. 2, ch. 24) to illustrate hybrid construction: "That illustrious man and great national ornament, Mr. Merdle, continued his shining course. It began to be widely understood that one who had done society the admirable service of making so much money out of it, could not be suffered to remain a commoner. A baronetcy was spoken of with confidence; a peerage was frequently mentioned" (Bakhtin, 1981, p. 306).

Bakhtin analyzed the hybrid construction involved in this excerpt as follows:

> We have here . . . fictive solidarity with the hypocritically ceremonial general opinion of Merdle. All the epithets referring to Merdle in the first sentence derive from general opinion, that is, they are the concealed speech of another. The second sentence— "it began to be widely understood," and so on—is kept within the bounds of an emphatically objective style, representing not subjective opinion but the admission of an objective and completely indisputable fact. The epithet "who had done society the admirable service" is completely at the level of common opinion, repeating its official glorification, but the subordinate clause attached to that glorification ("of making so much money out of it") are the words of the author himself (as if put in parentheses in the quotation). The main sentence then picks up again at the level of common opinion. We have here a typical hybrid con-

struction, where the subordinate clause is in direct authorial speech and the main clause is someone else's speech. The main and subordinate clauses are constructed in different semantic and axiological conceptual systems.   (Ibid.)

Bakhtin's analysis reveals the subtlety of semiotic devices that can bring voices into dialogic contact. In contrast to dialogue in the narrow sense, where the contribution of each separate voice is marked in the utterance form, the hybrid construction weaves voices together into an almost seamless web. One must examine such constructions very closely to determine "who is doing the talking" at each step. As in the example from *Little Dorrit,* there can be multiple shifts in voice or ideological perspective with no clear formal indication that such a shift has occurred. It is precisely by bringing voices into close contact in this way that they become "interanimated" and produce the sardonic effect intended by Dickens.

This brief review of Bakhtin's notion of the hybrid construction touches on the basic points about dialogicality noted earlier. On the one hand, the very existence of the voices involved and the form of their interanimation are inconceivable without the linguistic mechanisms harnessed to produce the ironic effect. On the other, the voices and their form of contact are sociohistorically specific. The effect intended by Dickens depends on the existence of a mercantile class and critics of this class in nineteenth-century industrial England. That is, the semantic and axiological conceptual systems that are brought into dialogic contact are sociohistorically situated. Furthermore, the particular form of interanimation in this case, a form that produces ironic humor, is peculiar to literary genres such as the English comic novel. According to Bakhtin (1981), such genres contrast with others, especially with the epic, where such mixing of author's and character's voices is minimized. Hence in addition to the voices involved, the semiotic mechanisms that make their dialogic relationship possible are sociohistorically specific.

My comments on Bakhtin have of necessity been brief (for further details see Holquist, 1981; Clark and Holquist, 1984; Wertsch, in press), but they do suggest a few ways to extend Vygotsky's approach such that the relationship between psychological processes and social institutional phenomena can be addressed. One way to integrate the ideas of the two theorists is to extend Vygotsky's claims about contextualized sign functioning, in particular, his notion of sense. By incorporating Bakhtin's ideas about voice and dialogicality into Vygotsky's account of sense, one has in essence expanded the notion of context and sign—context relationships beyond anything explicitly examined by Vygotsky. Sense is now viewed as being at least partly governed by the semiotic properties of voices and their interanimation. The voices and the form of their dialogic contact, in turn, are viewed as reflecting discourse properties peculiar to a specific sociohistorical setting. This is consistent with Vygotsky's remarks about sense in the final chapter of *Thinking and Speech* (1934a), but it is much more concrete in its specification of how sociohistorical forces are involved.

A second way in which Bakhtin's account of voices extends Vygotsky's notion of sense concerns the form of indexicality involved. As noted in chapters 4 and 5, Vygotsky's account of egocentric and inner speech rests squarely on an understanding of extralinguistic and intralinguistic context. The indexicality examined in this connection was referential; it always involved a relationship between a sign and a referent picked out by the use of that sign.

In Bakhtin's account of voices and dialogue, a form of nonreferential indexicality (Silverstein, 1976) is involved. Specifically, the "axiological belief system" of a speaker is indexed, but neither the speaker nor the perspective is referred to. For example, in the excerpt from *Little Dorrit* the voices are indexed by the presence of certain sign forms and contents, but the signs are not used to refer to the voices or to the individuals or group with whom they are associated.

In certain respects this issue of ideological perspective is closely related to that of referential perspective outlined in chapter 6. Common to both types of perspective taking is the issue of how a speaker externally or internally represents objects and events. Just as one must use some referential perspective when speaking of objects and events, one must also use some ideological perspective. The fact that certain voices seem to be ideologically neutral to a particular audience corresponds with what I termed a "common referring expression" in chapter 6. In both cases the seeming neutrality of the means of representation stems from a particular sociohistorical setting; given another such setting, the expression may not at all appear to be neutral or natural.

By taking into account certain of Bakhtin's ideas, it becomes apparent that the speech which is internalized carries with itself a great deal of sociohistorically specific ideological baggage. The voices to which a speaker is exposed in social life determine certain fundamental aspects of how reality can be represented in inner speech. Regardless of whether or not individuals are aware of this, a Bakhtinian extension of Vygotsky's account of contextualized sign functioning suggests that intrapsychological semiotic mediation is heavily influenced by this history of social institutional forces.

I have limited my discussion to three of the potential questions raised by the extension of Vygotsky's account of human consciousness in light of social institutional phenomena. The first question drew on Leont'ev's theory of activity; the second and third focused on Vygotsky's theory of semiotic mediation. In one case I argued that the decontextualization of mediational means may reflect a set of macrosociological forces that lead toward abstract categorization. Whereas this issue grows out of latent potentials of language concerned with decontextualization, the third question I raised focused on the other latent potential Vygotsky saw, namely, one based on contextualized sign functioning.

I should emphasize that all three of these potential questions are just that—potential questions. They represent the types of issues that must be raised if one wishes to reach Vygotsky's goal of creating a sociohistorical account of mind. In general, these issues concern ways in which the sociohistorical milieu wherein individuals function can influence their mental processes. They also call for the investigator to examine influences of this milieu on his or her theoretical and empirical research. The fact that I have raised these questions does not mean that I have posed them in the right way or that there might not be others. These are issues for future research.

Because he did not raise such questions himself, Vygotsky did not produce a fully sociohistorical account of mind. It is essential to recognize, however, that he did produce a psychology that is compatible with such an account. This is a major accomplishment because in this respect his approach differs from many others. Unlike theoretical frameworks that isolate psychology from semiotically mediated, human social interaction, Vygotsky's approach forges an inherent link between them. For this reason his approach allows one to relate individual psychology to sociohistorical context. Indeed, it is for this reason that human consciousness can be understood at all according to Vygotsky.

Throughout my account of Vygotsky's ideas, I have stressed the inherently cross-disciplinary (in a sense, even nondisciplinary) nature of his enterprise. In carrying out this enterprise he invoked ideas from philosophy, psychology, social theory, linguistics, literary analysis, and ethnology. As noted in the first chapter, the absence of this kind of broad vision today has produced a crisis in the social sciences. Instead of integrating theoretical and empirical findings from various disciplines, we have created isolated areas of inquiry that in some cases could not be integrated if we tried.

Why was Vygotsky able to operate with such a vision when today, after a half-century of "progress," we seem unable to do so? I have argued that the answer lies partly in Vygotsky's individual genius, a genius that owed a great deal to the rich intellectual setting of his childhood. The primary reason, however, lies in the sociohistorical milieu created by the Russian Revolution. A vision such as his is perhaps possible only in the kind of setting that existed in the USSR between the 1917 Revolution and Vygotsky's death. In this respect, Vygotsky was a product of his time.

It may strike many as ironic that Vygotsky's ideas should appear so fruitful to people removed from him by time, space, and political system. Instead of viewing this as paradoxical, however, it should perhaps be seen as a straightforward example of how human genius can transcend historical, social, and cultural barriers.

Notes

1. Vygotsky: The Man and His Theory

1. Vygotsky changed his name from Vygodsky in the early 1920s because he believed that it derived from the name of the town Vygotovo, where his family had its origins. Other members of his family, such as his daughters and his cousin David Vygodsky (to be mentioned later), retained the "d" in the spelling of their name.

2. The circumstances that led Levitin to find Dobkin provide an interesting story in themselves (see p. 14 of Levitin, 1982). The German invasion of World War II left nothing of what had once been the town of Gomel. For this reason Levitin (October 6, 1981—conversation) had been pessimistic about obtaining detailed information on Vygotsky's youth until he found Dobkin in Moscow.

3. There is some confusion over Vygotsky's date of birth since a different calendar was used prior to 1918 in Russia. According to the "old style" calendar, the date was November 5.

4. In addition to German and Russian, Vygotsky studied Latin and Greek and read Hebrew, French, German, and English. According to his daughter (October 16, 1981—conversation), he refused to speak in English (and perhaps other non-native languages as well) because his pronunciation did not live up to his own high standards. From comments such as these by Koffka (see Harrower, 1983), however, it seems that at least in the case of German, Vygotsky's communication skills were quite adequate.

5. In particular, opportunities for Jews changed for a period of about two decades following the 1917 Revolution.

6. The written version of this presentation was published as "Consciousness as a Problem in the Psychology of Behavior" (1925).

7. *Defectologia* is the Russian term used in the USSR for research on a wide range of disabilities (such as hearing impairment, mental retardation, blindness).

8. The full title of this volume is *Myshlenie i rech': Psikhologicheskie issledovaniya* [Thinking and speech: Psychological investigations]. The 1962 abridged English translation of this volume is titled *Thought and Language*. Russian clearly distinguishes between thought *(mysl')* and thinking *(myshlenie)* and between language *(yazyk)* and speech *(rech')*. Therefore the title *Thinking and Speech* will be used throughout this volume when referring to Vygotsky's 1934 work.

9. Vygotsky often shaved his head during certain times of the year. According to his daughter (October 16, 1981—conversation), this had nothing to do with illness or any fad such as that followed at the time by the Futurists. Rather, he simply thought it an appropriate way to stay cool during the summer.

10. The term "genetic" (Russian *geneticheskii*) is used throughout this volume. In all cases it is used in connection with developmental processes (as in ontogenetic or phylogenetic) rather than with genes, genetic codes, and the like.

11. The term "mental" is used as the translation of *psikhicheskii* throughout this volume unless otherwise noted. This term contrasts with "psychic" and "psychological," which are sometimes employed as translations. I have avoided "psychic" because of its inappropriate connotations in English, and "psychological" because I wish to reserve it as a translation of *psikhologicheskii*. "Psychological" tends to be used by Soviet scholars in connection with the science of mind, whereas "mental" is preferred for the object of study. In English, "psychological" often covers both meanings.

12. Semiotics is the science of signs. It includes linguistics as one of its branches. I use the broader term "semiotics" throughout this volume because Vygotsky's concern was with nonlinguistic as well as linguistic signs.

2. Vygotsky's Genetic Method

1. This volume includes three chapters. As the authors explain in the foreword, Vygotsky wrote the first two chapters, and Luria wrote the third. All quotations used here come either from the introduction or from the first two chapters.

2. Vygotsky's emphasis on decontextualization led him to focus on the development of concepts or abstract word meanings in his analysis of mediational means in social history. Abstract word meaning is only one of two major emphases in Vygotsky's semiotic analysis. The other is inner speech. Vygotsky noted in passing that inner speech emerges only at later stages of sociocultural change, but he failed to develop this claim to any significant extent. Therefore I shall not go into it here.

3. In Soviet psychology the use of the term "methodology" *(metodologiya)* is not restricted such that it refers only to issues of experimental design and the analysis of empirical data. It has a much broader application, namely, to the metatheoretical issue of what constitutes appropriate and valid theories.

3. The Social Origins of Higher Mental Functions

1. The distinction between external and internal processes in Vygotsky's account cannot be equated with the distinction between interpsychological and intrapsychological processes, because Vygotsky identified a type of functioning (egocentric

speech) that is both external and intrapsychological. His analysis recognized external interpsychological processes, external intrapsychological processes, and internal intrapsychological processes.

2. A more literal translation of the Russian term here *(interpsikhicheskii)* would be "interpsychic" or "intermental." However, because Vygotsky occasionally employed the term *interpsikhologicheskii* and because others such as Cole, John-Steiner, Scribner, and Souberman (see Vygotsky, 1978) have already used the term "interpsychological," I shall continue that practice here. These same points apply to Vygotsky's term *intrapsikhicheskii*.

3. The Russian term is *zona blizhaishego razvitiya*. The Russian *blizhaishego* is the superlative form of *blizkii* ("close"). Hence a more literal translation would be "zone of closest" or "nearest development." I shall follow the established practice of using "zone of proximal development" here, however.

4. The term "instruction" is a translation of the Russian *obuchenie,* a term that has sometimes been translated as "learning" (for example, Vygotsky, 1978, ch. 6). The inconsistent translation practice derives from the fact that there is no completely satisfactory English equivalent for *obuchenie;* it refers to the integrated activity of instructional interaction in which both teaching and learning are involved. Hence a more accurate, but entirely too cumbersome, translation might be "teaching-learning process." In English, "instruction" is often understood as focusing primarily on teaching, but since it may be understood to cover both teaching and learning, it seems to be the most appropriate translation for my purposes.

5. In this case Vygotsky's use of *obuchenie* seems to focus primarily on the learning aspect.

6. This word is a translation of *obuchenie*.

4. Vygotsky's Semiotic Analysis

1. The English term "unconditional" rather than the more commonly used "unconditioned" is employed in this volume. Like Toulmin (1978), I believe this is a better English equivalent for the Russian term *bezuslovnyi*.

2. Several years after Vygotsky's death the Prague school linguist J. Mukařovský (1977) reexamined Yakubinskii's ideas. He pointed out that the difference between monologue and dialogue does not correspond to a difference in functional languages as defined in the Formalist tradition. Rather, he emphasized that one must view monologue and dialogue as ends of a dynamic polarity that are seldom found in practice. Instead of purely dialogic or purely monologic speech, one almost always finds that characteristics of both are involved.

3. The term "indicatory" rather than "indicative" is sometimes used as the English translation of *ukazatel'naya*.

4. I use the term "reference" here because it is widely accepted in the Fregean tradition. A more literal translation of *predmetnaya otnesennost',* however, would be "object relatedness." This latter translation reflects Husserls's terminology.

5. Kohlberg, Yaeger, and Hjertholm (1968) found that during an early period in the development of egocentric speech, the proportion of total speech it comprises

actually increases. This curvilinear growth pattern is consistent with Vygotsky's notion of functional differentiation of speech functions but cannot be reconciled with Piaget's account of egocentric speech.

6. The Russian term here is *znachenie*. Therefore this term is now being used in a more general way than in the distinction between meaning and sense. I have made a practice of always using "meaning" for *znachenie,* but a more general term such as "signification" could also be employed here. If it were, it would be an overarching term for sense and meaning more narrowly interpreted.

5. Extending Vygotsky's Semiotic Analysis

1. Quine has noted in his accounts of reference that the objects about which we can speak are by no means limited to physical entities. While he sees physical objects playing an essential role in early forms of reference, his account also concerns how we speak "of attributes, number, sets, all sorts of abstract objects" (1973, p. 81).

2. There is no definite or indefinite article in Russian. Hence in Vygotsky's example *(Chasy upali),* no commitment to the definiteness of the referent was encoded.

3. In actuality, pitch and stress organization of the utterance would probably change in the two contexts outlined by Vygotsky. Hence even in this case, some aspect of the form would probably reflect the context in which it was used.

6. Semiotic Mechanisms in Vygotsky's Genetic Law of Cultural Development

1. I use the terms "objects" and "events" throughout this chapter when dealing with situation definitions. Although most of the objects and events examined are in the spatiotemporal context of the interlocutors involved, they need not be. They may also be abstract and/or removed from the speech context.

7. Units of Psychological Functioning

1. Much of Vygotsky's conceptualization about units, including his analogies based on chemistry (compare Vygotsky, 1962, p. 3), owe a great deal to R. Müller-Freinfels (compare Vygotsky, 1971, p. 205).

2. In actuality, each of the steps is a goal-directed action in its own right. Therefore this case actually involves an action made up of actions or subactions. However, the overall action has a unique psychological status that cannot be equated with the sum of the component actions. Since my ultimate concern is with the overall action, I shall follow the practice of labeling it with "action" and the three subactions "strategic steps." Furthermore, when I speak of the action of constructing the puzzle in accordance with the model, I am really concerned with the action of inserting a single piece. That is, I am concerned with the successful execution of one episode rather than with the entire task. Thus a hierarchical structure of actions is involved in the task setting I have chosen to examine. What I am calling an action is actually comprised of several strategic steps that could be

construed as actions in their own right. In addition, the action itself is only part of the larger task of making the entire puzzle (something that also could be construed as an action).

8. Mind and Society

1. It is worth noting in this connection that Leont'ev and Vygotsky differed in the importance they placed on semiotic mediation in their theories. It played a much more central role for Vygotsky than it did for Leont'ev. Hence Vygotsky's account of social history is grounded in changes in forms of mediation (see chapter 2), whereas Leont'ev's rests more heavily on the socioeconomic forces outlined by Marx.

The use of this term is one of the points at which Leont'ev does not follow Vygotsky's semiotic orientation. Whereas sense *(smysl)* for Vygotsky (see chapter 4) is a property of contextualized signs, Leont'ev employed this term to deal with the relationship between two levels of analysis in his approach (action and activity), neither of which need be semiotic in any essential way.

2. In what follows, I shall be interested in ideal typical versions of these activities in Western society. These ideal types are seldom if ever achieved in actual practice, but they serve as a target representation with which such practice may be compared.

3. The type of setting I have in mind is that found in Western educational institutions where abstract, reflective thinking is encouraged. This is one of the literacy practices outlined by Scribner and Cole (1981).

4. However, Bronfenbrenner (1979a) has noted that this is perhaps more a reemergence rather than an initial appearance of such interest.

5. Although there is no evidence that Leont'ev was influenced by Lukács, it is worth noting that in his critique of psychology (for example, Leont'ev, 1981) he focused on problems (such as "contemplation" as outlined in Marx's First Thesis on Feuerbach) very similar to those Lukács had raised several decades earlier in his critique of philosophy.

6. While Vygotsky often incorporated the notion of labor into his writings, he almost always had in mind a transhistorical notion of concrete labor. Marx and Lukács were primarily concerned with a second moment of labor that is historically specific to capitalism—abstract labor (see Postone, 1983).

7. In accordance with the comments of Clark and Holquist (1985), I am assuming that Bakhtin was the author of this work.

8. Although some authors (for example, Ivanov, 1976; Pomorska, 1978) claim otherwise, Clark and Holquist (1985) have concluded that Vygotsky and Bakhtin were neither personally acquainted nor influenced by one another's work. In my opinion, the similarities in their ideas derive from a common intellectual milieu and familiarity with many of the same works, in particular, Yakubinskii (1923).

Bibliography

Adorno, T. (1967) Sociology and psychology. *New Left Review* 46: 67–80.

—— (1968) Sociology and psychology, II. *New Left Review* 47: 9–19.

Akhutina, T. V. (1975) *Neirolingvisticheskii analiz dinamicheckoi afazii* [The neurolinguistic analysis of dynamic aphasia]. Moscow: Izdatel'stvo Moskovskogo Gosudarstvennogo Universiteta.

—— (1978) The role of inner speech in the construction of an utterance. *Soviet Psychology* 16 (3): 3–30.

Arns, F. J. (1980) Joint problem solving activity in adult–child dyads: A cross-cultural study. Diss.: Northwestern University.

Bakhtin, M. M. (1968) *Rabelais and His World*. Cambridge, Mass.: MIT Press.

—— (1981) *The Dialogic Imagination*. Ed. M. Holquist. Austin: University of Texas Press.

—— (1984) *Problems of Dostoevsky's Poetics*. Ed. and trans. C. Emerson. Minneapolis: University of Minnesota Press. Orig. pub. in Russian, 1929.

Bartlett, F. C. (1932) *Remembering: A Study in Experimental and Social Psychology*. Cambridge: Cambridge University Press.

Bates, E. (1976) *Language and Cognition: The Acquisition of Pragmatics*. New York: Academic Press.

Berg, E. E. (1970) L. S. Vygotsky's theory of the social and historical origins of consciousness. Diss.: University of Wisconsin.

Bernstein, L. E. (1979) Language as a product of dialogue. Northwestern University. Typescript.

Bibler, V. S. (1975) *Myshlenie kak tvorchestvo* [Thinking as creation]. Moscow: Izdatel'stvo Politicheskoi Literatury.

—— (1981) Vnutrennyaya rech' v ponimanii L. S. Vygotskogo (Eshche raz o predmete psikhologii) [Inner speech in L. S. Vygotsky's conceptualization (once again on the object of psychology)]. In *Nauchnoe tvorchestvo L. S. Vygotskogo i sovremennaya psikhologiya*. Tezisy dokladov vsesoyuznoi konferentsii, Moskva,

23–25 iyunya 1981 [The scientific work of L. S. Vygotsky and contemporary psychology. Theses of presentations of an all-union conference, Moscow, 23–25 June 1981]. Moscow: Akademiya Pedagogicheskikh Nauk SSSR.

—— (1983–84) Thinking as creation: Introduction to the logic of mental dialogue. *Soviet Psychology* 22 (2): 29–54.

Binet, A. (1969) The perception of lengths and numbers. In R. H. Pollack and M. W. Brenner, eds., *The Experimental Psychology of Alfred Binet*. New York: Springer.

Bloom, L. (1973) *One Word at a Time: The Use of Single-Word Utterances before Syntax*. The Hague: Mouton.

Bower, T. G. R. (1974) *Development in Infancy*. San Francisco: Freeman.

Bowerman, M. (1976) Semantic factors in the acquisition of rules for word use and sentence construction. In D. Morehead and A. Morehead, eds., *Normal and Deficient Child Language*. Baltimore: University Park Press.

—— (1978) The acquisition of word meaning: An investigation into some current conflicts. In N. Waterson and C. Snow, eds., *Development of Communication: Social and Pragmatic Factors in Language Acquisition*. New York: Wiley.

—— (1980) The structure and origin of semantic categories in the language-learning child. In M. L. Foster and J. Brandes, eds., *Symbol as Sense*. New York: Academic Press.

Bozhovich, L. I. (1977) The concept of the cultural-historical development of the mind and its prospects. *Soviet Psychology* 26 (1): 5–22.

—— (1979) Stages in the formation of the personality in ontogeny. *Soviet Psychology* 27 (3): 3–24.

—— (1980) Stages in the formation of personality in ontogeny. *Soviet Psychology* 28 (3): 36–52.

—— (1980–81) Stages in the formation of personality in ontogeny. *Soviet Psychology* 29 (2): 61–79.

Bozhovich, L. I.; L. S. Slavina; and T. V. Dovitskaya. (1976) Psikhologicheskie issledovaniya vol'nogo povedeniya [Psychological investigations of voluntary behavior]. *Voprosy psikhologii* [Problems of psychology], no. 4.

Breines, P. (1972) Praxis and its theorists: The impact of Lukács and Korsch in the 1920's. *Telos* 11: 67–103.

Bronfenbrenner, U. (1977) Toward an experimental ecology of human development. *American Psychologist* 32: 513–531.

—— (1979a) *The Ecology of Human Development: Experiments by Nature and Design*. Cambridge, Mass.: Harvard University Press.

—— (1979b) Contexts of child rearing: Problems and prospects. *American Psychologist* 34 (10): 844–850.

Broughton, J. M. (1981) Piaget's structural developmental psychology: V. Ideology-critique and the possibility of a critical developmental theory. *Human Development* (24): 382–411.

Brown, A. L., and R. Ferrara. (1985) Diagnosing zones of proximal development. In Wertsch (1985).

Brown, A. L., and L. A. French. (1978) The zone of proximal development: Implications for intelligence testing in the year 2000. *Intelligence* 3: 255–277.

Brown, R. (1970) How shall a thing be called? In R. Brown, ed., *Psycholinguistics*. New York: Free Press.

Bruner, J. S. (1962) Introduction. In Vygotsky (1962).

—— (1975a) The ontogenesis of speech acts. *Journal of Child Language* 2: 1–20.

—— (1975b) From communication to language: A psychological perspective. *Cognition* 3: 255–287.

—— (1976) Psychology and the image of man. *Times Literary Supplement*, December 17.

—— (1981) Intention in the structure of action and interaction. In L. P. Lipsitt, ed., *Advances in Infancy Research*, vol. 1. Norwood, N.J.: Ablex.

Bruner, J. S.; R. Olver; and P. Greenfield. (1966) *Studies in Cognitive Growth*. New York: Wiley.

Brushlinskii, A. V. (1979) The interrelationship of the natural and the social in human mental development. *Soviet Psychology* 27 (4): 36–52.

Buck-Morss, S. (1975) Socio-economic bias in Piaget's theory and its implications for the cross-cultural controversy. *Human Development* 18: 35–49.

—— (1977) *The Origin of Negative Dialectics: Theodor W. Adorno, Walter Benjamin, and the Frankfurt Institute*. New York: Free Press.

Bühler, C. (1927) *Soziologische und psychologische Studien uber das erste Lebensjahr* [Sociological and psychological studies of the first year of life]. Jena: G. Fischer.

Burks, A. W. (1949) Icon, index and symbol. *Philosophy and Phenomenological Research* 9: 673–689.

Campione, J. C.; A. L. Brown; R. A. Ferrara; and N. R. Bryant. (1984) The zone of proximal development: Implications for individual differences and learning. In Rogoff and Wertsch (1984).

Chafe, W. L. (1974) Language and consciousness. *Language* 50:111–133.

—— (1976) Givenness, contrastiveness, definiteness, subjects, topics, and point of view. In C. N. Li, ed., *Subject and Topic*. New York: Academic Press.

Chomsky, N. (1957) *Syntactic Structures*. Cambridge, Mass.: MIT Press.

—— (1965) *Aspects of a Theory of Syntax*. Cambridge, Mass.: MIT Press.

—— (1981) *Lectures on Government and Binding*. Dordrecht: Foris.

Clark, E. V. (1979) Building a vocabulary: Words for objects, actions, and relationship. In P. Fletcher and M. Garman, eds., *Language Acquisition: Studies in First Language Development*. Cambridge: Cambridge University Press.

Clark, H. H., and J. S. Begun. (1971) The semantics of sentence subjects. *Language and Speech* 14: 34–46.

Clark, H. H., and S. E. Haviland. (1977) Comprehension and the given-new contract. In R. O. Freedle, ed., *Discourse Production and Comprehension*. Norwood, N.J.: Ablex.

Clark, K., and M. Holquist. (1985) *M. M. Bakhtin: Life and Works*. Cambridge, Mass.: Harvard University Press.

Cole, M. (1979) Afterword. In Luria (1979).

—— (1985) The zone of proximal development: Where culture and cognition create each other. In Wertsch (1985).

Cole, M., and J. S. Bruner. (1971) Cultural differences and inferences about psychological processes. *American Psychologist* 26: 867–876.

Cole, M., and S. Scribner. (1974) *Culture and Thought: A Psychological Intro-duction*. New York: Wiley.

——— (1978) Introduction. In Vygotsky (1978).

Cook, W. A. (1979) *Case Grammar: Development of the Matrix Model*. Washington: Georgetown University Press.

Dasen, P. R., ed. (1977) *Piagetian Psychology: Cross-Cultural Contributions*. New York: Gardner Press.

Davydov, V. V. (1972) *Vidy obobshcheniya v obuchenii* [Forms of generalization in instruction]. Moscow: Pedagogika.

Davydov, V. V., and L. A. Radzikhovskii. (1985) Vygotsky's theory and the activity-oriented approach to psychology. In Wertsch (1985).

Dobrogaev, S. (1947) *Rechevye refleksi* [Speech reflexes]. Moscow: Izdatel'stvo Akademii Nauk SSSR.

Donaldson, M. (1978) *Children's Minds*. Glasgow: Fontana.

Dubois, J., and L. Irigaray. (1970) Experimental methods in psycholinguistics. In P. L. Garvin, ed., *Method and Theory in Linguistics*. The Hague: Mouton.

Eckensberger, L. H., and J. A. Meacham. (1984) The essentials of action theory: A framework for discussion. *Human Development* 27 (3–4): 166–172.

Egorova, T. V. (1973) *Osobennosti zapominaniya i myshleniya v shkol'nikakh razrushitel'nogo razvitiya* [Peculiarities of memory and thinking in develop-mentally backward school children]. Moscow: Izdatel'stvo Moskovskogo Go-sudarstvennogo Universiteta.

Eikhenbaum, B. M. (1965) The theory of the "formal method." In L. T. Lemon and M. J. Reis, eds., *Russian Formalist Criticism: Four Essays*. Lincoln: University of Nebraska Press. Orig. pub. 1927.

Elagina, M. C. (1977) *Poyavlenie rechi detei v protsesse sotrudnichestva c vroslymi* [The emergence of young children's speech in the process of cooperation with adults]. Diss. abstract (kandidatskaya): Moscow.

El'konin, D. B. (1972) Toward the problem of stages in the mental development of the child. *Soviet Psychology* 10: 225–251.

Emerson, C. (1983) The outer word and inner speech: Bakhtin, Vygotsky, and the internalization of language. *Critical Inquiry* 10 (2): 245–264.

Engels, F. (1940) *Dialectics of Nature*. New York: International Publishers.

Farwell, C. B. (1977) The primacy of goal in the child's description of motion and location. *Stanford Papers and Reports on Child Language Development* 13: 126–133.

Ferrara, R. A.; A. L. Brown; and J. C. Campione. (1983) Children's learning and transfer of inductive reasoning rules: A study of proximal development. University of Illinois. Typescript.

Fillmore, C. J. (1968) The case for case. In E. Bach and R. T. Harms, eds., *Universals in Linguistic Theory*. New York: Holt, Rinehart, and Winston.

Firbas, J. (1966) On defining the theme in functional sentence analysis. *Travaux linguistiques de Prague* 1: 267–280.

Frege, G. (1960) On sense and reference. In P. Geach and M. Black, trans., *The Philosophical Writings of Gottlob Frege*. Oxford: Oxford University Press.

Gal'perin, P. Ya. (1959) Razvitie issledovanii po formirovaniyu umstvennykh deistvii [The development of research on the formation of mental actions]. In

Psikhologicheskaya nauka v SSSR [Psychological science in the USSR], vol. 1. Moscow: Izdatel'stvo Akademii Pedagogicheskikh Nauk RSFSR.

—— (1960) Neskol'ko raz'yasnenii k gipoteze umstvennykh deistvii [Some interpretations of the hypothesis of mental actions]. *Voprosy psikhologii* [Problems of psychology] 6 (4): 141–148.

—— (1965) *Osnovnye rezul'taty issledovanii po probleme "Formirovanie umstvennykh deistvii i ponyatii"* [Fundamental results from the investigation of the problem "The formation of mental actions and concepts"]. Moscow: Izdatel'stvo Moskovskogo Gosudarstvennogo Universiteta.

—— (1966) K ucheniyu ob interiorizatsii [The teaching of internalization]. *Voprosy psikhologii* [Problems of psychology], no. 6, pp. 25–32.

—— (1969) Stages in the development of mental acts. In M. Cole and I. Maltzman, eds., *A Handbook of Contemporary Soviet Psychology*. New York: Basic Books.

—— (1977) *Vvedenie v psikhologii* [Introduction to psychology]. Moscow: Izdatel'stvo Moskovskogo Gosudarstvennogo Universiteta.

—— (1984) Letter to J. G. Blanck, March 29, 1984, private collection.

Geertz, C. (1973) *The Interpretation of Cultures*. New York: Basic Books.

Gelman, R., and C. R. Gallistel. (1978) *The Child's Understanding of Number*. Cambridge, Mass.: Harvard University Press.

Ginsburg, H. P. (1982) *Children's Arithmetic*. Austin, Tex.: Pro Editions.

—— (1982) The development of addition in the contexts of culture, social class, and race. In T. P. Carpenter, J. M. Moser, and T. A. Romberg, eds., *Addition and Subtraction: A Cognitive Perspective*. Hillsdale, N.J.: Erlbaum.

Ginsburg, H. P., and B. S. Allardice. (1984) Children's difficulties with school mathematics. In B. Rogoff and J. Lave, eds., *Everyday Cognition: Its Development in Social Context*. Cambridge, Mass.: Harvard University Press.

Ginsburg, H. P.; J. K. Posner; and R. L. Russell. (1981) The development of mental addition as a function of schooling and culture. *Journal of Cross-Cultural Psychology* 12: 163–178.

Goffman, E. (1974) *Frame Analysis*. New York: Harper and Row.

Goody, J. (1977) *The Domestication of the Savage Mind*. Cambridge: Cambridge University Press.

Goudena, P. P. (1982) Social aspects of private speech of young children during cognitive tasks. Paper presented at the Tenth World Congress of Sociology, Mexico City.

—— (1983) Private speech: An analysis of its social and self-regulative functions. Diss.: University of Utrecht.

Goudena, P. P., and F. H. R. Leenders. (1980) Exporatief onderzoek naar aspekten van private taal. [Exploratory research on aspects of private speech]. Utrecht: Internal report, IPAW.

Goudge, T. A. (1950) *The Thought of C. S. Peirce*. New York: Dover.

—— (1965) Peirce's index. *Transactions of the C. S. Peirce Society* 2 (Fall).

Greenfield, P. M., and J. H. Smith. (1976) *The Structure of Communication in Early Language Development*. New York: Academic Press.

Greenfield, P. M., and P. G. Zukow. (1978) Why do children say what they say when they say it?: An experimental approach to the psychogenesis of presupposition. In K. Nelson, ed., *Children's Language,* vol. 1. New York: Gardner Press.

Griffin, P., and M. Cole. (1984) Current activity for the future: The zo-ped. In Rogoff and Wertsch (1984).

Habermas, J. (1979) Toward a reconstruction of historical materialism. In J. Habermas, *Communication and the Evolution of Society.* Trans. T. McCarthy. Boston: Beacon Press.

Halliday, M. A. K. (1967) Notes on transitivity and theme in English, II. *Journal of Linguistics* 3: 199–244.

Halliday, M. A. K., and R. Hasan. (1976) *Cohesion in English.* London: Longman.

Hanfmann, E., and J. Kasanin. (1937) A method for the study of concept formation. *Journal of Psychology* 3: 521–540.

Harrower, M. (1983) *Kurt Koffka: An Unwitting Self-Portrait.* Gainesville: University Presses of Florida.

Hickmann, M. (1980a) Creating referents in discourse: A developmental analysis of linguistic cohesion. In J. Kreiman and A. Ojeda, eds., *Papers from the Parasession on Pronouns and Anaphora: Sixteenth Regional Meeting of the Chicago Linguistic Society.* Chicago: Chicago Linguistic Society.

——— (1980b) The context dependence of linguistic and cognitive processes. In M. Hickmann, ed., *Proceedings of a Working Conference on the Social Foundations of Language and Thought.* Chicago: Center for Psychosocial Studies.

——— (1982) The development of narrative skills: Pragmatic and metapragmatic aspects of discourse cohesion. Diss.: University of Chicago.

——— (1985) The implications of discourse skills in Vygotsky's developmental theory. In Wertsch (1985).

Holquist, M. (1981) The politics of representation. In S. Greenblatt, ed., *Allegory in Representation: Selected Papers from the English Institute.* Baltimore: Johns Hopkins University Press.

Holquist, M., and C. Emerson. (1981) Glossary. In Bakhtin (1981).

Holzkamp, K. (1973) *Sinnliche erkenntnishistorischer Ursprung und gesellschaftliche Funktion der Warnehmung* [The social function of perception and its origins in the history of sense cognition]. Frankfurt: Atheneum.

Hundeide, K. (1985) The tacit background of children's judgments. In Wertsch (1985).

Husserl, E. (1900) *Logische Untersuchungen,* 2 vols. Halle: Max Niemeyer. Published in English as *Logical Investigations,* 2 vols. Trans. J. N. Findlay. New York: Humanities Press, 1970.

Il'enkov, E. V. (1977) *Dialectical Logic: Essays on Its History and Theory.* Moscow: Progress Publishers.

Ivanov, V. V. (1971) Afterword. In Vygotsky (1971).

——— (1974) The significance of M. M. Bakhtin's ideas on sign, utterance, and dialogue for modern semiotics. In H. Baran, ed., *Semiotics and Structuralism: Readings from the Soviet Union.* White Plains, N.Y.: International Arts and Sciences Press.

——— (1976) *Ocherki po istorii seimotiki v SSSR* [Essays on the history of semiotics in the USSR]. Moscow: Izdatel'stvo Nauka.

———— (1977) The role of semiotics in the cybernetic study of man and collective. In D. P. Lucid, ed., *Soviet Semiotics: An Anthology*. Baltimore: Johns Hopkins University Press.

Jakobson, R. O. (1960) Concluding statement: Linguistics and poetics. In T. A. Sebeok, ed., *Style in Language*. Cambridge, Mass.: MIT Press.

James, C. T. (1972) Theme and imagery in the recall of active and passive sentences. *Journal of Verbal Learning and Verbal Behavior* 11: 205–211.

James, D. (1972) Some aspects of the syntax and semantics of interjections. In *Papers from the Eighth Regional Meeting, Chicago Linguistic Society*. Chicago: Chicago Linguistic Society.

James, W. (1904) Does consciousness exist? *Journal of Philosophy, Psychology, and Scientific Methods* 1: 477–491. Reprinted in W. James, ed., *Essays in Radical Empiricism*. Cambridge, Mass.: Harvard University Press, 1976.

Joravsky, D. (in preparation) *Russian Psychology*.

Karmiloff-Smith, A. (1979) *A Functional Approach to Child Language*. Cambridge: Cambridge University Press.

Kaye, K. (1982) *The Mental and Social Life of Babies*. Chicago: University of Chicago Press.

Kaye, K., and R. Charney. (1980) How mothers maintain "dialogue" with two-year-olds. In D. Olson, ed., *The Social Foundations of Language and Thought: Essays in Honor of Jerome S. Bruner*. New York: Norton.

Koffka, K. (1934) *Osnovy psikhicheskogo razvitiya* [Foundations of mental development]. Moscow and Leningrad: Sotsekgiz.

Kohlbergh, L., and J. V. Wertsch. (in press) Language and the development of thought. In L. Kohlberg, ed., *Developmental Psychology and Early Education*. New York: Longman.

Kohlberg, L.; J. Yaeger; and E. Hjertholm. (1968) Private speech: Four studies and a review of theories. *Child Development* 39: 691–736.

Köhler, W. (1921a) *Intelligenzpruefungen an Menschenaffen* [Intelligence testing of great apes]. Berlin: J. Springer.

———— (1921b) Zur Psychologie des Schimpansen [On the psychology of chimpanzees]. *Psychologische Forschung* no. 1, pp. 2–46.

———— (1925) *The Mentality of Apes*. New York: Harcourt, Brace.

Kozulin, A. (1984) *Psychology in Utopia: Toward a Social History of Soviet Psychology*. Cambridge, Mass.: MIT Press.

Laboratory of Comparative Human Cognition. (1983) Culture and cognitive development. In W. Kessen, ed., *Mussen's Handbook of Child Psychology*, 4th ed., vol. 1. New York: Wiley.

Lave, J. (1977a) Tailor-made experiments and evaluating the intellectual consequences of apprenticeship training. *Quarterly Newsletter of the Institute for Comparative Human Development* 1: 1–3.

———— (1977b) Cognitive consequences of traditional apprenticeship training in West Africa. *Anthropology and Education Quarterly* 8: 177–180.

Lee, B. (1985) The intellectual origins of Vygotsky's semiotic analysis. In Wertsch (1985).

Lemon, L. T., and M. J. Reis, eds. and trans. (1965) *Russian Formalist Criticism: Four Essays*. Lincoln: University of Nebraska Press.

Lenin, V. I. (1927) *Materialism and Empirico-Criticism: Critical Notes Concerning a Reactionary Philosophy*. London: M. Lawrence.

Leont'ev, A. A. (1970) Social and natural in semiotics. In J. Morton, ed., *Biological and Social Factors in Psycholinguistics*. Urbana: University of Illinois Press.

—— (1981) Sign and activity. In Wertsch (1981a).

Leont'ev, A. N. (1948) Review of O. I. Skorokhodova, *Kak ya vosprinimayu okruzhayushchii mir* [How I perceive the surrounding world]. *Sovetskaya pedagogika* [Soviet pedagogy], no. 3.

—— (1959) *Problemy razvitiya psikhiki* [Problems in the development of mind]. Moscow: Izdatel'stvo Moskovskogo Gosudarstvennogo Universiteta. Published in English as *Problems in the Development of Mind*. Moscow: Progress Publishers, 1982.

—— (1971) Preface. In Vygotsky (1971).

—— (1975) *Deyatel'nost', soznanie, lichnost'* [Activity, consciousness, personality]. Leningrad: Izdatel'stvo Politicheskoi Literaturi. Published in English as *Activity, Consciousness, and Personality*. Englewood Cliffs, N.J.: Prentice-Hall, 1978.

—— (1981) The problem of activity in psychology. In Wertsch (1981a).

Leont'ev, A. N., and A. R. Luria. (1956) Vygotsky's outlook on psychology. In Vygotsky (1956).

Levina, R. E. (1981) L. S. Vygotsky's ideas about the planning function of speech in children. In Wertsch (1981a).

Levitin, K. (1982) *One Is Not Born a Personality: Profiles of Soviet Education Psychologists*. Moscow: Progress Publishers.

Lisina, M. I. (1974) *Vliyanie obshcheniya s vzroslymi na razvitie rebenka v techenii pervogo goda zhizni* [The influence of social interaction with adults on the development of the child during the first half year of life]. In *Razvitie obshcheniya v doshkol'nikakh* [The development of social interaction in preschoolers]. Moscow: Pedagogika.

—— (1978) Mekhanizmy izmeneniya dominantnoi deyatel'nosti detei v techenii pervykh semi let zhizni [Mechanisms of changing the dominant activity of children during the first seven years of life]. *Voprosy psikhologii* [Problems of psychology] 5: 73–78.

Longacre, R. E. (1983) *The Grammar of Discourse*. New York: Plenum.

Lucy, J. (1981) An empirical approach to the Whorfian question. Paper presented at the Northwestern University Psycholinguistics Colloquium, Evanston, Ill., 18 November 1981.

—— (1985) Whorf's view of the linguistic mediation of thought. In E. Mertz and R. J. Parmentier, eds., *Semiotic Mediation: Sociocultural and Psychological Perspectives*. New York: Academic Press.

Lukács, G. (1971) *History and Class Consciousness: Studies in Marxist Dialectics*. Cambridge, Mass.: MIT Press.

Luria, A. R. (1971) Towards the problem of the historical nature of psychological processes. *International Journal of Psychology* 6 (4): 259–272.

—— (1975a) *Osnovnye problemy neirolingvistiki* [Basic problems of neurolinguistics]. The Hague: Mouton.

—— (1975b) *Ob istoricheskom razvitii poznavatel'nykh protsessov* [The historical development of cognitive processes]. Moscow: Izdatel'stvo Nauka. Published in English as *Cognitive Development: Its Cultural and Social Foundations*. Cambridge, Mass.: Harvard University Press, 1976.

—— (1978) Comment. In Vygotsky (1978).

—— (1978) *The Making of Mind: A Personal Account of Soviet Psychology*. Ed. M. Cole and S. Cole. Cambridge, Mass.: Harvard University Press.

—— (1981) *Language and Cognition*. Ed. J. V. Wertsch. New York: Wiley Intersciences.

Lyons, J. (1977) *Semantics*, vols. 1 and 2. Cambridge: Cambridge University Press.

Malinowski, B. (1960) The problem of meaning in primitive languages. In C. K. Ogden and I. A. Richards, eds., *The Meaning of Meaning*. London: Routledge and Kegan Paul.

Marx, K. (1959) Theses on Feuerbach. In L. S. Feuer, ed., *Marx and Engels: Basic Writings on Politics and Philosophy*. Garden City, N.Y.: Doubleday.

—— (1977) *Capital: A Critique of Political Economy*, vol. 1. Trans. B. Fowkes. New York: Vintage Books.

McCawley, J. D. (1968) The role of semantics in a grammar. In E. Bach and R. T. Harms, eds., *Universals in Linguistic Theory*. New York: Holt.

McLane, J. B. (1981) Dyadic problem solving: A comparison of child–child and mother–child interaction. Diss.: Northwestern University.

Mead, G. H. (1924–25) The genesis of the self and social control. *International Journal of Ethnoscience* 35: 251–277.

—— (1934) *Mind, Self, and Society from the Standpoint of a Social Behaviorist*. Chicago: University of Chicago Press.

Medvedev, P. N./M. M. Bakhtin. (1978) *The Formal Method in Literary Scholarship: A Critical Introduction to Sociological Poetics*. Baltimore: Johns Hopkins University Press.

Mehan, H. (1979) *Learning Lessons*. Cambridge, Mass.: Harvard University Press.

Morris, C. (1971) Foundations of the theory of signs. In O. Neurath, R. Carnap, and C. Morris, eds., *Foundations of the Unity of Science: Toward an International Encyclopedia of Unified Science*, vol. 1. Chicago: University of Chicago Press.

Mukařovský, J. (1977) Two studies on dialogue. In J. Burbank and P. Steiner, eds. and trans., *The Word and Verbal Art: Selected Essays by Jan Mukařovský*. New Haven: Yale University Press.

Nelson, K. (1973) Some evidence for the cognitive primacy of categorization and its functional basis. *Merrill-Palmer Quarterly* 19: 21–39.

Olson, D. R. (1970) *Cognitive Development: The Child's Acquisition of Diagonality*. New York: Academic Press.

—— (1977) From utterance to text: The bias of language in speech and writing. *Harvard Educational Review* 47: 257–281.

—— (1980) Some social aspects of meaning in oral and written language. In D. R. Olson, ed., *The Social Foundations of Language and Thought*. New York: Norton.

Pavlov, I. P. (1941) The conditioned reflex. In W. H. Gantt, ed. and trans., *Lectures on Conditioned Reflexes*, vol. 2. London: Lawrence and Wishart.

Peirce, C. S. (1931–1935) *Collected Papers of Charles Sanders Peirce*. Ed. C. Hort-shorne and P. Weiss. Cambridge Mass.: Harvard University Press.

Piaget, J. (1923) *Le langage et la pensée chez l'enfant*. Paris. Published in English as *The Language and Thought of the Child*. New York: Harcourt Brace, 1926. Published in Russian as *Rech' i myshlenie rebenka*. Moscow and Leningrad: Gosizdat, 1932.

—— (1952) *The Origins of Intelligence in Children*. New York: International Universities Press.

Pomorska, K. (1978) Mixail Baxtin and his verbal universal. *PTL: A Journal for Descriptive Poetics and Theory of Literature* 3: 379–386.

Postone, M. (1983) The present as necessity: Towards a reinterpretation of the Marxian critique of labor and time. Diss.: Johann Wolfgang Goethe-Universität, Frankfort am Main.

Potebnya, A. A. (1913) *Mysl' i yazyk* [Thought and language]. Khar'kov: Ti-pografiya "Mirnyi Trud."

Quine, W. V. O. (1960) *Word and Object*. Cambridge, Mass.: MIT Press.

—— (1973) *The Roots of Reference*. La Salle, Ill.: Open Court Publishing.

Radzikhovskii, L. A. (1979) Osnovnie stadii nauchnogo tvorchesta L. S. Vy-gotskogo [Fundamental stages in Vygotsky's scientific work]. Diss. (kandidat-skaya): Moscow State University.

Rahmani, L. (1973) *Soviet Psychology: Philosophical, Theoretical, and Experimental Issues*. New York: International Universities Press.

Rogoff, B. (1981) Schooling and the development of cognitive skills. In H. C. Triandis and A. Heron, eds., *Handbook of Cross-Cultural Psychology*, vol. 4. Boston: Allyn and Bacon.

Rogoff, B.; C. Malkin; and K. Gilbride. (1984) Interaction with babies as guidance in development. In Rogoff and Wertsch (1984).

Rogoff, B., and J. V. Wertsch, eds. (1984) *Children's learning in the "zone of proximal development,"* no. 23. In *New Directions for Child Development*. San Francisco: Jossey-Bass, 1984.

Rommetveit, R. (1974) *On Message Structure: A Framework for the Study of Language and Communication*. New York: Wiley.

—— (1979a) Deep structure of sentence versus message structure: Some critical remarks on current paradigms, and suggestions for an alternative approach. In Rommetveit and Blakar (1979).

—— (1979b) Language games, syntactic structure and hermeneutics: In search of a preface to a conceptual framework for research on language and human communication. In Rommetveit and Blakar (1979).

—— (1979c) On the architecture of intersubjectivity. In Rommetveit and Blakar (1979).

—— (1979d) On negative rationalism in scholarly studies of verbal communication and dynamic residuals in the construction of human intersubjectivity. In Rommetveit and Blakar (1979).

—— (1979e) On the relationship between children's mastery of Piagetian cognitive operations and their semantic competence. In Rommetveit and Blakar (1979).

—— (1979f) The role of language in the creation and transmission of social representations. University of Oslo. Typescript.

—— (1979g) On "meanings" of situations and social control of such meaning in human communication. Paper presented at the Symposium on the Situation in Psychological Theory and Research, Stockholm.

—— (1985) Language acquisition as increasing linguistic structuring of experience and symbolic behavior control. In Wertsch (1985).

Rommetveit, R., and R. M. Blakar, eds., (1979) *Studies of Language, Thought and Verbal Communication*. London: Academic Press.

Rubinshtein, S. L. (1946) *Osnovy obshchei psikhologii* [Foundations of general psychology]. Moscow: Uchpedgiz.

—— (1957) *Bytie i soznanie* [Being and consciousness]. Moscow: Izdatel'stvo Akademii Nauk, SSSR.

Rubtsov, V. V. (1981) The role of cooperation in the development of intelligence. *Soviet Psychology* 19 (4): 41–62.

Russac, R. J. (1978) The relation between two strategies of cardinal number: Correspondence and counting. *Child Development* 49: 728–735.

Sakharov, L. (1930) O metodakh issledovaniya ponyatii [Methods of investigating concepts]. *Psikhologiya* [Psychology] 3 (1).

Sammarco, J. G. (1984) Joint problem-solving activity in mother–child dyads: A comparative study of normally achieving and language disordered preschoolers. Diss.: Northwestern University.

Sapir, E. (1921) *Language: An Introduction to the Study of Speech*. New York: Harcourt, Brace, and World.

Saxe, G. B. (1977) A developmental analysis of notational counting. *Child Development* 48: 1512–1520.

—— (1981) Body parts as numerals: A developmental analysis of numeration among the Oksapmin in Papua, New Guinea. *Child Development* 52: 306–316.

—— (1982a) Culture and the development of numerical cognition: Studies among the Oksapmin of Papua, New Guinea. In C. J. Brainerd, ed., *Children's Logical and Mathematical Cognition*. New York: Springer-Verlag.

—— (1982b) Developing forms of arithmetical thought among the Oksapmin of Papua, New Guinea. *Developmental Psychology* 18 (4): 583–594.

Saxe, G. B.; M. Gearhart; and S. R. Guberman. (1984) The social organization of early number development. In Rogoff and Wertsch (1984).

Saxe, G. B., and J. Posner. (1983) The development of numerical cognition: Cross-cultural perspectives. In H. P. Ginsburg, ed., *The Development of Mathematical Thinking*. New York: Academic Press.

Schaeffer, B.; V. H. Eggleston; and J. L. Scott. (1974) Number development in young children. *Cognitive Psychology* 6: 357–379.

Scinto, L. F. M. (in press) *Oral and Written Language Norms and the Growth of the Mind*. New York: Academic Press.

Scribner, S. (1977) Modes of thinking and ways of speaking. In P. N. Johnson-Laird and P. C. Wason, eds., *Thinking: Readings in Cognitive Science*. New York: Cambridge University Press.

———— (1984) Cognitive studies of work. *Quarterly Newsletter of the Laboratory of Comparative Human Cognition* 6 (1, 2): 1–46.

———— (1985) Vygotsky's uses of history. In Wertsch (1985).

Scribner, S., and M. Cole. (1973) Cognitive consequences of formal and informal education. *Science* 182: 553–559.

———— (1981) *The Psychological Consequences of Literacy.* Cambridge, Mass.: Harvard University Press.

Seve, L. (1978) *Man in Marxist Theory and the Psychology of Personality.* Sussex: The Harvester Press.

Shklovskii, V. B. (1914) *Voskreshenie slova* [The resurrection of the word]. Petersburg.

Sigel, I. E. (1970) The distancing hypothesis: A causal hypothesis for the acquisition of representational thought. In M. R. Jones, ed., *Miami Symposium on the Prediction of Behavior, 1968: Effects of Early Experience.* Coral Gables: University of Miami Press.

———— (1979) On becoming a thinker: A psychoeducational model. *Educational Psychologist* 14: 70–78.

———— (1982) The relationship between parental distancing strategies and the child's cognitive behavior. In L. M. Laosa and I. E. Sigel, eds., *Families as Learning Environments for Children.* New York: Plenum.

Sigel, I. E., and R. R. Cocking, (1977) Cognition and communication: A dialectic paradigm for development. In M. Lewis and L. A. Rosenblum, eds., *Interaction, Conversation, and the Development of Language: The Origins of Behavior,* vol. 5. New York: Wiley.

Sigel, I. E., and A. McGillicuddy-Delisi. (1984) Parents as teachers of their children: A distancing behavior model. In A. D. Pellegrini and T. D. Yawkey, eds., *The Development of Oral and Written Language: Readings in Developmental and Applied Psycholinguistics.* Norwood, N.J.: Ablex.

Sigel, I. E., and R. Saunders. (1979) An inquiry into inquiry: Question asking as an instructional model. In L. G. Katz, ed., *Current Topics in Early Childhood Education,* vol. 2 Norwood, N.J.: Ablex.

Silverstein, M. (1976) Shifters, linguistic categories, and cultural description. In K. Basso and H. Selby, eds., *Meaning in Anthropology.* Albuquerque: University of New Mexico Press.

———— (1977) Cognitive implications of a referential hierarchy. University of Chicago. Typescript.

———— (1980) Cognitive implications of a referential hierarchy. Paper presented at Max-Planck-Institut für Psycholinguistik, Nijmegen, The Netherlands, November 20.

———— (1985) The functional stratification of language and ontogenesis. In Wertsch (1985).

Sinclair, J., and R. Coulthard. (1975) *Towards an Analysis of Discourse: The English Used by Teachers and Pupils.* London: Oxford University Press.

Smirnov, A. N. (1975) *Razvitie i sovremennoc sostoyanie psikhologicheskoi nauki v SSSR* [The development and present status of psychology in the USSR]. Moscow: Izdatel'stvo Pedagogika.

Stern, C., and W. Stern. (1928) *Die Kindersprache. Eine psychologische und sprach-*

theoretische Untersuchung [Child language: a psychological and speech-theoretic investigation]. Leipzig: J. A. Barth.

Sugarman, S. (1983) *Children's Early Thought: Developments in Classification.* Cambridge: Cambridge University Press.

Toulmin, S. (1978) The Mozart of psychology. *New York Review of Books,* September.

Tucker, R. C. (1971) *The Soviet Political Mind: Stalinism and Post-Stalin Change.* New York: Norton.

Tulviste, P. (1978a) On the origins of theoretic syllogistic reasoning in culture and in the child. In *Problems of Communication.* Tartu, USSR: Tartu University Press.

—— (1978b) O teoreticheskikh problemakh istoricheskogo razvitiya myshleniya [Theoretical problems of the historical development of thinking]. In L. I. Antsiferova, ed., *Printsip razvitiya v psikhologii* [The principle of development in psychology]. Moscow: Izdatel'stvo Nauka.

Valsiner, J. (1984) Construction of the zone of proximal development in adult–child joint action: The socialization of meals. In Rogoff and Wertsch (1984).

Varshava, B. E., and L. S. Vygotsky. (1931) *Psikhologicheskii leksikon* [Psychological dictionary]. Moscow: Uchpedgiz.

Vetrova, V. V. (1975) Vliyanie slushaniya rechi vzroslykh na razvitie rechi detei [The influence of hearing adult speech on young children's verbal development]. Diss. abstract (kandidatskaya): Moscow.

Vlasova, T. A. (1972) New advances in Soviet defectology. *Soviet Education* 14: 20–39.

Vlasova, T. A., and M. S. Pevzner, eds. (1971) *Deti c vremennoi otstalost'yu razvitiya* [Children with temporary retardation in development]. Moscow: Pedagogika.

Voloshinov, V. N. (1973) *Marxism and the Philosophy of Language.* Trans. L. Matejka and I. R. Titunik. New York: Seminar Press. Orig. pub. in Russian, 1929.

—— (1976) *Freudianism: A Marxist Critique.* New York: Academic Press.

Vygotsky, L. S. (1925) *Psikhologiya iskusstvo* [The psychology of art]. Published in English as *The Psychology of Art.* Trans. Scripta Technica, Inc. Cambridge, Mass.: MIT Press, 1971.

—— (1929) The problem of the cultural development of the child. *Journal of Genetic Psychology* 36: 415–434.

—— (1931a) Diagnostika razvitiya i pedologicheskaya klinika trudnogo detstva [The diagnosis of development and the pedological clinic for difficult childhood]. Published as L. S. Vygotsky, *Diagnostika razvitiya i pedologicheskaya klinika trudnogo detstva* [The diagnosis of development and the pedological clinic for difficult childhood]. Moscow: Izdatel'stvo Eksperimental'nogo Defektologicheskogo Instituta, 1936.

—— (1931b) Istoriya razvitiya vysshikh psikhicheskikh funktsii [The history of the development of higher mental functions]. In L. S. Vygotsky, *Razvitie vysshikh psikhicheskikh funktsii* [The development of higher mental functions]. Moscow: Izdatel'stvo Akademii Pedagogicheskikh Nauk RSFSR, 1960.

—— (1932) Lektsii po psikhologii [Lectures on psychology]. In L. S. Vygotsky, *Razvitie vysshikh psikhicheskikh funktsii* [The development of higher mental functions]. Moscow: Izdatel'stvo Akademii Pedagogicheskikh Nauk RSFSR, 1960.

—— (1934a) *Myshlenie i rech': Psikhologicheskie issledovaniya* [Thinking and speech: Psychological investigations]. Moscow and Leningrad: Gosudarstvennoe Sotsial'no-Ekonomicheskoe Izdatel'stvo.

—— (1934b) Problema obucheniya i umstvennogo razvitiya v shkol'nom vozraste [The problem of instruction and cognitive development during the school years]. In L. S. Vygotsky, *Umstvennoe razvitie detei v protsesse obucheniya* [Cognitive development in children in the process of instruction]. Moscow and Leningrad: Uchpedgiz, 1935.

—— (1934c) Thought in schizophrenia. *Archives of Neurology and Psychiatry* 31 (5): 1063–1077.

—— (1956) *Izbrannye psikhologicheskie issledovaniya* [Selected psychological investigations]. Moscow: Izdatel'stvo Akademii Pedagogicheskikh Nauk SSSR.

—— (1960) *Razvitie vysshykh psikhicheskikh funktsii* [The development of higher mental functions]. Moscow: Izdatel'stvo Akademii Pedagogicheskikh Nauk.

—— (1962) *Thought and Language*. Cambridge, Mass.: MIT Press.

—— (1972) Problema periodizatsii etapov v detskom vozraste [The problem of stage periodization in child development]. *Voprosy psikhologii* [Problems of psychology] 2: 114–123.

—— (1977) Iz tret'ryadei L. S. Vygotskogo [From the notebooks of L. S. Vygotsky]. *Vestnik Moskovskogo Universiteta: Seriya psikhologii* [Moscow University record: Psychology series] 15: 89–95.

—— (1978) *Mind in Society: The Development of Higher Psychological Processes*. Ed. M. Cole, V. John-Steiner, S. Scribner, and E. Souberman. Cambridge, Mass.: Harvard University Press.

—— (1979) Consciousness as a problem in the psychology of behavior. *Soviet psychology* 17 (4): 3–35. Orig. pub. as Soznanie kak problema psikhologii povedeniya [Consciousness as a problem in the psychology of behavior]. In K. N. Kornilov, ed., *Psikhologiya i marksizm* [Psychology and Marxism]. Moscow and Leningrad: Gosizdat, 1925.

—— (1981a) The instrumental method in psychology. In Wertsch (1981a).

—— (1981b) The genesis of higher mental functions. In Wertsch (1981a).

—— (1981c) The development of higher forms of attention in childhood. In Wertsch (1981a).

—— (1982a) *Sobranie sochinenii, Tom pervyi: Voprosy teorii i istorii psikhologii* [Collected works, vol. 1: Problems in the theory and history of psychology]. Moscow: Izdatel'stvo Pedagogika.

—— (1982b) *Sobranie sochinenii. Tom vtoroi: Problemy obshchei psikhologii* [Collected works, vol. 2: Problems of general psychology]. Moscow: Izdatel'stvo Pedagogika.

—— (1983a) *Sobranie sochinenii. Tom tretii. Problemy razvitiya psikhiki.* [Collected works, vol. 3: Problems in the development of mind]. Moscow: Izdatel'stvo Pedagogika.

—— (1983b) *Sobranie sochinenii, Tom pyatyi: Osnovy defektologii* [Collected works, vol. 5: Foundations of defectology]. Moscow: Izdatel'stvo Pedagogika.

———— (1984a) *Sobranie sochinenii, Tom chetvertyi: Detskaya psikhologiya* [Collected works, Vol. 4: Child psychology]. Moscow: Izdatel'stvo Pedagogika.

———— (1984b) *Sobranie sochinenii. Tom shestoi. Nauchnoe nasledstvo.* [Collected works, vol. 6: Scientific legacy]. Moscow: Izdatel'stvo Pedagogika.

Vygotsky, L. S., and A. R. Luria. (1930) *Etyudy po istorii povedeniya: Obez'yana, primitiv, rebenok* [Essays in the history of behavior: Ape, primitive, child]. Moscow and Leningrad: Gosudarstvennoe Izdatel'stvo.

Weber, M. (1968) *On Charisma and Institution Building: Selected Papers.* Ed. S. N. Eisenstadt. Chicago: University of Chicago Press.

———— (1978) *Economy and Society: An Outline of Interpretive Sociology.* Ed. G. Roth and C. Wittich. Berkeley: University of California Press.

Werner, H. (1957) The concept of development from a comparative and organismic point of view. In D. Harris, ed., *The Concept of Development.* Minneapolis: University of Minnesota Press.

———— (1961) *Comparative Psychology of Mental Development.* New York: Science Press.

Wertsch, J. V. (1979a) From social interaction to higher psychological processes: A clarification and application of Vygotsky's theory. *Human Development* 22 (1): 1–22.

———— (1979b) The regulation of human action and the given-new organization of private speech. In G. Zivin, ed., *The Development of Self-Regulation through Private Speech.* New York: Wiley.

———— (1980a) Semiotic mechanisms in joint cognitive activity. Paper presented at the Joint US–USSR Conference on the Theory of Activity, Institute of Psychology, USSR Academy of Sciences, Moscow.

———— (1980b) The significance of dialogue in Vygotsky's account of social, egocentric, and inner speech. *Contemporary Educational Psychology* 5: 150–162.

————, ed. (1981a) *The Concept of Activity in Soviet Psychology.* Armonk, N.Y.: M. E. Sharpe.

———— (1981b) Trends in Soviet cognitive psychology. *Storia e critica della psicologia* 2 (2): 219–295.

———— (1984) The zone of proximal development: Some conceptual issues. In Rogoff and Wertsch (1984).

————, ed. (1985) *Culture, Communication, and Cognition: Vygotskian Perspectives.* New York: Cambridge University Press.

———— (in press) The semiotic mediation of mental life: L. S. Vygotsky and M. M. Bakhtin. In E. Mertz and R. J. Parmentier, eds., *Semiotic Mediation: Psychological and Sociocultural Perspectives.* New York: Academic Press.

Wertsch, J. V., and M. Hickmann. (in press) A microgenetic analysis of problem-solving in social interaction. In M. Hickmann, ed., *Social and Functional Approaches to Language and Thought.* New York: Academic Press.

Wertsch, J. V.; G. D. McNamee; J. G. McLane; and N. A. Budwig. (1980) The adult–child dyad as a problem solving system. *Child Development* 51: 1215–1221.

Wertsch, J. V.; N. Minick; and F. J. Arns. (1984) The creation of context in joint problem solving. In B. Rogoff and J. Lave, eds., *Everyday Cognition: Its Development in Social Contexts.* Cambridge, Mass.: Harvard University Press.

Wertsch, J. V., and J. G. Sammarco. (1985) Social precursors to individual functioning: The problem of units of analysis. In R. A. Hinde and A. N. Perret-Clermont, eds., *Interindividual Relations and Cognitive Development.* Oxford: Oxford University Press.

Wertsch, J. V., and P. J. Schneider. (1979) Variations of adults' directives to children in a problem solving situation. Northwestern University. Typescript.

Wertsch, J. V., and C. A. Stone. (1978) Microgenesis as a tool for developmental analysis. *Quarterly Newsletter for the Laboratory of Comparative Human Cognition* (University of California, San Diego) 1 (1): 8–10.

———— (1985) The concept of internalization in Vygotsky's account of the genesis of higher mental functions. In Wertsch (1985).

Whorf, B. L. (1956) *Language, Thought and Reality: Selected Writings of Benjamin Lee Whorf.* Cambridge, Mass.: MIT Press.

Yakubinskii, L. P. (1916) O zvukah poeticheskogo yazyka [On the sounds of poetic language]. *Poetika: Sborniki po teorii poeticheskogo yazyka* [Poetics: Collections on the theory of poetic language]. Petrograd.

———— (1923) *O dialogicheskoi rechi* [On dialogic speech]. Petrograd: Trudy Foneticheskogo Instituta Prakticheskogo Izucheniya Yazykov.

Youniss, J. (1983) Beyond ideology to the universals of development. In D. Kuhn and J. A. Meacham, eds., *On the Development of Developmental Psychology.* Munich: Karger, Basel.

Zhirmunskii, V. A. (1921) Zadacjo poetiki [The task of poetics]. In *Voprozy teoiri literatury* [Problems of the theory of literature], no. 39.

Zinchenko, P. I. (1939) Problema neproizvol'nogo zapominaniya [The problem of involuntary memory]. *Nauchnye zapiski Khar'kovskogo gosudarstvennogo pedagogicheskogo instituta inostrannykh yazykov* [The scientific record of the Khar'kov State Pedagogical Institute of Foreign Languages], vol. 1. Published in English as The problem of involuntary memory. *Soviet Psychology* 22, no. 2 (1983–84): 55–11.

———— (1981) Involuntary memory and the goal directed nature of activity. In Wertsch (1981a).

Zinchenko, V. P. (1985) Vygotsky's ideas about units for the analysis of mind. In Wertsch (1985).

Zinchenko, V. P., and V. M. Gordon (1981) Methodological problems in the psychological analysis of activity. In Wertsch (1981).

Name Index

Ach, N., 99
Adorno, T., 2
Akhutina, T. V., 55, 125
Allardice, B. S., 48, 50
Aristotle, 4
Arns, F. J., 164, 165, 167, 181–182,
    207, 213, 215
Ashpiz, S., 4

Bakhtin, M. M., 224–229, 237
Bartlett, F. C., 192
Bates, E., 65
Begun, J. S., 137
Bekhterev, V. M., 185, 187
Bely, A., 7
Berg, E. E., 81
Bernstein, L. E., 123
Bibler, V. S., 112
Binet, A., 48
Blakar, R. M., 159
Blok, A. A., 7
Blonskii, P. P., 20
Bloom, L., 102
Bloomfield, L., 130
Boas, F., 130
Bower, T. G. R., 44
Bowerman, M., 102
Bozhovich, L. I., 12, 189

Breines, P., 218
Brentano, F., 186
Bronfenbrenner, U., 67, 216, 237
Broughton, J. M., 223
Brown, A. L., 69, 70, 164
Brown, R., 170
Bruner, J. S., 1, 44, 50, 59, 74, 102,
    133, 217
Brushlinskii, A. V., 197–198
Bryant, N. R., 69, 70
Buck-Morss, S., 219, 223
Budoff, M., 70
Budwig, N. A., 164
Bühler, C., 93
Bühler, K., 13, 125
Bunin, I. A., 7
Burks, A. W., 98

Campione, J. C., 69, 70
Chafe, W. L., 141–142, 144
Charney, R., 74
Chelpanov, G. I., 10
Chomsky, N., 130, 132
Clark, E. V., 133
Clark, H. H., 137
Clark, K., 228, 237
Cocking, R. R., 71
Cole, M., 14, 19, 24, 33, 36, 37, 38,

Cole (*cont.*)
39, 40, 57, 75, 193, 217, 235, 237
Cook, W. A., 132

Dasen, P. R., 50
Davydov, V. V., 43, 73, 196, 200–201, 206
Descartes, R., 201–202, 222
Dickens, C., 227–228
Dobkin, S., 3, 4, 5, 6, 7, 8, 9, 233
Dobrogaev, S., 92
Donaldson, M., 26
Dostoevsky, F. M., 7, 226
Dovitskaya, T. V., 189
Dubois, J., 136

Eckensberger, L. H., 211
Eggleston, V. H., 52
Egorova, T. V., 68
Eikhenbaum, B. M., 82
Eizenshtein, S. M., 13
Elagina, M. C., 44
El'konin, D. B., 12, 75, 203
Emerson, C., 112, 226
Engels, F., 8, 28, 29, 77, 199

Farwell, C. B., 134
Ferrara, R. A., 69, 70, 164
Feuerbach, L., 199
Fillmore, C. J., 132
Firbas, J., 141
Frege, G., 130, 168, 235
French, L. A., 69
Freud, S., 8, 13

Gallistel, C. R., 52
Gal'perin, P. Ya., 9, 12, 66, 200
Gearhart, M., 75
Geertz, C., 29, 30, 56
Gelman, R., 52
Gesell, A., 13
Gilbride, K., 74
Ginsburg, H. P., 48, 49, 50, 51, 53, 54
Goffman, E., 203
Gogol', N. V., 126
Goody, J., 36, 217
Goudena, P. P., 119, 120

Goudge, T. A., 98
Greenfield, P. M., 50, 102, 134, 135, 145, 146
Griffin, P., 75
Guberman, S. R., 75

Habermas, J., 2, 30
Halliday, M. A. K., 141, 153
Hanfmann, E., 105, 106
Harrower, M., 233
Hasan, R., 153
Hegel, G. W. F., 8
Heine, H., 3
Hickmann, M., 98, 149–150, 154–155, 166
Hjertholm, E., 116, 121, 235
Holquist, M., 226, 228, 237
Holzkamp, K., 206
Humboldt, W. von, 85
Hundeide, K., 159
Husserl, E., 97, 235

Il'enkov, E. V., 201–202
Irigaray, L., 136
Ivanov, V. V., 13, 82, 112, 237

Jaensch, E. R., 24
Jakobson, R. O., 82, 84, 136
James, C. T., 137
James, W., 7, 200
Janet, P., 92
John-Steiner, V., 235
Joravsky, D., 89

Kant, I., 222–223
Karmiloff-Smith, A., 146–149, 150
Kasanin, J., 105, 106
Kaye, K., 74
Koffka, K., 13, 21, 72, 233
Kohlberg, L., 43, 116, 121, 143, 235
Köhler, W., 13, 27, 45
Kornilov, K. N., 8, 10
Kotelova, Yu. V., 100
Kozulin, A., 11, 64, 199, 202

Laboratory of Comparative Human Cognition, 216

Seve, L., 32, 58
Shchedrovitskii, G. P., 2
Shklovskii, V. B., 82
Sigel, I. E., 71
Silverstein, M., 98, 102, 129–131,
    135–137, 140, 144–145, 154,
    156, 169, 176, 229
Simmel, G., 218–219
Slavina, L. S., 12, 189
Smekhova, R., 7
Smirnov, A. N., 30, 202
Smith, J. H., 134, 135
Souberman, E., 235
Spinoza, B., 7, 200–202
Stalin, J., 14
Stern, C., 96, 99
Stern, W., 96, 99
Stone, C. A., 55, 64, 65
Sugarman, S., 44, 102

Thorndike, E. L., 22, 72
Tolman, E. C., 192
Tolstoy, L. N., 7, 87
Toulmin, S., 8, 235
Tucker, R. C., 11, 14
Tulviste, P., 38, 41
Tyuchev, F., 7

Valsiner, J., 74
Varshava, B. E., 197
Vetrova, V. V., 44
Vlasova, T. A., 68
Voloshinov, V. N., 224–226
Vossler, K., 140
Vygodsky, D., 7, 233
Vygotskaya, G. L., 3, 13

Weber, M., 218–219, 222–223
Werner, H., 55
Wertsch, J. V., 43, 55, 64–66, 72,
    75, 113, 122, 142–145, 159, 162–
    166, 169–171, 173–179, 182,
    202, 207, 213, 215, 228
Whorf, B. L., 137, 138

Yaeger, J., 116, 121, 235
Yakubinskii, L. P., 81, 84, 85, 86, 87,
    88, 113, 123, 235, 237
Youniss, J., 223

Zaporozhets, A. V., 12
Zinchenko, P. I., 12, 200
Zinchenko, V. P., 63, 185, 192, 200,
    205–206, 208
Zukow, P. G., 145–146

Subject Index

Mental functions (*cont.*)

tary, 45, 49–50, 52; elementary and higher, 24–27, 42; higher, 36–39, 52, 54, 62, 94, 104, 110, 115, 150–151, 156, 189–190; relationships among, 189–192, 196; rudimentary, 31–32, 49, 51, 57

Metapragmatic uses of speech, 155

Metasemantic function of language, 156

Method, experimental-developmental, 18

Moscow, 5–7, 8, 9–10, 12, 13, 233

Motives and goals, 212–214

Pavlovian theory, 15, 25, 97

Perception, 24, 112

Phenotype, 17

Pragmatic presupposition, 144–146

Predicativity, 122–123, 140. *See also* Subject and predicate, grammatical and psychological

Prolepsis, 216. *See also* Intersubjectivity

Psychological Institute (Moscow), 8, 10

Qualitative change, 19–24, 28–29, 33, 41, 47, 80, 96, 151, 159

Rationalization, 218–219

Reductionism: behavioristic, 28; biological, 20–21, 42–43; individualistic psychological, 1–2, 59–60; social or cultural, 1–2, 43, 47–48, 60

Referentiality, 129–130; discourse, 139–145, 198; propositional, 130–139, 198

Referential perspective, 167–177, 229. *See also* Referring expressions

Referring expressions, 170–175; common, 170, 173–174; context-informative, 171, 173–175; deictic, 171, 173–175

Reflection, 188–189

Regulation, 127, 132; other-, 119, 163–166, 178–182; self-, 25–26,

110–111, 115–116, 119, 125, 129, 150–152, 163–166; voluntary, 25–27, 65

Reification, 218–219, 221, 223

Retardation, 18, 47

Russian Revolution (1917), 3, 7, 10, 231

Second signal system, 81, 89–92

Sense, 95, 124–127, 196–197, 212, 224–225, 229, 236–237; infusion of, 126

Shanyavskii People's University (Moscow), 6–7

Signs, 15, 16

Sign-sign and sign-object relationships, 89, 103, 108–110, 123, 139, 153, 196, 229

Sign types and sign tokens, 98, 105–106, 108, 131, 133, 139, 153–154, 156, 168, 223–224

Situation definition. *See* Intersubjectivity

Social institutions, 59–60, 74–75, 209–218, 224, 228, 230

Social interaction, 15, 26, 60, 66, 80, 86, 91, 95–96, 107, 111–113, 152

Social relations, 58, 61

Speech functions, 84–85, 88–89; communicative and intellectual, 93–94, 114, 125; dialogic, 65, 112–113, 123, 225–229; dialogic and monologic, 85–88, 235; differentiation of egocentric from social, 117–121; egocentric, 108, 111–127, 143–144, 158, 163–164, 177, 224, 229, 234–236; egocentric and socialized in Piagetian theory, 114–115; indicative and symbolic, 96–99, 235; inner, 108, 110, 112, 121–127, 158, 177, 210, 223–230, 234; labeling, 111; poetic and practical language, 83–84; regulative, 140 (*see also* Regulation); signaling and signification, 89–92; social and individual, 92–93, 111, 115; social contact or

Speech functions (*cont.*)
phatic, 93; spoken versus written, 86; written, 86, 123. *See also* Explanatory principles: speech
Speech production, 125
Stalinist purges, 10
Subject and predicate, grammatical and psychological, 122, 140–144
Symbolists, 83

Theme and rheme, 141. *See also* Subject and predicate, grammatical and psychological
Thinking, 24, 61, 99, 112, 116–117, 201–202; abstract reasoning, 38; categorization, 34, 37–38; syllogistic reasoning, 35, 37
Tools, 78; physical (technical), 15, 22–23, 27–28, 77, 79; psychological, 22–23, 27, 32, 77–81

Units of analysis, 192–208, 236; activity theory, 199, 202–208, 210–

211; word meaning, 185, 192–198, 205–207, 236; versus elements, 193–195

Volition, 25, 61
Voluntary control, 26, 103–104
Vygotskian school, 9. *See also* Activity theory

Word meaning, 236; and reference, 97, 107, 129 (*see also* Referentiality); complexes, 101–102, 104–107; everyday concepts (spontaneous), 102–104; scientific concepts (genuine), 102–104, 125, 152–153, 156, 217; development of, 97–108; pseudoconcepts, 105–107; unorganized heaps, 100–101. *See also* Sense; Units of analysis: word meaning

Zone of proximal development, 61, 67–75, 159, 161–162, 235